World Urbanization 1950-1970: Volume I

KINGSLEY DAVIS

World Urbanization 1950-1970
Volume I: Basic Data for Cities,
Countries, and Regions

KINGSLEY DAVIS

Price—$3.00

Institute of International Studies
University of California, Berkeley

© 1969 by the Regents of the University of California

ACKNOWLEDGMENTS

Any study that tries to provide and utilize comparative data for all the world's countries will necessarily demand skills, manpower, and resources beyond those of a single individual. The present study is no exception. It is the product of many hands and of generous support. I take pleasure in acknowledging both kinds of assistance.

First let me cite those research assistants who worked directly on the project. None was associated with the study throughout, since the beginning in 1965 to the present, but several participated long enough to play an important role in its completion. They are as follows:

Patricia Matsushita (now Mrs. Day). She was longest in service on the project and grew to be a much admired leader in data collection and estimation.

Nancy Wang. A statistician, Mrs. Wang did the programming and data processing during the last seven months preceding publication of Volume I. She also served as an acute critical analyst of the data.

Mark H. Skolnick. Until he left in the summer of 1968 to enter graduate school, Mr. Skolnick played a versatile role on the project. He was computer expert, data compiler, and idea man.

James Mulherin. A valuable worker in the early stages of the project, Mr. Mulherin's initials are on many pages of notes in our endless files.

Maura McDowell (now Mrs. Kealey). Another assistant who participated in the early stages of the project and whose initials are on many pages of notes, Mrs. Kealey was at the time a graduate student in history.

Virginia Stibbs. In the last stages of the work Miss Stibbs helped greatly in an editorial capacity, and her first-hand knowledge of many Asian countries and cities was most useful.

Kwan-hwa Chen. A graduate student in demography, Miss Chen was with the project for nearly a year and was always willing to do what needed to be done.

v

Eileen Rusky. Although she came late to the project, Mrs. Rusky soon proved her worth as a research assistant and an apprentice in data processing.

To all of these co-workers I am grateful for their industry, skill, and initiative.

Several persons not directly involved in the research contributed in other ways to the project. Eduardo E. Arriaga, senior member of IPUR's research staff, gave both encouragement and valuable professional advice. Nancy Donovan, editor for the Institute of International Studies, always responded to our pleas for editorial help as we struggled to put together the manuscript of this unorthodox type of book; and Judith Clark, our own bookkeeper and administrative aide, supervised and did most of the offset typing for the book. Finally, Cleo C. Stoker, Administrative Services Officer of the Institute, had the least to do directly with the project but a great deal to do with the long-run welfare and efficiency of our research unit.

On the all-important financial side, the work has been supported mainly by the Institute of International Studies from funds generously furnished by the Ford Foundation for comparative investigations. Insofar as Latin American countries are dealt with, support has come from a grant of the Rockefeller Foundation in behalf of IPUR's comparative demographic research on Latin America. In truth, it is difficult to exclude any major source of financing since the office began in 1956. At that time the Ford Foundation enabled us to get started with a five-year grant of substantial size. The continuing work of the office is an indirect product of that initial support. I am most pleased to acknowledge both the direct and the indirect support that the Ford and Rockefeller Foundations have given us.

Needless to say, responsibility for the accuracy or inaccuracy of the materials presented, both in the text and in the tables, is mine alone.

Kingsley Davis

Berkeley, California
March 31, 1969

TABLE OF CONTENTS

LIST OF TABLES IN THE INTRODUCTORY CHAPTERS

Chapter I

THE NATURE AND PURPOSE OF THE BASIC DATA

The purpose of this volume is to provide essential data on urbanization and the growth of cities throughout the world. Its main feature is the series of tables--numbered from A to H--which follow the introductory chapters. These tables provide information for all countries and regions of the globe at the same three dates--1950, 1960, and 1970. The volume thus constitutes a sourcebook of worldwide statistics on rural and urban populations, on the number and size of cities, and on indices of urbanization and change, all made comparable in regard to time.

The introductory chapters acquaint the reader with the contents and underlying methodology of the tables. In addition, each major table is preceded by a separate explanation of its particular data. In Table A, furthermore, there is a three-digit code that helps one to assess the quality of the data for each country, and at the end of the volume there are "Notes on Special Sources, Definitions, and Procedures for Particular Countries."

With the explanations and codes provided, the reader can utilize and interpret the data in the tables. The book thus stands by itself. However, as the title page indicates, it is the first volume of a two-volume series. The companion volume is devoted to an analysis of the data contained in the tables--an analysis emphasizing the world as a whole and the relation of urbanization to economic development.

Some Principles Underlying the Effort

There are a few guidelines, or principles, concerning the nature and purpose of the task which underlie our effort to provide basic information on world urbanization. Three of these merit discussion before I turn to more specific questions concerning methods and procedures.

World Coverage

One idea concerns the desirability of world coverage. Years ago, when I was at Columbia University, I felt that the study of urbanization, like many other fundamental processes of change in human society, requires at least some basic information that covers the entire world. Otherwise, the investigator is forced to deal with selected samples without a basis for judging their degree of bias. My studies of broad aspects of urbanization have thus long been designed to provide at least certain basic information on a global scale.[1]

The achievement of world coverage, however, poses problems. Since data on the location of people come mainly from censuses, the first difficulty is that some countries have not had a census. This is true of fewer countries than is commonly supposed,[2] but unfortunately the question is not simply whether or not the country has had a census. Even the countries that have had a census may not have had enough of them, or had them at the right time or for the right population. Comparison requires a proper basis, and the study of change requires serial information.

Since census-taking is not universal and since countries that do take censuses take them on different dates, world coverage entails a great amount of estimation if the data are to be comparable as to time and suitable for the study of change. The

---

[1]Some previous studies growing out of this effort are the following: "The World Distribution of Urbanization" (with Hilda Hertz), Bulletin of the International Statistical Institute, Vol. 33 (1951), Part 4, pp. 227-242; "Urbanization and the Development of Pre-Industrial Areas" (with Hilda Hertz), Economic Development and Cultural Change, Vol. 3 (October 1954), pp. 6-26; "The Origin and Growth of Urbanization in the World," American Journal of Sociology, Vol. 60 (March 1955) pp. 429-437; "Conventional versus Metropolitan Data in the International Study of Urbanization" (with Jack P. Gibbs), American Sociological Review, Vol. 23 (October 1958), pp. 504-514; The World's Metropolitan Areas (with others; Berkeley: University of California Press, 1959); "The Urbanization of the Human Population," Scientific American, Vol. 213 (September 1965), pp. 40-53.

[2]During the period 1945-54 approximately 78 per cent of the world's inhabitants were enumerated at least once in a national census, and during the period 1955-64 approximately 67 per cent were so enumerated, according to the United Nations Demographic Yearbook, 1962, p. 1. The decline in the percentage from the earlier to the later period is due to China. More countries took a census around 1960 than did so around 1950, but the fact that the world's biggest country, Mainland China, took a census in 1953 but did not take one around 1960 greatly inflated the proportion of the earth's population enumerated "around 1950" compared to "around 1960."

investigator must be willing to take some risks. He must be prepared to use estimates liberally, both those made by others (officially or unofficially) and those made by himself.

Not all urban phenomena are equally subject to estimation. Estimates of individual city populations are more numerous and easier to make, for example, than estimates of a nation's total urban population. Again, estimates of the sheer number of people in a country or a city are easier to find, or to make, than estimates of the peoples' characteristics, such as their age and sex distribution. Accordingly, in the effort of our research office to gain world coverage, we have confined ourselved to certain types of urban data for which such coverage is feasible-- that is, for which estimates could be found or made with some chance of being near the truth. The types of data contained in the tables are described in the next section below. Despite their limited range, they represent indispensable information. They provide the broadest facts about urbanization and cities, and thus offer a framework, or background, for other facts and questions. In other words, the basic data which are in these tables form a logical prerequisite to any comparative study of urbanization, regardless of how narrow the questions or how diversified the additional data incorporated. Also, the world- wide tables afford a means of judging the representativeness of any limited sample of countries.

Comparability in Time

A second leading idea--genuine comparability as to time-- became an operating principle of the project early in 1965. At that time, after many years of checking on the character and speed of world urbanization, I decided that not only world coverage, but world coverage at particular common dates, was desirable. It was then that work on the series of tables pub- lished here began.

Previously, my practice and that of other investigators was to compile urban data for different countries at approxi- mately the same date. This procedure made it possible to use data from censuses in different countries even though the enum- erations were not for the same year. This practice had serious drawbacks, however. It made it difficult to compare rates of change, to summarize data for entire regions or for the world as a whole, or to determine when complete coverage had or had not been achieved.

Although the advantages of common dates for international data are indisputable, in practice the task proves burdensome. It causes less trouble and delay than the other requirement, world coverage, but it does entail a large amount of estimation.

3

Critical Data Assemblage

A third guideline underlying the present work is that international data suitable for comparative research cannot be assembled in an off-hand manner but must be scrutinized and, when necessary, rejected or adjusted. Because electronic computers make the manipulation of data relatively cheap in time and money, the demand for data to put into the computers has grown commensurately. The demand is sometimes met on an indiscriminate basis. Investigators may take the entries they find in various compendia, such as the Demographic Yearbook or the Statistical Yearbook of the United Nations and subject the data to statistical manipulation without critical assessment. The footnotes in the secondary source may be ignored; the entries may all be assumed to be equally valid; the omission of countries for which no entries are given may cause no anxiety. The uncritical use of international statistics encourages the multiplication of data banks and tertiary collections drawn from secondary sources. By what might be called the "law of false purification of transferred data," the more a given statistic gets transferred from one publication to another, the more it tends to lose any qualifications it had to start with, and the more the conclusions drawn from it seem laws of nature.[3]

The tables in this volume doubtless contain many errors but they represent at least an effort in responsible data assemblage. The figures taken from others have been checked and accepted, rejected or adjusted. Our estimates and projections have been examined by more than one person and checked against alternative possibilities. Attention has been paid to internal consistency, and the process of assembling and utilizing the data has been linked with work on the theory and concepts of urbanization. An effort has been made to give an account of our methods of estimation and projection, and to code the data so as to give an idea of the trustworthiness of the information for each country. Our aim is to make comparative research on urbanization as exact as possible.

------

[3]Further remarks on international data for comparative research will be found in K. Davis, "Problems and Solutions in International Comparison for Social Science Purposes," Population Reprint Series, No. 273 (University of California, Institute of International Studies, 1968). First published in Spanish in America Latina (Jan.-March 1965).

The Content of the Tables

As mentioned above, each of the eight major data tables is preceded by an "Explanation." The present section is not meant to repeat the explanations but instead to give a brief view of the material in the entire series of tables.

The first thing to note is that the figures in the series can be classified on two different axes. First, there are absolute versus relative figures. The relative figures are rates, ratios, and proportions derived solely from the absolute figures in the tables. In turn, the absolute figures themselves are of two kinds: prime data and derived data. The prime data are the initial inputs assembled as the basis for everything else, while the derived figures are obtained from the prime data by subtraction or addition. The rates and ratios are based on absolute numbers of both kinds, being obtained from them by some kind of formula involving division. All of the absolute figures, whether prime or derived, are given for all three dates, and so are the relative figures except for the rates of change which are given for each of the two decades. Let us describe the absolute and the relative figures separately.

Absolute Figures

The prime data for each country consist of the following: the area (in square kilometers), the total population, the urban population, the population of each city of 100,000 or more. The absolute figures which are derived from these prime entries are the rural population, the town population, the total city population, the number of cities, the number and population of cities by size-class. The absolute figures for each country are summed to get totals for each region.

Schematically organized, the absolute figures in the tables can be represented by the diagram on the following page. Only the items in capital letters are prime data, the other numbers being derived from them.

With this diagram, one can readily see how the derived figures are obtained from the prime entries. The rural figure is obtained by subtracting the urban population from the total population. The town population is obtained by subtracting the total city population from the total urban population. Since we define a city as a place having 100,000 or more inhabitants, this means that what we call towns are urban places having less than 100,000. We did not compile data on individual towns because such places are not only more numerous than large ones, but also

DATA INCLUDED IN TABLES FOR EACH COUNTRY AND REGION

AREA	TOTAL POPULATION										
	Rural Population	TOTAL URBAN POPULATION									
		Class I "Towns"	Cities								
			INDIVIDUAL CITIES (100,000+)			Number of Cities			Population of Cities		
			NAME	TYPE	POPULATION	Class II	Class III	Class IV	Class II	Class III	Class IV

Class I: Under 100,000; Class II: 100,000–500,000;
Class III: 500,000–1,000,000; Class IV: 1,000,000+.

6

more difficult to find data for or to estimate in the absence of data. We therefore have to content ourselves with giving the combined population of all towns in each country, derived as indicated. On the other side of the urban category--the cities, or places of 100,000 or more--the information is sufficiently available to allow the individual places to be identified. Our tables thus give for each country the name and population of each city of 100,000 or more, as well as their combined population. Furthermore, we can sum up, for each country and region, the number of cities and the city population falling in each size-class. To avoid clumsy column headings, we have adopted the convention of designating the four urban size-classes referred to in the tables by Roman numerals. Class I embraces the towns (all urban places under 100,000 in population); Class II, the cities of 100,000 to 500,000; Class III, the cities of 500,000 to 1,000,000; and Class IV, the cities of 1,000,000 or more.

It is possible to derive more absolute figures from our prime data than are shown in the tables. For instance, the countries can be grouped in other ways than by regions, and sums computed for the new groupings; or the regions can be combined into continental areas, or redivided into different regions. An investigator can, of course, use the data in whatever way he wishes, in accord with his special interests.

Rates and Ratios

The potential use of the absolute figures is not fully realized until one examines the various indices, rates, ratios, and equations that can be derived from the absolute figures. The tables in the present volume contain only a few of the extremely numerous relative values that can be derived. Some of these are standard measures of one or another aspect of urbanization.

The relative data in the tables fall into four classes. First there are the proportions: the percentage of the total population which lives in rural places, in all urban places, in towns, in all cities, in each of three size-classes of city. Second there are the growth rates: the growth of the total, rural, urban, town, city, city-class, and individual city populations during each of the two decades, 1950-60 and 1960-70. Third there are the density averages: the average density of the entire population in the country or region, and the approximate average density of the rural population. Fourth there are the special indices: the rank of each of the hundred largest cities in the world and the degree of primacy of the biggest city in each country.

Most of these relative measures require no explanation, but
some do. The growth rates are calculated geometrically; they show
the average annual percentage increase during the given decade.
The approximate rural density, which is the rural population divided by the entire national territory, is a very rough indicator
of man-land relationships in the non-urban sphere. It is a less
valuable measure than agricultural density, but unfortunately the
latter cannot be derived from our data, whereas the approximate
rural density can be. Finally, there is the index of first-city
primacy, which is obtained by dividing the population of the
biggest city in each country by the combined population of the
next three. Our office has computed this index only for those
countries that have four or more cities of 100,000 or more.

The Sources of the Data

Since all the other figures in the tables are derived from
the prime data, the question of sources concerns only the prime
entries. As might be guessed, a great many of the prime figures
do not come directly from any source: they are estimates or projections made by us. When I speak of sources, then, I am speaking of the documents from which we obtained either the entries
found in our tables or other figures which we used in estimating
or computing the entries.

Our first source in assembling the prime data was the
Demographic Yearbook of the United Nations. This fundamental
compendium of international information publishes figures for
the total area of each country, midyear estimates for the total
population, and, for countries that have had censuses, figures
on the urban population (along with the "urban" definition).
It also publishes census data and official estimates of the population of all national capitals, regardless of size, and of all
other cities of 100,000 or more. In doing so, it gives the
population for both the city proper and the urban agglomeration
when these are available. Finally, the Yearbook occasionally
includes grouped data for the population of inhabited localities
classified by size, along with a code indicating the type of
"locality." At times this information helps us to determine
the urban population when other data are lacking. All told,
the Demographic Yearbook has proved an invaluable source.

For additional data we have turned to other secondary
sources, such as The Statesman's Yearbook, America en Cifras,
Outre Mer, The World's Metropolitan Areas, the United Nations'
Population and Vital Statistics Report, and other international
compendia and atlases, including those devoted to particular
regions. Very often, in addition, we found ourselves consulting

8

the statistical documents of the country in question--census volumes, national statistical yearbooks, provincial or city yearbooks, and demographic articles and monographs. Frequently one source was checked against another.

In its working tables and notes, the research staff carried along a reference to the source for every figure. This made possible the two quality codes given in Table A. It also helped in the preparation of the "Special Notes" at the end of the volume, where sources with respect to problematic cases are generally mentioned.

In the nature of the case, since this volume is being published in 1969, all of our 1970 figures are projections. These were entirely made in our research office on the basis of the most recent data we could find in December, 1968. The methodology and procedures for making the projections are described in Chapter III. As for the 1950 and 1960 figures, they are of course census figures whenever possible, but since a majority of the world's countries did not take a census in those exact years, the figures are mostly estimates. Except for the figures on the total population of each country, which come mostly from the Demographic Yearbook, the overwhelming majority of the 1950 and 1960 estimates are our own. The raw materials for making the estimates come from the types of sources mentioned above, but the mode of dealing with the materials varied according to the exigencies of each case at hand. The methodology and procedures for making the projections are described in Chapter III; first, however, the problems of defining terms must be discussed.

Chapter II

PROBLEMS OF DEFINITION

A book providing information on urban phenomena must necessarily pay attention to the meaning of terms describing those
phenomena. Although adequate conceptual definitions cannot be
conveyed apart from a theoretical frame of reference and are
therefore dealt with in the second volume, the operational definitions can be discussed here. The two key terms are the <u>urban</u>
population and the <u>city</u> population.

The Definition of "Urban"

There are two standard criticisms of the traditional urban
definition. One is that it varies from one country to another
and thus renders the data non-comparable. The second is that it
turns a continuum into a dichotomy and thus oversimplifies and
distorts comparisons of the degree of urbanization. Both criticisms need serious consideration. Let us begin with the second
one.

The Dichotomy Criticism

Whatever its social meaning, there can be no doubt that the
urbanity of a place is at least partially a function of its size,
and vice versa. Since human settlements vary in size from isolated farmsteads to huge city agglomerations, they vary also in
how urban they are. It is obviously arbitrary, therefore, to
designate a single point in the continuum as the dividing line
between rural and urban. It is like employing "literacy" as a
measure of the degree of education. Nevertheless, this is what
the so-called "urban definition" does, as ordinarily conceived.
Stipulating the smallest place that will be called urban, it
relegates all lesser settlements to the rural category and all
greater ones to the urban class. Frequently, however, additional
criteria are introduced. For instance, places "having an urban
character" or "enjoying a political status" as the capital of a
district or province may be treated as urban regardless of size,
while other places are included only if they reach or exceed the
minimum size. Such additional criteria may be realistic and
useful, but they do not meet the fundamental criticism that a

10

dichotomy is being used when a continuum actually exists. Even
if political functions are recognized as conveying urban status,
it is still true that some political towns have more political
functions than others.

There is no definitive answer to the criticism. All that
can be said is that the dichotomy is useful for some purposes
but, due to its deficiencies, not for all purposes. We commonly
use dichotomous measurements and find them useful, even though
reality presents us with a scale. A person "has a fever" or he
does not have a fever. It is raining or it is not raining. Life
would be difficult without such simple devices, and so would the
study of urbanization. In most cases there are additional indices and measurements if we need to go further in the matter,
and that is certainly true in the field of knowledge considered
here. Our data on cities represent a supplementary body of information about urbanization. We do not have to depend solely
upon the urban-rural dichotomy.

Comparability of "Urban"

The other criticism, to the effect that the urban definition
varies from one country to another, is more serious from the
standpoint of comparative study. Fortunately, it is open to em-
pirical test with precisely the kind of materials we have in our
tables. Admittedly, no one could claim that our data on the urban population, or anyone else's for that matter, are strictly
comparable among different countries. They are not exactly comparable and should not be used to compare individual nations
without taking the definitions into account. On the other hand,
it would be a mistake to exaggerate the degree of incomparability
or to reject the data entirely as having no utility. The toler-
ance-level for international differences of definition differs
markedly with the particular research purpose at hand. It
therefore pays to ask just how comparable the urban data are.
To try to answer this question with respect to our data, I shall
first explain our actual procedures and then examine the evidence
as contained in the results of applying the urban definition code.

IPUR's Preference for the National Definition. The practice
in our office has been to accept each country's own definition of
"urban" unless there is reason to believe it is a clear distortion. In other words, we have not sought to impose a uniform
minimum size on the data. Our reason for this is not solely
convenience but also fidelity to the truth. The smallest place
which has what are ordinarily regarded as urban characteristics
--commerce, modern industry, predominantly non-agricultural
employment--does in fact vary according to the national economic
and demographic situation. For instance, cultivation of rich

and well watered (often irrigated) land by labor-intensive methods, in countries that are densely populated and economically underdeveloped, typically produces large agricultural villages, the population of which may well exceed 4,000 or even 5,000. On the other hand, a highly industrial country with well-capitalized agriculture may have towns of only a few hundred inhabitants which are nevertheless commercially and industrially developed and hence urban in the usual social and economic meaning of that term. Since countries tend to exercise some common sense in their statistical services, their own mode of classifying their people deserves respect. Only in extreme or bizarre cases, then, do we feel we should alter the official definition.

The Urban Definition Code and What It Shows

Concerning each country's definition of "urban," there are three questions that can be asked: First, does the country have a a formal definition, or is the definition unknown or of such a character (e.g., an indirect estimate) that it cannot be specified? Second, if the country has a known definition, does the definition state a minimum size of place that is to be called urban? Third, if a minimum size is stated, what is the minimum?

Years ago the United Nations discussed the comparability of urban definitions[1] but, to my knowledge, did not differentiate these three questions and made no tabulation of countries with respect to them. In the present study we have coded each country in a manner designed to answer the questions. (The urban-definition code is the last digit in the three-digit code under the name of each country in Table A.) The results of the coding are of considerable interest.

Countries With and Without an Urban Definition. The first question is answered by Code No. 9 versus the rest of the code numbers. This number, the last item at the "worst" end of the scale, designates countries for which no definition could be found or for which, due to the nature of the estimate, no definition could be implied or assumed. Many of these were countries which had no census and hence no data to which a definition could be applied. As the accompanying table (Table 1) shows, there were 19 countries, nearly 9 per cent of all countries, that

---

[1] Demographic Yearbook, 1952, pp. 9-11. See also, Data on Urban and Rural Population in Recent Censuses (Lake Success: United Nations, 1950). The latter publication was too early to include analyses of definitions used in censuses taken around 1950.

Table 1

CODING OF WORLD'S COUNTRIES WITH RESPECT TO URBAN
DEFINITION, 1950 AND 1960

| Code Number | Definition of "Urban" | COUNTRIES[1] | | POPULATION | | | |
		Number	Per Cent	1950 (000's)	Per Cent	1960 (000's)	Per Cent
0	Under 1,000	4	1.9	15,046	0.6	17,483	0.6
1	1,000 - 1,999	7	3.3	38,816	1.6	49,886	1.6
2	2,000 - 2,999	27	12.6	430,180	17.2	504,919	16.8
3	3,000 - 4,999	11	5.1	21,864	0.9	27,980	0.9
4	5,000 - 7,499	21	9.8	551,423	22.0	667,316	22.2
5	7,500 - 9,999	1	0.5	999	----	1,349	----
6	10,000 - 19,999	1	0.5	27,977	1.1	30,431	1.0
7	20,000+	1	0.5	83,419	3.3	93,419	3.1
8	Minimum not stated or not available	122	57.0	1,194,678	47.8	1,439,360	47.8
9	No definition; indirect estimate	19	8.9	137,492	5.5	180,516	6.0
TOTAL		214	100.0	2,501,894	100.0	3,012,659	100.0

[1] The countries have the same code in 1950 and 1960. However, there are subcategories of Code No. 8 that involve a difference of one country (see Table 3).

received Code No. 9. However, they were in general small countries, and this meant that they comprised a smaller proportion of the world's population than they comprised of the world's nations. From the standpoint of having a definition, then, the data are in better shape than might have been expected.

Definitions With and Without a Minimum Size. Omitting the countries without a definition, we can now ask about the ones among the remainder which fail to specify a minimum size of urban place. Such countries were coded No. 8, and from Table 1 it looks as though they numbered 122 or a whopping 63 per cent of the 195 countries that had an urban definition. It also looks as though in both 1950 and 1960 they embraced 51 per cent of the combined population in countries with an urban definition. However, there are two facts not shown in Table 1 which modify this finding. One is that China is among the countries coded No. 8. There is evidence that China does not adhere to any size-limit rigidly but does have in mind a flexible limit of 2,000.[2] If we code China No. 2 instead of No. 8, without making any other change, then the countries without a size-limit in their urban definition had only 27 per cent of the combined population in all countries having an urban definition at all. The other qualification about Code No. 8 is that it includes all the countries that were 100-per-cent urban or 100-per-cent rural. These are countries for which a lower size-limit to the urban category is not relevant, and they numbered 28 in 1950 and 27 in 1960.[3] Although these are

---

[2]Ullman cites an official publication stating in 1955 that towns of fewer than 2,000 inhabitants may be classified as urban if their inhabitants are engaged in commerce and industry. Later, however, to judge by another publication he cites, the tendency was to define small towns as urban only when they have a town government. The 1953 census classed 920 towns of less than 2,000 as urban, with a combined population of 1.2 million. This was slightly more than 2 per cent of the entire urban population. Morris B. Ullman, Cities of Mainland China: 1953 and 1958 (Washington, D.C.: Bureau of the Census, Series P-95, No. 59, August 1961), pp. 4-10.

[3]They were distributed in 1960 as follows:

	Number of Countries	Population (Millions)
100-per-cent Urban	8	5.12
100-per-cent Rural	19	2.66

small countries and thus do not greatly influence the population distribution, they obviously have an important effect on the sheer proportion of countries not having a size-limit in their definition. The findings with respect to size-limit versus no size-limit in the urban definition of relevant countries can be summarized as follows for 1960. The proportions for 1950 are almost identical.

	Countries	Population (Millions)
With China Coded 8		
All Relevant Countries	168	2,824.4
With Minimum Size	73	1,392.8
Per Cent with Minimum Size	43.5	49.3
With China Coded 2		
All Relevant Countries	168	2,824.4
With Minimum Size	74	2,062.8
Per Cent with Minimum Size	44.0	73.0

In sum, among the relevant countries with definitions, the proportion with a stipulated minimum size is substantial, especially when viewed in terms of population.

Concentration of Size-Limits Among Countries with Size Definitions. If the comparability of definitions with respect to the size of the smallest place admitted as "urban" is to be gauged, it can be done only with the countries that do in fact specify a minimum size in their urban definition. These are the countries coded 0 through 7, and as we have just shown there are 73 of them (74, if China is counted).

Among these countries it turns out that the minimal sizes are concentrated within a narrow range. Some 80 per cent of the countries, representing 86 per cent of the entire population of the group of 73, define urban places in such a way as to be coded 2, 3, or 4. In other words, the overwhelming majority of countries with a minimum-size urban definition specify a minimum somewhere within the range from 2,000 to 7,500 inhabitants (see Table 2, opposite).

If China is given code 2, the proportion of countries whose minima fall within the 2,000 to 7,500 range is raised to 81 per

15

Table 2

DISTRIBUTION OF COUNTRIES WITH A MINIMUM SIZE IN
THEIR URBAN DEFINITION, 1950 AND 1960

Code Number	Definition of "Urban"	Percentage of Countries [1]	PERCENTAGE OF POPULATION [1] 1950	1960
0	Under 1,000	5.5	1.3	1.3
1	1,000 - 1,999	9.6	3.3	3.6
2	2,000 - 2,999	35.6	35.8	35.2
3	3,000 - 4,999	15.1	1.9	2.0
4	5,000 - 7,499	28.8	47.1	47.9
5	7,500 - 9,999	1.4	0.1	0.1
6	10,000 - 19,999	1.4	2.4	2.2
7	20,000+	2.7	8.1	7.7
TOTAL		100.0	100.0	100.0

[1] The absolute figures for each of the seven codes are
given in Table 1. The total number of countries coded with
one or the other of the first seven codes is 73; their total
population in 1950 was 1,169,723,500; and in 1960 it was
1,392,783,000.

16

cent, and the proportion of the population is raised to 90 per cent.

With or without China, our finding bespeaks more inter-national comparability in the urban definition than is generally recognized. There is little reason to believe that among the countries for which we could find no definition in quantitative terms (countries coded No. 8) or for which the nature of the estimate allowed no specific definition (countries coded No. 9) the situation is much different. In most of them the "urban population" is probably in fact equal to the number of people living in places above a size that falls somewhere between 2,000 and 7,500.

Just how comparable this clustering of minima makes the various nations, however, depends on the significance of the 2,000-to-7,500 range. If a large portion of the urban population falls in that range, then two countries may each have a minimum within the range and yet have their apparent difference in degree of urbanization be heavily influenced by the difference in defi-nition. To test this possibility, we can take the United States in 1910 as being somewhat typical of the world as a whole today with respect to urbanization. At that date the urban population --defined as the inhabitants of places of 2,500 and over--was 45.7 per cent of the total United States population.[4] If the definition had been different, restricting the urban category to places of 7,500 and over, the proportion urban would have been approximately 39 per cent. The difference is substantial, but it introduces an error of only seven percentage points. In Ireland in 1956, the proportion urban when "urban" is defined as towns of 2,000 or over was 43.2 per cent; when "urban" is defined as towns of 7,500 and over, the proportion was 35.8 per cent.[5] Again the difference is substantial, but it is only one-fourteenth of the entire urbanization scale. The reason the difference is not greater is that the fraction of the population living in places in the 2,000-to-7,500 range is small. In the United States in 1910, the proportion of the population who lived in towns of 2,500 to 7,500 was 6.3 per cent; in Ireland in 1956 the propor-tion in towns of 2,000 to 7,500 was 7.4 per cent.

---

[4]Computed from Statistical Abstract of the United States, 1946, p. 13.

[5]Computed from United Nations Demographic Yearbook, 1962, p. 389.

Actually, the differences in the minimum-size definitions may reflect, at least in part, variations among countries in the relation of urban characteristics to sheer size. If a country with big rural villages does not call a place urban until it reaches 5,000 inhabitants, while a country with small urban towns calls them urban if they have 2,000 people, who is to say that the definitions differ? While no one would contend that there is an underlying standard concept of "urban" expressing itself in all countries, it nevertheless seems probable that the definitions have more similarity, in a socio-economic sense, than reliance upon a universally fixed numerical definition would provide.

Utility of the Rural-Urban Data. We conclude that the objuctions to using the rural-urban dichotomy in comparative international study, although in part true and deserving of attention, are not so devastating as to require abandonment of the data. To ignore rural-urban statistics because they have deficiencies would be a case of throwing the baby out with the bath. Although individual countries should not be compared with one another without looking at their definitions, the data on the rural-urban division are useful in comparing regions and in comparing countries grouped according to cultural and/or economic characteristics. With the definition code provided in Table A, it is possible to discern whether or not there is a systematic bias in group comparisons and, if there is, to work out an approximate correction for it. Furthermore, the data on the urban population are extremely useful in analyzing social and economic change, either for a single country or for a region or a class of countries. Census officials tend to use the same definition of "urban" fairly consistently in successive censuses; in our data we have made a strenuous effort to keep the definition constant for the three dates included.

As stated already, the degree of urbanization in a country need not be judged solely by the proportion of its population stated to be urban. The population in cities not only offers additional information about the urban structure but also provides an alternative index of the degree of urbanization. When data on cities are used in conjunction with statistics on the rural-urban distribution, the two kinds of information afford a double check on the validity of comparisons.

The Definition of "City"

Cities, however, present their own problem of operational definition. The problem is not a lack of a standard minimum size; we have solved that issue by arbitrarily defining a city as any place with 100,000 or more inhabitants. We could have

set the minimum at 50,000 or even at 20,000, but we wanted information on _individual_ cities as well as on cities collectively,
and such information, as indicated in Chapter I, is hard to
obtain or to estimate for places below 100,000.

The real problem in defining a city concerns the boundary.
When a town has fewer than 100,000 people, it normally has municipal boundaries that come near to including all of the town's
inhabitants, with the consequence that the political entity can
be safely taken as the demographic and ecological unit. In such
a town land is still comparatively cheap and the municipal
boundaries have usually been generously drawn or redrawn; furthermore, the center is not very crowded or overtaxed, with the result that citizens have not been driven to move out beyond the
city limits. In the main urban settlements, however, the growth
of population and technology that has characterized most nations
and cities in modern times has long since caused the old political
boundaries to be overrun. In these settlements people have
sought to escape overcrowding and higher taxes in the central city
by moving to nearby satellite areas, and often this process has
resulted in the coalescence of what were once separate towns or
cities. The process of suburbanization has gone further in
countries with a high level of living, because advanced technology does two things: it allows continued participation in
city life even when one's residence is miles away, and it encourages dispersal by increasing the noise, congestion and
pollution at the center. Although local and national controls
over land ownership and housing may dampen the centrifugal
movement, the pressures are such that the movement tends to occur
anyway in one form or another, and it is particularly character-
istic of the larger places.

The fact that it is mainly larger places that are affected
by the transcendance of political boundaries can be illustrated
by data from the United States, the country where suburbanization
is most unrestrained and abundant. The Bureau of the Census in
this country delimits urbanized areas, which are composed of one
or more central (political) cities having a population of 50,000
or more, together with "surrounding closely settled incorporated
places and unincorporated areas" that meet certain criteria of
density and contiguity.[6] The minimum possible size of these
"urbanized areas" is, by definition, 50,000. By publishing
figures on both the central city (or city proper) and the surrounding "fringe," the census shows where the spillover from city

---

[6]Census of Population, 1960, Vol. 1, Part A, _Number of
Inhabitants_, p. xviii.

boundaries is greatest. The figures according to the magnitude of population in the whole urbanized area are shown in the second column of the accompanying table (Table 3).

The Urbanized Area versus the Metropolitan Area

Our preference would of course be to provide data on urbanized areas for the whole world—that is, to give for each city the population of its entire zone of actual urban settlement more or less as the United States does with its "Urbanized Area" concept. This unit, which we abbreviate as "UA," would include the whole population centered on the central city, or city proper (abbreviated as "CP"). It would include the urban population interacting on a day-to-day basis, as judged by such criteria as density, contiguity, daily movement, and occupational structure. However, even the United States census, which pioneered in this effort, has found this concept difficult to apply because the boundaries shift continuously. It has also been of limited analytic usefulness because the boundaries correspond with no other units for which statistical data are available. The Census Bureau has consequently maintained and put to more use another type of unit, the "Standard Metropolitan Statistical Area," which is composed of political areas (counties) that surround the central city and meet certain criteria. This is an easier concept to apply, because the boundaries of the subunits remain fixed and do not have to be redelimited at every census; but it has the disadvantage that some rural people are inevitably included in the metropolitan area, whereas this is not the case, at least theoretically, with the urbanized area. The difference in population between the UA and the MA delimitation for the same unit is noramlly not great, precisely because the extra rural people included in the MA are not densely settled compared to the urban mass. Certainly the difference is not normally so large as the difference between the central city, or city proper, and either the MA or the UA.[7] But the main point is that the urbanized area concept, though preferable in principle, is so difficult to apply that we could not expect most countries to provide data in terms of it.

---

[7] These concepts and the problems of application have been more fully discussed in K. Davis et al., The World's Metropolitan Areas (Berkeley: University of California Press, 1959), pp. 6-33. That book gives the results of an effort to delimit MA's for as many of the world's cities as possible for dates around 1950.

Table 3

PROPORTION OF POPULATION IN THE "FRINGE" OF UNITED STATES
"URBANIZED AREAS" AND "STANDARD METROPOLITAN STATISTICAL
AREAS," BY SIZE OF AREA

Population of the UA or the SMSA	URBANIZED AREAS		METROPOLITAN AREAS	
	Number of Areas	Per Cent of Population in Fringe	Number of Areas	Per Cent of Population in Fringe
50,000 to 75,000	30	8.8	8	12.7
75,000 to 100,000	30	18.7	14	27.5
100,000 to 250,000	85	28.5	89	43.2
250,000 to 500,000	31	36.2	48	51.0
500,000 to 1,000,000	21	36.5	29	47.3
1,000,000 to 3,000,000	11	51.5	19	57.4
3,000,000+	5	43.3	5	43.9

Source: United States, Census of Population, 1960, Vol. 1,
Part A, Number of Inhabitants, pp. xxvi, 1-40 to 1-49, 1-117 to
1-118. The "fringe" is defined as that part of the UA or of the
SMSA lying outside the central city or cities.

Many countries do attempt to designate a larger unit than
the city proper, but in doing so they apparently pursue the easier
path of delimiting it in terms of ready-made fixed political
areas which surround or are contiguous to the central city and
usually are more extensive than the total urbanized zone.
Accordingly, although these larger units are frequently called
by some such term as "Urban Agglomerations" or "Greater Such
and Such," they appear to approximate the MA rather than the UA
concept. One indication that they are really MA's is that the
fringe often has a higher proportion of the alleged UA's total
population when the unit is small than when it is large. This
should not occur in UA's, as was shown above, but may easily
occur in MA delimitations because MA's, by including surrounding
and contiguous territory, inevitably include rural inhabitants.
When the central city is small, the added rural areas frequently
loom large in relation to it, whereas if the central city is big,
the rural areas do not have much weight, relatively speaking.
This point is partially illustrated in Table 3, already referred
to, where the percentage of fringe inhabitants is much greater
in the SMSA's (as seen in the last column) than it is in the
UA's, especially in the smaller size-classes. In the American
MA's the fringe proportion is not negatively associated with the
size of the MA, but its positive association is less close and
less regular than it is for the UA's. In certain other countries,
as will be seen in a moment, the fringe proportion declines
steeply as the size of the alleged UA gets greater.

The United Nations, in giving the population (when available) of capital cities and of all cities of 100,000 or more,
provides data for both the city proper and for the greater urban
zone when both can be obtained. It calls the greater urban zone
an "Urban Agglomeration." I have gone along with this usage,
changing the name to "Urbanized Area" (which fortunately has the
same initials), but I have done so with misgivings because of my
belief that most of these UA's are in fact metropolitan areas of
one sort or another. The Demographic Yearbook tries to alert the
reader to the cases in which the UA data are of a metropolitan
character, but in numerous instances it evidently lacks information on the exact composition of the wider urban unit. The
United Nations clearly has a preference for the kind of unit I
call an urbanized area, because its definition is as follows:

The urban agglomeration has been defined as including
the suburban fringe or thickly settled territory lying
outside of, but adjacent to, the city boundaries.[8]

---

[8]Demographic Yearbook, 1967, p. 24.

I have the same preference but must acknowledge that many of the
units designated as UA's in the tables in this volume, a majority
of them taken from the Demographic Yearbook, are actually MA's.
In a sizable number of cases this use of MA data is deliberate;
if we have no UA information, strictly defined, but do have what
we know are MA data, the latter is used.[9] The practice is jus-
tifiable because, if the MA is competently delimited, the error
involved is not great. In nearly all cases the error of taking
an MA for a UA is far less than taking a City Proper for either
one. An attempt to standardize the city units completely would
have delayed this publication by years. Needless to say, an
effort has been made to spot and modify overextended "Urban
Agglomerations." References to procedures used in problem cases
will be found in the "Special Notes" at the end of the volume.

Indirect evidence that the UA's as listed in the Demographic
Yearbook are often in fact MA's can be obtained by seeing whether
or not the proportion in the fringe rises as the size of the
alleged UA declines. By this test, South Africa's UA's are well
delimited, those of Holland are questionable, and those of Turkey
are poorly delimited, as the following tabulation shows:[10]

PER CENT IN FRINGE

Population of "UA"	Turkey (1965)	South Africa (1960)	Netherlands (1966)
Over 500,000	14.6	37.0	23.2
200,000 to 500,000	29.8	24.4	38.9
Under 200,000	39.6	13.2	20.3

The relative importance of the fringe surely depends not
only on how the surrounding zone is extended but also on how the
City Proper, or central city, is delimited. The city proper may
be an old walled area that has not been changed for centuries, or
it may be one that was recently determined. If recently

---

[9]For example, much use was made of the MA delimitations in
our book, The World's Metropolitan Areas, for information per-
taining to 1950.

[10]Computed from the Demographic Yearbook, 1967, Table 6.

determined, the reason may be that the city is new or that the government wanted the boundaries to include the whole urbanized area. In either case, the fringe will be small in relation to the central city unless the entire so-called UA is delimited in an unreasonable manner. In some instances the city proper is ridiculously small, which makes the fringe absurdly large. According to the <u>Demographic Yearbook</u> for 1967, the city proper of Adelaide, Australia, had 18,580 inhabitants in 1966, while the total UA had 726,930. The city proper of Melbourne had 75,709, while its UA had 2,108,499. The "fringe" in Adelaide held 97.4 per cent of the urbanized area, and in Melbourne it held 96.4 per cent.

Our tables give only one population for each city.[11] This is the population of the UA whenever that population or an approximation to it could be found or estimated. Otherwise the CP population is given. In those tables that list the cities by name, an asterisk appears by the name of those that are UA's. Actually, the UA's constitute a majority, especially among the larger places. Of the total number of cities in the world with 100,000 or more inhabitants, 75 per cent were delimited as UA's in 1950, 72 per cent in 1960, 68 per cent in 1970. The proportion goes down slightly from one census to the next because of the rapid addition of new cities, many of which are in underdeveloped countries and many of which have not yet had time to have the UA area delimited. In terms of population, the proportion of city inhabitants who live in places delimited as UA's was 84 per cent in 1950, 82 in 1960 and 80 in 1970. The population is more weighted in the direction of UA's than is the number of places because it is the bigger urban aggregates that are more frequently designated as UA's.

---

[11]There were only a few exceptions when both were given in order to have comparable units at the beginning and end of each decade.

Chapter III

METHODS OF ESTIMATION FOR 1950 AND 1960

In discussing the sources of the data in Chapter I, I mentioned that most of the estimates for 1950 and 1960, at least for
the urban population, are our own, and that all of the projections
for 1970 are ours. The raw materials for making the estimates
and projections normally came from the types of sources previously
described. Although the mode of dealing with the raw materials
varied according to the exigencies of each case, there were nevertheless certain standard procedures that could be adopted in most
cases. When in particular instances the information available
did not allow application of these procedures, or when the procedures gave dubious or conflicting results, special stratagems
had to be used. In this chapter I shall describe the main methods
of estimating the 1950 and 1960 figures, when such estimates were
necessary. The next chapter will consider the methods of projection for 1970.

Methods of Making Estimates for 1950 and 1960

The necessity of making estimates for 1950 and 1960 arose
from the fact that countries frequently lack census data for one
or both of those years. This being the problem, our methods of
estimation centered chiefly on handling census data for other
years to derive approximate information for 1950 and 1960 and
dealing with cases having no census data at all. The procedures
can best be understood if each population category is dealt with
separately. I shall begin with the total population of each
nation.

The Total Population

In many ways the total population was the easiest statistic
to obtain, the reason being that the United Nations publishes
midyear estimates for most countries of the world. These are
usually official figures, but they may also be unofficial ones
calculated by the United Nations itself. Ordinarily we accepted
these midyear estimates for 1950 and 1960 when the country had
no census within the year. If the country did have a census in
the target year, we took the census figure regardless of the

25

time of year when it was taken. (In such cases, our urban data would be from the same census and hence would jibe in exact date with the total population.)

One type of problem occurred independently of whether or not there had been a census--namely, a change of the national boundaries. This problem was met in the present study by assigning each country its 1960 boundaries throughout. In general, we did not concern ourselves with the question of whether the population was de facto or de jure, but took the census figure or estimate as given in the source. However, we did make an effort to include all elements in the nation. Thus if a segment of the population--say, an ethnic or nationality group--was not included in the census, we tried to find an estimate of the size of that group, or made an estimate ourselves, so as to include it in the figure for the total population. A particularly difficult question arose when the country had officially estimated a certain percentage of underenumeration in its census. Whether or not such a "correction factor" was allowed depended on whether or not it made sense in the light of other data for the same country. The question of double-counting--when two countries apparently included the same people in their population--was less troublesome.

More serious than the problems just mentioned were the cases in which the official midyear estimates seemed to be unreasonable or in which no estimate was given at all. There were a number of cases in which the estimate for one year was incompatible with another, yielding rates of change impossible to explain. Furthermore, although in the 1967 Demographic Yearbook there were only five countries for which no population estimate for 1960 appeared, in the 1966 Yearbook--the most recent issue in which 1950 midyear estimates were published--there were 45 countries for which no population estimate was given for 1950. These various problem cases called for special treatment.

In a typical dubious case, the estimate for a given date would differ from one issue of the Demographic Yearbook to another, or the series in the Yearbook would have a bar at a certain certain date representing a break in the comparability of the series, or we ourselves would find a discontinuity. Such breaks could result from boundary changes, an alteration of the basis for estimation, or a failure to readjust old estimates after a census was finally taken. In some of these hard cases, especially if no census at all had ever been taken, our estimating procedure had to be largely guesswork; in other cases reasonable adjustments could be reached.

Fortunately, the problem cases with respect to the total population were relatively few. This can be seen by examining the distribution of the countries according to the total-population code.

The Total-Population Code. The code for the total population is the first digit in the code number under each country's name in Table A, and the code values are described in the explanation for that table. Briefly, the code states whether or not the national population figure is from a census for the year in question and, if not, how many years away from the nearest census it is. Failing any census at all, the code states whether the estimate is judged to be fairly good or quite uncertain. The best estimate can normally be made when two censuses are available; consequently, the code differentiates between the countries in which only one census could be used and those in which two or more were available; and, for both of these groups, it states how many years away the nearest census was. The code is meant to be graduated--that is, the most reliable figures are coded 0, the most unreliable are coded 8, with an approximate progression in between.

The distribution of the world's countries according to the total-population data code is shown for 1950 and 1960 in Table 4. The most interesting thing about the distribution, and one that is reassuring, is the heavy concentration of countries in the first three categories. In 1950 there were 145 countries that were coded 0, 1, or 2, meaning that they either had a census in 1950 or did not have one then but had the advantage of having had at least two censuses at other times, the closest one being four years or less from 1950. These 145 countries represented 68 per cent of all countries in 1950. In 1960 the picture was even better: the number of countries in the first three categories was 158, or 74 per cent of all the countries. If a country falls into one of the first three code categories, it is one in which the figure for the total population is likely to be reasonably accurate. In both 1950 and 1960, the concentration of the world's people in countries that have this good rating on the total-population scale was only slightly less than the concentration in sheer number of countries, as Table 5 brings out. At both dates over 60 per cent of the world's inhabitants lived in countries that fell in the first three codes.

At the other end of the scale there is a concentration of countries on Code No. 8. These are countries, mostly in Asia and Africa, for which the quality of the figure for the total population has to be regarded as very poor. Fortunately, these are mostly small countries. In 1950, although they constituted 11 per cent of all the countries in the world, they included only 3 per cent of the population; and in 1960 they comprised 10 per cent of the countries and 3 per cent of the population.

27

Table 4

DISTRIBUTION OF THE WORLD'S COUNTRIES ACCORDING
TO THE TOTAL-POPULATION CODE, 1950 AND 1960

Code Number	Meaning of Code	1950		1960	
		Number of Countries	Per Cent of all Countries	Number of Countries	Per Cent of all Countries
0	Census in year in question	54	25.2	77	36.0
1	Two censuses, closest 1-2 years from date	46	21.5	55	25.7
2	Ibid., closest 3-4 years	45	21.0	26	12.1
3	Ibid., closest 5+ years	14	6.5	4	1.9
4	One census, 1-2 years from date	2	0.9	8	3.7
5	One census, 3-4 years from date	4	1.9	5	2.3
6	One census, 5+ years from date	21	9.8	11	5.1
7	No census, fair estimate	5	2.3	7	3.3
8	No census, uncertain estimate	23	10.7	21	9.8
TOTAL		214	100.0	214	100.0

Table 5

DISTRIBUTION OF THE WORLD'S PEOPLE ACCORDING TO
THE TOTAL-POPULATION CODE, 1950 AND 1960

Code Number/1	1950		1960	
	Population (000's)	Per Cent of Total	Population (000's)	Per Cent of Total
0	543,153	21.7	760,231	25.2
1	722,358	28.9	973,362	32.3
2	208,479	8.3	131,872	4.4
3	96,555	3.9	21,314	0.7
4	1,863	0.1	230,245	7.6
5	561,054	22.4	42,086	1.4
6	266,864	10.7	727,543	24.1
7	21,276	0.9	28,599	0.9
8	80,293	3.2	97,407	3.2
TOTAL/2	2,501,894	100.0	3,012,659	100.0

1/ The meaning of the code is given in Table 3.

2/ The figures do not always add to totals because of
rounding.

29

Since China is one of the countries with only one census (taken in 1953), its influence on the distribution of the world's population with respect to the total-population code is to make the distribution somewhat worse than it would be if China were not included. Table 6 shows the proportion of the world's population falling in each code when China is removed. The omission reduces Code No. 5 in 1950 from 22.4 per cent to 0.05 per cent, and it reduces Code No. 6 in 1960 from 24.1 to 2.5 per cent.

Table 6

DISTRIBUTION OF THE WORLD'S PEOPLE ACCORDING TO THE
TOTAL-POPULATION CODE, 1950 AND 1960, WITHOUT CHINA

Code Number	PER CENT OF TOTAL POPULATION	
	1950	1960
0	28.0	32.5
1	37.2	41.6
2	10.7	5.6
3	5.0	0.9
4	0.1	9.8
5	0.1	1.8
6	13.7	2.5
7	1.1	1.2
8	4.1	4.2
TOTAL	100.0	100.0
BASE (000's)	1,941,894	2,342,659

On the other hand, removal of China substantially increases the percentage of the total population located in countries coded 0, 1, and 2, the good codes. It puts 76 per cent of the world's 1950 population and 80 per cent of the 1960 population in such countries.

Estimating the Urban Population in 1950 and 1960

The cases in which we had to make our own estimate of the total population were relatively few, but there were many in

30

which we had to estimate the _urban_ population. The reason is
that annual estimates of the urban population are not regularly
made by national statistical offices or published in statistical
abstracts and compendia, as is done with respect to the total
population.

The easiest type of case was one in which the target date
was bracketed by two censuses, because then, if both censuses
provided statistics on the urban population, the estimate could
be made by simple interpolation. Such interpolations were done
either with the absolute urban population or with the proportion
urban, depending on whether or not irregularities of growth could
have been expected in the total or the urban population due to
historical events.

If the target date was preceded by two censuses but not
followed by any census at all, or if it was followed by two censuses but not preceded by one that was close or accurate enough
to be used, we made an estimate by forward or backward extrapolation. The accuracy of these extrapolations is largely a function
of the length of time involved, which is a matter covered in the
urban-population code to be discussed in a moment.

In some cases the country in question had a census or two
but did not report on the urban population as such. In these
instances, if data were supplied on inhabited places by size, we
could define the urban population at the time of the census
according to our best judgment as to what the minimum size of
urban place in that country should be. If, however, the only
information available on specific places was for places too large
to permit this procedure--say, places 20,000 or more--we then
had to estimate the urban population at the census date on the
basis of a ratio of places that size to the total urban population. Such a ratio was usually obtained from data on a country
or countries roughly similar in character to the one under consideration.

If the country had had only one census, the lack of a trend
for extrapolation was a serious handicap in arriving at an estimate of the urban population. If the one census had occurred on
neither of the two target dates, then the difficulty arose with
respect to two estimates and not just one. The estimates made
with the help of only one census had two kinds of trend data to
serve as crutches: the growth of the total population (normally
not estimated by us) and estimates, censuses, or sample surveys
for one or more of the nation's larger cities or towns. We
assumed in principle that the urban population would not grow
more slowly than the total population nor faster than the big-
city population. Sometimes we took the ratio of urban to total

population growth as found in neighboring countries at a similar
level of development as a basis for estimating the urban growth
in the country at hand. If we had estimates or survey data on
the largest cities at other dates than the census, we could use
their growth as indicative of the trend of the entire urban population, but we modified that trend if it appeared to us on other
grounds that the smaller urban places might not be growing that
fast.

The hardest cases were by all odds the countries that had
not had a census at all in recent decades. Here we were thrown
back almost entirely on total population estimates and estimates
of cities and towns for different dates. The latter had to be
assessed as to probable accuracy in whatever way possible and
adjusted if necessary. With estimates for the total population
and the largest city or cities, we usually calculated the entire
urban population on the basis of ratios found in other countries
of a similar character but with better data.

The Urban-Population Code. The code for the urban population, represented by the second digit of the code series in Table
A, has the same meaning as the total-population code, except that
in this instance it applies to the urban population. The code
classifies the countries according to whether they had a census
with urban population data in the target year; or if not, whether
they had one or two censuses with such data at other dates and,
if so, how near the closest census was to the target date. The
results of the coding are shown in the accompanying table (Table
7). They indicate in the last two columns, that in 1950 over 31
per cent of the world's urban population, and in 1960 over 36
per cent, lived in countries that had a census with usable urban
data during the year. The table also shows that nearly three-
fourths of the urban people in 1950, and over four-fifths of
those in 1960, were in countries coded 0, 1, or 2. At the other
end of the scale, there were less than one-fifth of the world's
countries which had had no census at all with usable urban data.
Fortunately, however, these countries were on the average quite
small; they therefore accounted for a very small share of the
total urban population--1.4 per cent in 1950 and 2.1 per cent in
1960.

China plays a big role in the distribution of the world's
urban people according to the urban-population code, although
not quite so big as she played with respect to the total-population code. With China removed, as shown in Table 8, Code No. 5
is drastically decreased in 1950, and in 1960 Code No. 6 is
drastically decreased, with a consequent rise in the proportion
in the other codes. As a result, the distribution looks better,
because in the world apart from China, the proportion of people

Table 7

DISTRIBUTION OF WORLD'S COUNTRIES AND URBAN PEOPLE
ACCORDING TO URBAN-POPULATION CODE

Code Number/1		PERCENTAGE OF COUNTRIES		PERCENTAGE OF URBAN POPULATION	
		1950	1960	1950	1960
0	Census during year	23.4	31.3	36.1	36.7
1	Two censuses, closest 1-2 years	19.2	24.3	26.1	40.0
2	Ibid., closest 3-4 years	19.2	9.3	11.6	3.7
3	Ibid., closest 5+ years	5.1	0.9	11.2	0.6
4	One census, 1-2 years	0.5	4.2	----	2.1
5	One census, 3-4 years	3.3	3.7	8.8	1.7
6	One census, 5+ years	9.8	7.0	4.7	13.5
7	No census, fair estimate	0.5	1.4	----	----
8	No census, poor estimate	19.2	17.8	1.4	1.8
TOTAL PERCENTAGE		100.0	100.0	100.0	100.0
BASE		(214)	(214)	(706,383)/2	(993,718)/2

1/ The code categories are the same as those in Tables 4 and 5, except that they are with reference to the urban rather than the total population.

2/ Thousands.

in countries coded 0 to 2 rises to 81 per cent in 1950 and 90 per cent in 1960. Without China, the only "bad" codes with sizable populations in them are Nos. 3, 6, and 8; together these included 19 per cent of the urban population in 1950 but only 5.3 per cent in 1960.

Table 8

DISTRIBUTION OF THE WORLD'S URBAN INHABITANTS
ACCORDING TO URBAN-POPULATION CODE,
1950 AND 1960, WITH CHINA OMITTED

Code Number/1	PERCENTAGE OF URBAN POPULATION	
	1950	1960
0	39.6	41.3
1	28.6	45.1
2	12.8	4.1
3	12.3	0.7
4	----	2.3
5	0.1	1.9
6	5.1	2.6
7	----	----
8	1.6	2.0
TOTAL	100.0	100.0
BASE (000's)	644,693	882,856

1/The description of each code number is in the preceding table.

All told, analysis of the materials in terms of the urban-population code indicates data of better quality than I had expected. It is hard to believe that sheer lack of census information could greatly distort the accuracy of the figures on the urban population of the world, given sound estimates.

Sampling Bias that Would Result from Lack of World Coverage. In view of the numerous comparative studies done with only the "countries for which data are available," it seems worthwhile to use our material to get an idea of the bias such a practice

leads to. Suppose, for example, that an investigator were inter-
ested in the relationship between urbanization and fertility, and
he decided to utilize data from the countries that had a census
in 1960 or within two years of it. These would be the countries
coded No. 0, 1, or 4 in our tables. How representative would
they be?

The countries that would fall in the investigator's sample
would be unrepresentative of the world as a whole. As Table 9
shows, they would contain 79 per cent of the world's urban population, as against 45 per cent of the world's rural population.

Table 9

PROPORTION OF WORLD'S NATIONS, CITIES, AND POPULATION
IN THE GROUP OF COUNTRIES THAT HAD A CENSUS (WITH
URBAN DATA) WITHIN TWO YEARS OF 1960

| | Number of Countries | POPULATION | | | | | Number of Cities |
		Total	Rural	Urban	Town	City	
Per Cent							
In Sample	59.8	63.1	55.4	78.8	76.8	80.1	79.6
In Non-Sample	40.2	36.9	44.6	21.2	23.2	19.9	20.4
All Countries	100.0	100.0	100.0	100.0	100.0	100.0	100.0
BASE	(214)	(3,013)	(2,019)	(994)	(405)	(588)	(1,301)

The bias with respect to the city population would be even
greater, for the countries included in the sample would have 80
per cent of the world's cities and city population, while those
outside the sample would have only 20 per cent. Furthermore, as
can be seen in Table 10, the average size of country, the approximate rural density, and all other characteristics that our data
allow us to measure would be very different as between the sample and the universe. The proportion urban would be 41 per cent
in the sample but only 19 per cent in the non-sample.

Looked at another way, the sample would unequally represent
countries having different degrees of urbanization. For instance,
among all countries with less than 20 per cent of their population

35

Table 10

URBAN CHARACTERISTICS OF COUNTRIES THAT DID AND DID NOT HAVE
A CENSUS (WITH URBAN DATA) WITHIN TWO YEARS OF 1960

	WEIGHTED AVERAGES[1]		
	Sample	Non-Sample	World
Area (000's)	707.5	521.5	632.7
Population (000's)	14,857.5	12,917.4	14,077.8
Density			
Overall	21.0	24.8	22.3
Approximate Rural	12.4	20.1	14.9
Per Cent			
Rural	58.8	81.0	67.0
Urban	41.2	19.0	33.0
City	24.8	10.5	19.5

[1] Each country is weighted by its population. The averages
are obtained by using in each computation the totals for the
entire group of countries.

urban, the sample would contain 51 per cent of the nations and 44 per cent of the population; whereas, among countries with more than 60 per cent of their population urban, the sample would hold 81 per cent of the nations and 96 per cent of the population. In the latter group, the sample would contain 97 per cent of the cities and 98 per cent of the city population.

Not only would such a sample be unequally representative of the countries stratified according to degree of urbanization, but there is no reason to believe that within each stratum, whatever the quantitative degree of representation, the selection would be random. The very fact that one country with 15 per cent of its population urban has had a census near 1960 whereas another country with the same degree of urbanization has not had one is suggestive of other differences between the two. In short, if one tried to assess the relationship between urbanization and another variable such as fertility, the use of such a sample as I have described--the most frequent kind of sample, be it re-membered--would be extremely prejudicial.

Estimating City Populations in 1950 and 1960

The city population of each country presents fewer problems of estimation than the urban population does. For one thing, as mentioned already, it is possible to deal with cities individu-ally, whereas this is not possible for the smaller urban places. By considering as cities only those places with 100,000 or more inhabitants, we escape a large part of the burden of estimation for 1950 and 1960, because census figures and estimates by others (both official and unofficial) are frequently available for places of that size. Occasionally governments take special municipal censuses, and often they prepare official estimates for inter-censal years. For those cities for which our office has had to make estimates, the ordinary procedures of interpolation or extra-polation could usually be employed. Practically never were figures (estimated or enumerated) totally lacking for a particu-lar city, but a problem did occasionally arise from conflicting or wild estimates. In such instances, our procedure was to examine implied growth rates, search for an explanation of abnormal rates, compare the rates with those of other cities in the same country, and try to assess the reliability of the sources from which different figures came. As a general check on the figures for individual cities, their sum (the total city popula-tion in each country) was a useful figure to look at. Since cities normally account for a good share of the urban population --a share that varies according to the degree of urbanization-- the city/urban ratio is a statistic that can signal a possible error. When the ratio seemed too high or too low to be plausible in the circumstances of the nation at the time, we checked our methods of making the urban and city estimates.

The most taxing problem in estimating city populations concerned the unit itself. Wishing to refer to the urbanized area rather than the city proper whenever possible, we frequently found ourselves trying to estimate that part of the UA--the fringe--lying beyond the city proper. Virtually never did we make such an attempt without having the data for the two parts of the UA at <u>some</u> time, but armed with such information, we usually tried to estimate the fringe population for another date when we had only the CP population. The estimation was frequently done by viewing the fringe growth in relation to the CP growth as being similar to that of other cities in the same country. If such comparative data did not exist, the growth of the fringe was estimated with other elements of the situation in mind, such as the approximate size of the city, the economic level of the country, the degree of crowding in the CP, and the growth of the urban population in general. The "Special Notes" at the end of the volume explain what we did in many such cases.

The City Population and the Urban Data Code. The census data on cities came overwhelmingly from the same censuses that gave the total population and the urban population as a whole. For this reason the tables in this volume have no separate code for the city population but simply treat the urban-population code as applicable to them. According to this code, the cities of the world and the world's population are distributed as shown in Table 11.

If the distribution of population in this table is compared to that for the total urban population in Table 7 above, it will be seen that it is much the same. However, since the code has not been specifically applied to the city population, it does not reveal the probable truth--namely, that the city data are superior to the urban data. Not only are there the occasional municipal censuses previously referred to, but the intercensal estimates made for most cities of the world are often of excellent quality. The estimates, whether official or unofficial, can be reasonably accurate because of the very features of city life that lend themselves to human accounting--features such as utility installations, rationing cards, legal records, building permits, tax records, address directories, etc. Of course, the less educated the population and the less advanced the government and economy, the poorer may be the basis of estimation, but even so, the sheer fact of having the people in a restricted area that is well-mapped and known at first-hand by the officials, and the dependence of the population on common services and collective records make the estimation of the population a reasonable enterprise.

Table 11

DISTRIBUTION OF CITY POPULATION BY URBAN-POPULATION CODE

Code Number[1]	PERCENTAGE OF CITIES		PERCENTAGE OF CITY POPULATION	
	1950	1960	1950	1960
0	34.3	37.4	37.9	39.1
1	27.6	40.0	26.9	39.0
2	9.6	4.0	10.7	3.1
3	12.2	0.9	9.8	0.5
4	----	2.1	----	2.0
5	10.4	1.7	10.1	1.4
6	4.4	11.1	3.7	13.4
7	----	0.1	----	----
8	1.6	2.6	1.0	1.4
TOTAL PERCENTAGE	100.0	100.0	100.0	100.0
BASE	(961)	(1301)	(404,536)[2]	(588,272)[2]

[1] The code categories are the same as those in Table 7.

[2] Thousands.

39

China's effect on the distribution of the _city_ population according to the urban code (Table 12) is much the same as its effect on the distribution of the urban population. For 1950, omission of China greatly reduces the proportion of the city population in Code 5 and increases the proportion slightly in other codes, and in 1960 it reduces the proportion in Code 6. Since these are among the poorer codes, the net effect is to increase the proportion in the good codes. Over 80 per cent of the city population in 1950, and over 90 per cent in 1960, were in countries coded 0, 1, or 2. On the whole the city population of the world is known with fair accuracy.

The Rural and the Town Population

As explained in Chapter I, the rural and town populations in our tables are derived data. This means that their accuracy is dependent on the accuracy of the prime figures from which they come. The rural population, being derived by subtracting the urban from the total population, is just as accurate as these figures, in combination, are; and the town population, obtained by subtracting the city population from the total urban, is as accurate as those figures are. The error in each case is the algebraic sum of the errors in the two numbers from which it is derived. However, the relative error may be much greater. If, for instance, the total population of a country were really 150,000, and the urban population were 100,000, the rural population would be 50,000. Now, if the _reported_ total population were 10 per cent less, and the urban population 10 per cent more, the algebraic sum of the two relative errors would be -20 per cent. But the relative error in the _rural_ figure is not -20 per cent but -50 per cent. Use of the figures for the rural and town population must be made always with this potentiality for residual error in mind. In general, precisely because of this potentiality, we have used the rural and the town population as a check on our estimates for the total population and the urban population, when we have had to make them. This has meant inspection of the derived figures and, upon occasion, adjustment of the original data, but a margin of extra uncertainty in the derived figures, in comparison to the prime data, is undeniable.

The town population is derived from two numbers--the total urban and the city population--which are both judged in terms of the urban-population code. The distribution of the world's town population according to this code would be about the same as the distribution of the world's urban population. The rural population, however, is derived from two figures judged by different codes. Furthermore, since the rural sector tends to loom larger in the more backward countries, its distribution on these codes

Table 12

DISTRIBUTION OF CITY POPULATION BY URBAN-POPULATION
CODE, CHINA OMITTED

Code Number[1]	PERCENTAGE OF CITIES		PERCENTAGE OF CITY POPULATION	
	1950	1960	1950	1960
0	38.3	41.4	42.1	44.5
1	30.7	44.3	29.9	44.4
2	10.7	4.4	11.9	3.5
3	13.6	1.0	10.9	0.6
4	----	2.3	----	2.3
5	0.1	1.9	----	1.6
6	4.9	1.8	4.1	1.5
7	----	0.1	----	----
8	1.7	2.9	1.1	1.6
TOTAL PERCENTAGE	100.0	100.0	100.0	100.0
BASE	(862)	(1177)	(363,981)[2]	(516,981)[2]

[1] The code categories are the same as those in Table 7.

[2] Thousands.

41

Table 13

DISTRIBUTION OF RURAL POPULATION BY URBAN-POPULATION CODE

Code Number/1		PERCENTAGE OF RURAL POPULATION		PERCENTAGE OF RURAL POPULATION, CHINA OMITTED	
		1950	1960	1950	1960
0	Census during year	14.4	16.5	19.9	22.8
1	Two censuses, closest 1-2 years	29.3	33.9	40.5	46.9
2	Ibid., closest 3-4 years	7.5	4.9	10.4	6.8
3	Ibid., closest 5+ years	6.2	0.6	8.5	0.9
4	One census, 1-2 years	----	5.0	----	7.0
5	One census, 3-4 years	27.8	1.7	0.1	2.3
6	One census, 5+ years	7.5	30.0	10.4	3.2
7	No census, fair estimate	0.4	0.2	0.6	0.3
8	No census, poor estimate	6.9	7.1	9.5	9.8
TOTAL	PERCENTAGE	100.0	100.0	100.0	100.0
BASE		(1,795,511)/2	(2,018,941)/2	(1,297,201)/2	(1,459,803)/2

1/ The code categories are the same as those in Table 7.

2/ Thousands.

is likely to be different from that of the total population and especially from that of the urban population. This turns out to be true when the rural population is tabulated according to the codes, as Table 13 shows.

Conclusion

The preceding account of the estimation procedures, together with the analysis of the data in terms of the two quality codes, should give the reader an overall understanding of the 1950 and 1960 figures in the tables. Further insight is provided in the explanations of each major table, and also in the notes at the end of the volume. All that remains by way of introduction to the tables is a description of the projecting methods used in obtaining the figures for 1970.

Chapter IV

THE METHODOLOGY OF THE 1970 PROJECTIONS

When assemblage of the primary data for 1950 and 1960 was
complete (December, 1968), the year 1970 lay in the future. All
the figures for 1970 in this volume are therefore projections
based on past trends. They are also figures for which our research office must take responsibility.

The materials available for making the projections varied
in quality, quantity, and recency--not only from one country to
another but also from one category of population to another.
For instance, it was generally easier to find recent information
(that is, near to 1970) about cities than about the entire urban
population, and to find more recent figures for the total population than for either the city or the urban population. All of
these variations in the raw material required somewhat different
projection techniques for the several categories of population;
accordingly, the following sections consider each category
separately.

Projecting the Total Population

The total population of each country was projected on the
basis of the growth trend shown by the most recent midyear estimate available at the time, in conjunction with an estimate a
few years earlier. Usually the most recent estimate was for
1967, and the earlier estimate was two to four years prior to
that. In most cases the latest midyear estimate came from the
United Nations' Population and Vital Statistics Report and the
earlier one from the Demographic Yearbook, 1967. Other sources
were used when figures in these sources were missing or seemed
to be questionable. In almost no instances did we have to fall
back on the 1950 and 1960 estimates in our tables to obtain a
growth trend.

One way of judging the projections for 1970 is to test the
world sum they yield. This sum comes to 3.605 billion. When
the United Nations' estimate of the world's population in 1967
is moved forward at the rate increase they give to this population,[1] 1.9 per cent per year, the 1970 figure comes out to be

---

[1] Demographic Yearbook, 1967, p. 97.

3.619 billion. If the rate of growth between our 1950 and 1960 sums for the world is applied to the 1960 sum, the resulting 1970 projection is 3.628 billion. The difference between either of these figures and the sum of our individual-country projections is less than 1 per cent.

Projecting the Urban Population to 1970

Given the projected total population of each country in 1970, the only additional information we needed to know to calculate the projected urban population was the proportion urban in 1970. We decided to utilize the 1950 and 1960 data on the percentage urban as a basis for projecting the percentage to 1970. At first it might seem that the proper way to do this would be to take the 1950-60 change in the percentage and apply it directly to the 1960 percentage to get the projected proportion in 1970. However, this alone would not suffice, because the rate of change in the proportion urban varies systematically according to the level already reached. A country that was 10 per cent urban in 1950 and 14 per cent in 1960, would have made a 40-per-cent gain in the proportion. If this were applied to the 14 per cent, it would yield a proportion of 19.6 per cent in 1970. But among the countries of the world, the rate of change in the proportion urban is somewhat slower when the starting level is 14 per cent than when the starting level is 10 per cent.

To get a more precise method of projecting the urban population, we therefore made provision for a variable correction factor to be applied to the 1950-60 rates of change in the urban percentage. The basis for computing the correction factor was established by determining, for all countries of more than zero and less than complete urbanization, the curvilinear relationship between the percentage urban in 1950 and the rate of change in that percentage by 1960. The curve shows that the lower the percentage urban in 1950, the faster the rate of change during the subsequent decade.

For a given country, then, the urban population in 1970 was obtained by a procedure involving the following steps:

(1) Calculating from our data the rate of change in the country's urban proportion during the decade from 1950 to 1960.

(2) Reading two values from the regression curve that plots for all countries the urban percentage in 1950 against the rate of change in that percentage during

the subsequent decade. These two values were:

(a) The rate of change when the percentage urban is that shown by the country in <u>1950</u>.

(b) The rate of change when the percentage urban is that shown by the country in <u>1960</u>.

(3) Obtaining the ratio between these two values--that is, between "a" and "b" above.

(4) Reducing the country's rate of change in proportion urban during 1950-60 by the value of this ratio-- that is, multiplying the value obtained in Step 1 by that obtained in Step 3.

(5) Applying the resulting rate of change (from Step 4) to the 1960 percentage urban in the country, to get the projected urban proportion in 1970.

(6) Multiplying the projected total population in 1970 (see previous section) by the projected percentage urban (from Step 5) to get the projected urban population in 1970.

In a few cases the results of the calculation were not accepted, either because they were inconsistent with other statistical information about the country after 1960 or because historical events did not seem to justify the use of the 1950-60 trend in such a direct way. However, in a great majority of cases the projected urban population seemed to be reasonable.

The assumption on which the projections are based is a conservative one. By using the regression curve alluded to, the pace of urbanization is implicitly claimed to be a bit slower in 1960-70 than it was in 1950-60. I think this assumption is correct, but the height-slope relationship on which it is based does relate to the earlier decade and not to the last one. It is conceivable that the entire pace of urbanization from given levels may have risen after 1960.

A general test of our projections of the urban population is provided by looking at the world as a whole. If we treat the world as if it were a single country, we can determine its projected urban population in 1970 by exactly the same procedures outlined above. The result can be compared with the summation of our individual-country projections for the entire world. This comparison, however, is not a real test of the conservative bias in our projections, because the treatment of the world as a single country still involves the assumption that the rate of change in the proportion urban diminishes as the proportion rises. If this assumption is dropped, the world can be given the same rate of change it experienced from 1950 to 1960 and the resulting projection is necessarily higher than the other one. The difference, however, is not large. Here are the world projections by the three methods:

	Millions
Sum of 1970 projections for individual countries	1,371.4
Projecting world as a unit:	
By same procedures as for individual countries	1,361.9
By straight extrapolation of 1950-60 change in urban proportion	1,389.0

The difference between the first two numbers is less than 1 per cent, as might be expected; the surprising thing is the small difference (1.3 per cent) between the first and third figures.

Projecting Each Country's Entire City Population

With respect to the city population, two approaches were possible: A projection for each country could be made by dealing with the country's city population as a whole, or it could be made by projecting the population of individual cities and then summing them to get the total city population of the country in 1970. We used both methods. The second method will be discussed in the next section on projections for individual cities; the first method will be described now.

The projection of the entire city population was made in the same way that the projection for the entire urban population was made. We began by computing the rate of change from 1950 to 1960 in the proportion of the country's population living in cities. This rate was then modified on the basis of a correction derived from a regression curve showing the relationship between the rate of rise in the city proportion during 1950-60 and the level of the starting proportion in 1950. The ratio of the two rates read from this line at the points indicated by the country's percentage urban in 1950 and 1960, gave the correction factor. In other words, the projection of each country's city population as a whole involved the same operational steps that the projection of the urban population involved, as described above.

47

The projection of each country's city population by this
method was checked by comparing it with the result obtained by
summing the projections for the individual cities within the
country. In case of discrepancy, the one or the other, or possibly both, would be modified according to our best judgment in
the light of whatever additional evidence could be assembled.
In no case, however, were the two figures allowed to go unrecon-
ciled. The city population for every country in 1970 is always
the sum of the individual cities within that country.

Projections for Individual Cities in 1970

The method of projecting the population of each city had
nothing to do with the projection of the urban or even the entire
city population. It was essentially similar to the method of
projecting the total population of each country. As in that case,
we took the most recent data available for the city, found comparable data a few years earlier, and extrapolated the growth
trend shown by the two figures to 1970. Population estimates
for most of the world's cities were available for a recent year
--usually 1965, 1966, or 1967.[2] In some instances we had to fall
back on earlier data or found such a paucity of recent information that we had to utilize our 1950 and 1960 figures to estab-
lish a growth trend; but on the whole the number of city population figures available after 1960 was gratifying.

A flaw in this technique of projecting the population of
individual cities--a flaw that did not occur with respect to
projections of the total population--was that when used by itself the method tended to cause us to overlook certain new cities.
If, for example, a country had eight cities above 100,000 according to the latest estimates (say, estimates for 1966) there is
obviously the possibility that a ninth or tenth city may have
reached the 100,000 status between 1966 and 1970. Since the
Demographic Yearbook lists cities only if they are 100,000 or
more (unless they are national capitals), and since our own
tables for 1950 and 1960 deal solely with cities of that size,
we had difficulty in testing all the potential towns of less than
100,000 to see if by 1970 they would qualify for inclusion. Although we caught a good share of such towns, we undoubtedly overlooked a portion of them. To evaluate our method, it is desirable
to try to estimate how many new cities may have been overlooked
in this way.

---

[2]The latest issue of the Demographic Yearbook available was
the 1967 volume, which listed the population of most of the
national capitals and cities of 100,000 or more.

Unfortunately, the estimation of the lost new cities is not easy. In utilizing the several possible methods, we have to avoid a trap. Inherent in the projections, as indicated already, is the assumption that urbanization proceeded at a slightly slower rate in 1960-70 than it did in 1950-60, simply because the world in 1960 had already apparently gone beyond the level when the fastest urbanization occurs. This fact must not be ignored in estimating the number of new cities overlooked in 1970. If, for instance, the world's entire city population is projected to 1970 simply by extrapolating the rise in the per-centage in cities between 1950 and 1960, the result is 850 million city dwellers in 1970. But if the city population of the world is projected in the same way as for individual countries--that is, with a correction factor derived from the regression line pre-viously described--the result is 834 million. The difference cannot be interpreted as a measure of city population lost by overlooking new cities, but is simply a function of two dif-ferent projection methods.

With this caution in view, an estimate of how many new cities were overlooked in the 1970 projections can be made by first assuming that the increase in new cities between 1960 and 1970 should be the same as it was during the previous decade, in relation to the cities of more than 250,000 at the end of each of the two decades. On this basis, the expected number of new cities in 1970 is 486, whereas we found only 302. Alternatively, the expected number of cities of 100,000 to 250,000 in 1970 can be predicted on the basis of the growth in this number during 1950-60. The difference between the expected and the actual number is the number of new cities overlooked. The loss, according to this method, is 185 new cities. However, the assumption of the second method, and to some extent of the first method, is that the 1950-60 rate of change will continue until 1970. If we modify the resulting estimate by the ratio of the two projections of the world's total city population given above (834 ÷ 850), we come out with 166 new cities lost.

By assigning an average population in 1970 to these new cities, we can figure out how many city people were presumably overlooked. Since most of these cities would have reached 100,000 only a short time before 1970, their average population in 1970 cannot be much more than that. If they had an average of 105,000 inhabitants in 1970, the city population overlooked would have been 17.4 million, or 2.09 per cent of the total city population actually shown in our tables for 1970.

This estimate must be viewed as high, because other means of estimation give a lower figure. For example, if certain new cities were inadvertently left out of the 1970 projections, they were nevertheless included in the urban population figures.

49

Therefore, the "town" population (obtained by subtracting the city population from the urban population) should be larger in 1970 than could be expected if the town population grew at the 1950-60 rate, modified by the curve ratio. The result of this calculation indicates that only 5.5 million of the people we project as being in towns in 1970 were really in cities of 100,000 or more. This would be less than 1 per cent of the city people projected for the world. The conclusion seems proper that in the 1970 projections between 50 and 175 new cities were overlooked, containing between 0.5 and 2.2 per cent of the city population. The people involved, however, were not lost from our data but simply misclasssified, because they appear in the total urban projection.

Regardless of world totals, in each country any discrepancy between the projection of the city population as a whole and the sum of the individual-city projections was cause for further investigation, as already indicated. One source of the discrepancy could be the failure to find all of the cities that were new by 1970, but there were also other possible sources, some exercising an influence in the opposite direction. For instance, if a country added no new cities during 1950-60 (which might be largely accidental), this fact would lower the projection of the combined city population below what it would have been had it been based on a longer time-span allowing the addition of new cities. Conversely, if a country happened to have an unusually large number of new cities crossing the 100,000 line during 1950-60, this would automatically make its projected 1970 city population abnormally high. If it received only the normal number of new cities during 1960-70, the projected city population would exceed the sum of the individual-city projections. Each country that showed a discrepancy of the kind mentioned required a case study to determine where the difficulty lay. The final figures that went into the tables, however, were consistent: the sum of the individual cities equalled the total city population.

Conclusion

Once the primary figures were projected to 1970, the other data for that year could be calculated from them. The primary information, it will be recalled, includes figures on the area, total population, urban population, and city populations of each country; the derived information includes absolute figures like the rural population and town population, as well as summaries for regions and classes of cities, ratios and averages, and growth rates. In other words, the projections for 1970 provide the same range of statistics that is available for 1950 and 1960, and they make it possible to calculate the same rates for the decade from 1960 to 1970 that were computed for the decade from 1950 to 1960.

The specific data projected for each country in 1970 will of course be superseded as censuses taken in and around that year provide more accurate information. In the meantime, the projections given here will provide at least an approximately true indication of the up-to-date progress and condition of urbanization around the world. The analysis in the second volume, based on these data, is aimed at giving an understanding of the principal trends and features of world urbanization, but the number of topics that can be explored with the materials far exceeds the compass of any single volume or any one investigator.

CONTINENTS, REGIONS, AND COUNTRIES IN THE
ORDER IN WHICH THEY APPEAR IN THE TABLES

AFRICA

Northern Africa: Algeria, Ifni, Libya, Morocco, Spanish North
Africa, Spanish Sahara, Sudan, Tunisia, United Arab Republic.

Western Africa: Cape Verde Islands, Dahomey, Gambia, Ghana,
Guinea, Ivory Coast, Liberia, Mali, Mauritania, Niger, Nigeria,
Portuguese Guinea, Saint Helena, Senegal, Sierra Leone, Togo,
Upper Volta.

Eastern Africa: Burundi, Comoro Islands, Ethiopia, French
Somaliland, Kenya, Madagascar, Malawi, Mauritius, Mozambique,
Reunion, Rwanda, Seychelles, Somalia, Southern Rhodesia, Tangan-
yika, Uganda, Zambia, Zanzibar.

Middle and Southern Africa: Angola, Basutoland (Lesotho), Bechu-
analand (Botswana), Cameroon, Central African Republic, Chad,
Congo (Brazzaville), Congo (Democratic Republic of), Gabon, Sao
Tome, South West Africa, Spanish Equatorial Guinea, Swaziland.

South Africa

NORTHERN AMERICA

Northern America: Bermuda, Canada, Greenland, St. Pierre and
Miquelon, United States.

LATIN AMERICA

Middle America: British Honduras, Canal Zone, Costa Rica, El
Salvador, Guatemala, Honduras, Mexico, Nicaragua, Panama.

Caribbean: Bahama Islands, Barbados Islands, Cayman Islands,
Cuba, Dominican Republic, Guadeloupe, Haiti, Jamaica, Leeward
Islands, Martinique, Netherlands Antilles, Puerto Rico, Trinidad
and Tobago, Turks and Caicos Islands, United States Virgin Islands, Windward Islands.

Tropical South America: Bolivia, Brazil, British Guiana,
Colombia, Ecuador, French Guiana, Peru, Surinam, Venezuela.

Temperate South America: Argentina, Chile, Falkland Islands,
Paraguay, Uruguay.

EAST ASIA

East Asia: China (Taiwan), China (Mainland), Hong Kong, North
Korea, South Korea, Macau, Mongolia, Ryukyu Islands.

Japan

SOUTH ASIA

Southeast Asia: Brunei, Burma, Cambodia, Indonesia, Laos, West
Malaysia, Maldive Islands, Philippines, Portuguese Timor, Sabah,
Sarawak, Singapore, Thailand, North Viet-Nam, South Viet-Nam,
West Irian.

Southwest Asia: Bahrain, Cyprus, Federation of South Arabia
(Southern Yemen), Gaza Strip, Iran, Iraq, Israel, Jordan, Kuwait,
Lebanon, Muscat and Oman, Qatar, Saudi Arabia, Syria, Trucial
Oman, Turkey, Yemen.

South Central Asia: Afghanistan, Bhutan, Ceylon, India, Kashmir-
Jammu, Nepal, Pakistan, Sikkim.

EUROPE

Northern Europe: Channel Islands, Denmark, Faeroe Islands, Fin-
land, Iceland, Ireland, Isle of Man, Norway, Sweden, United
Kingdom.

Western Europe: Austria, Belgium, France, Federal Republic of
Germany, Liechtenstein, Luxembourg, Monaco, Netherlands, Switzerland.

Eastern Europe: Bulgaria, Czechoslovakia, Eastern Germany,
Hungary, Poland, Romania.

Southern Europe: Albania, Andorra, Gibraltar, Greece, Holy See,
Italy, Malta and Gozo Islands, Portugal, San Marino, Spain,
Yugoslavia.

OCEANIA

Australia-New Zealand

Oceania: American Samoa, Christmas Island, Cocos Islands, Cook
Islands, Fiji, French Polynesia, Gilbert and Ellice Islands, Guam,
Johnston Island, Midway Island, Nauru, New Caledonia, New Guinea,
New Hebrides, Niue Island, Norfolk Island, Pacific Islands, Papua,
British Solomon Islands, Tokelau Islands, Tonga, Wake Island,
Western Samoa.

U.S.S.R.

Union of Soviet Socialist Republics

EXPLANATION

The first table of basic data on urbanization gives the
entire population, the rural and urban populations, and the city
population for each country of the world. It gives the actual
figures for 1950 and 1960, as contained in official censuses,
official estimates, or our own estimates for those years; and it
gives the projected figures for 1970. The 1970 projections are
all made by International Population and Urban Research on the
basis of the most recent information available in December, 1968.

The boundaries of each country are taken as those defined
in 1960. The definition of "urban" is normally that of the country itself; in some cases, however, we have changed the definition
for purposes of comparability, and in other cases, when no urban
data as such were available, we have used our own definition in
preparing estimates. The urban definition is coded in the last
digit of the two numbers given in parenthesis under the name of
each country (see below). It is assumed that the same definition
applies in 1970 as applied in 1960. The "rural" category is
equivalent to "non-urban"; hence, in each case, the sum of the
rural and urban populations equals the total population.

The term "city" denotes an urban place with 100,000 or more
inhabitants. The city population is therefore a part of the urban
population; the difference between the urban population as a whole
and the city population--a remainder designated by us as the
"town" population--is given in Table B. Whenever possible each
city of 100,000 or more is taken to be the entire built-up area
within which the inhabitants can be said to belong, economically
and socially, to one urban complex. In other words, insofar as
the information can be obtained, the city is defined as the
"urbanized area," "urban agglomeration," or "metropolitan area,"
rather than simply as the political city.

Both the urban and the city definitions, as far as humanly
possible, are made constant between 1950 and 1960, and in most
cases they are automatically made constant as between 1960 and
1970.

The figures shown for each subregion of the world are sum-
mations of the data for individual countries at each date.

The numbers in parentheses under each country's name for
1950 and 1960 are code numbers that help the reader to assess the
quality of the data. The first digit in each number refers to

the total population, the second to the urban population, and the third to the urban definition. The reason no code number is shown on the 1970 line is that the projections to 1970 are made variously on the basis of recent estimates or census figures or on the basis of the 1950-60 trend itself if no more recent data are available. Given the nature of the projections, the definition remains almost universally the same as in 1960 and hence does not need to be coded; furthermore, the 1970 total population is so frequently projected from two recent estimates made by the United Nations that it needs no coding, and the urban population for 1970 is normally projected from the data used for 1950-1960 and hence already coded.

In the codes, the numerical values of the first and second digits have the same meaning, although the first digit refers to the figure for the total population and the second to the figure for the urban population. The meanings of the scale--meanings which apply to both the first and second digits--are as follows:

0--Census data from a census taken during the year in question (1950 or 1960).

1--Interpolated or extrapolated from two censuses, the closest being 1-2 years.

2--Ibid., closest census 3-4 years.

3--Ibid., closest census 5+ years.

4--Interpolated or extrapolated from a census and official estimate, the census being 1-2 years from date.

5--Ibid., the census being 3-4 years from date.

6--Ibid., the census being 5+ years from date.

7--No census at all, our estimate is judged to be fairly good.

8--No census at all, our estimate is judged to be uncertain.

The last digit of the code indicates approximately the urban definition for the country in question. It specifies the range in which the minimum size of place defined as "urban" falls, or else reveals that no minimum size is, or can be, designated. The minimum size of course varies from one country to another;

the code does not specify the exact minimum, but simply the range within which the exact minimum is to be found. The ranges for each code are as follows:

0--Less than 1,000

1--1,000 - 1,999

2--2,000 - 2,999

3--3,000 - 4,999

4--5,000 - 7,499

5--7,500 - 9,999

6--10,000 - 19,999

7--20,000+

8--No minimum-size definition available, or 100 per cent urban, or 100 per cent rural.

9--No definition available; urban population estimated by indirect means.

Further explanations will be found in the introductory chapters and the "Special Notes" to this volume and in the analytical text that constitutes the second volume. It should be noted that the populations given here are rounded to the nearest thousand. Also, when the entry in a column is zero, a dash is used for ease in reading.

TABLE A

TOTAL, RURAL, URBAN AND CITY POPULATIONS*
(All Populations in Thousands)

REGION AND COUNTRY		TOTAL	RURAL	URBAN	CITY
NORTHERN AFRICA					
	1950	52,044	39,252	12,792	7,683
	1960	66,012	46,490	19,522	12,049
	1970	85,095	55,694	29,401	17,918
Algeria					
(118)	1950	8,920	6,737	2,183	1,062
(008)	1960	10,784	7,418	3,366	1,770
	1970	13,663	8,446	5,217	1,861
Ifni					
(008)	1950	38	30	8	---
(008)	1960	50	37	13	---
	1970	54	37	17	---
Libya					
(555)	1950	999	787	212	114
(225)	1960	1,349	1,017	332	288
	1970	1,850	1,329	521	483
Morocco					
(112)	1950	8,959	6,887	2,072	1,415
(002)	1960	11,640	8,253	3,387	2,200
	1970	15,519	10,035	5,484	3,718
Sp. North Africa					
(008)	1950	142	---	142	---
(008)	1960	153	---	153	---
	1970	165	---	165	---
Spanish Sahara					
(603)	1950	20	16	4	---
(003)	1960	24	14	10	---
	1970	48	16	32	---
Sudan					
(669)	1950	8,950	8,382	568	230
(559)	1960	11,770	10,912	858	320
	1970	15,631	14,328	1,303	450

*See explanation on preceding pages.

REGION AND COUNTRY		TOTAL	RURAL	URBAN	CITY
Tunisia					
(224)	1950	3,555	2,467	1,088	615
(224)	1960	4,157	2,618	1,539	648
	1970	4,882	2,764	2,118	1,085
U.A.R.					
(228)	1950	20,461	13,946	6,515	4,247
(008)	1960	26,085	16,221	9,864	6,823
	1970	33,283	18,739	14,544	10,321
WESTERN AFRICA					
	1950	58,619.	52,406	6,213	1,664
	1960	82,076	69,974	12,102	4,087
	1970	111,890	89,865	22,025	8,264
Cape Verde Islands					
(008)	1950	148	138	10	---
(008)	1960	200	187	13	---
	1970	245	222	23	---
Dahomey					
(888)	1950	1,570	1,435	135	---
(788)	1960	2,050	1,806	244	---
	1970	2,732	2,294	438	175
Gambia					
(118)	1950	263	244	19	---
(228)	1960	298	272	25	---
	1970	364	327	37	---
Ghana					
(114)	1950	4,845	4,156	689	173
(004)	1960	6,727	5,176	1,551	730
	1970	8,808	5,818	2,990	1,573
Guinea					
(784)	1950	2,250	2,131	119	---
(784)	1960	3,072	2,832	240	112
	1970	4,011	3,560	451	220
Ivory Coast					
(889)	1950	2,586	2,389	197	---
(889)	1960	3,230	2,719	511	180
	1970	4,288	·3,044	1,244	495

REGION AND COUNTRY		TOTAL	RURAL	URBAN	CITY
Liberia					
(689)	1950	860	818	42	---
(489)	1960	988	860	128	---
	1970	1,168	824	344	---
Mali					
(683)	1950	3,445	3,304	141	---
(073)	1960	4,140	3,893	247	130
	1970	5,010	4,581	429	225
Mauritania					
(883)	1950	712	697	15	---
(883)	1960	970	948	22	---
	1970	1,161	1,133	28	---
Niger					
(883)	1950	2,103	2,055	48	---
(883)	1960	2,876	2,800	76	---
	1970	3,845	3,727	118	---
Nigeria					
(229)	1950	30,500	26,500	4,000	1,305
(229)	1960	45,921	38,221	7,700	2,471
	1970	66,000	52,174	13,826	4,621
Portuguese Guinea					
(008)	1950	510	459	51	---
(068)	1960	521	450	71	---
	1970	531	435	96	---
Saint Helena					
(228)	1950	5	5	---	---
(228)	1960	5	5	---	---
	1970	5	5	---	---
Senegal					
(669)	1950	2,093	1,678	415	186
(049)	1960	3,110	2,380	730	358
	1970	3,958	2,877	1,081	600
Sierra Leone					
(289)	1950	2,004	1,829	175	---
(289)	1960	2,228	1,978	250	106
	1970	2,550	2,188	362	175

REGION AND COUNTRY		TOTAL	RURAL	URBAN	CITY
Togo					
(638)	1950	1,100	1,041	59	---
(008)	1960	1,440	1,301	139	---
	1970	1,851	1,546	305	180
Upper Volta					
(889)	1950	3,625	3,527	98	---
(889)	1960	4,300	4,146	154	---
	1970	5,363	5,110	253	---
EASTERN AFRICA					
	1950	59,828	56,502	3,326	812
	1960	76,251	70,558	5,693	2,114
	1970	97,242	87,662	9,580	4,709
Burundi					
(488)	1950	1,862	1,844	18	---
(688)	1960	2,908	2,861	47	---
	1970	3,544	3,451	93	---
Comoro Islands					
(688)	1950	165	159	6	---
(488)	1960	192	182	10	---
	1970	288	267	21	---
Ethiopia					
(889)	1950	16,000	15,050	950	392
(889)	1960	20,700	19,400	1,300	551
	1970	24,754	23,111	1,643	786
French Somaliland					
(388)	1950	57	38	19	---
(088)	1960	81	44	37	---
	1970	116	50	66	---
Kenya					
(113)	1950	6,018	5,706	312	135
(113)	1960	8,115	7,509	606	434
	1970	10,861	9,861	1,000	779
Madagascar					
(889)	1950	4,256	3,877	379	177
(889)	1960	5,393	4,810	583	250
	1970	6,864	5,973	891	432

REGION AND COUNTRY		TOTAL	RURAL	URBAN	CITY
Malawi					
(788)	1950	2,740	2,706	34	---
(788)	1960	3,490	3,398	91	---
	1970	4,429	4,189	240	174
Mauritius					
(114)	1950	479	337	142	---
(114)	1960	662	381	281	---
	1970	857	388	469	146
Mozambique					
(089)	1950	5,739	5,613	126	---
(089)	1960	6,579	6,339	240	178
	1970	7,373	6,934	439	325
Reunion					
(252)	1950	244	185	59	---
(162)	1960	337	230	107	---
	1970	457	276	181	---
Rwanda					
(188)	1950	2,050	2,048	2	---
(388)	1960	2,669	2,664	5	---
	1970	3,624	3,614	10	---
Seychelles					
(228)	1950	36	26	10	---
(008)	1960	42	31	10	---
	1970	50	34	16	---
Somalia					
(889)	1950	1,886	1,585	301	---
(889)	1960	2,010	1,610	400	---
	1970	2,941	2,228	713	200
Southern Rhodesia					
(613)	1950	2,652	2,396	256	108
(413)	1960	3,640	3,048	592	418
	1970	4,964	3,964	1,000	697
Tanganyika					
(178)	1950	7,733	7,498	235	---
(268)	1960	9,237	8,803	434	148
	1970	12,878	11,959	919	350

REGION AND COUNTRY		TOTAL	RURAL	URBAN	CITY
Uganda					
(169)	1950	5,199	5,097	102	---
(149)	1960	6,677	6,423	254	135
	1970	8,542	7,930	612	325
Zambia					
(668)	1950	2,440	2,123	317	---
(558)	1960	3,210	2,600	610	---
	1970	4,326	3,189	1,137	495
Zanzibar					
(118)	1950	272	214	58	---
(118)	1960	309	223	86	---
	1970	374	244	130	---
MIDDLE AND SOUTHERN AFRICA					
	1950	26,321	24,577	1,744	454
	1960	31,487	27,832	3,655	1,407
	1970	38,297	32,412	5,885	2,293
Angola					
(004)	1950	4,145	3,898	247	142
(064)	1960	4,831	4,439	392	225
	1970	5,515	4,917	598	335
Basutoland (Lesotho)					
(228)	1950	588	584	4	---
(228)	1960	724	716	8	---
	1970	964	948	16	---
Bechuanaland (Botswana)					
(228)	1950	369	294	75	---
(228)	1960	483	382	101	---
	1970	649	509	140	---
Cameroon					
(789)	1950	4,200	3,984	216	---
(789)	1960	4,700	4,312	388	153
	1970	5,839	5,091	748	343
Central African Rep.					
(884)	1950	1,072	995	77	---
(884)	1960	1,230	1,062	168	---
	1970	1,585	1,207	378	180

REGION AND COUNTRY		TOTAL	RURAL	URBAN	CITY
Chad					
(688)	1950	2,580	2,523	57	---
(588)	1960	3,070	2,941	129	---
	1970	3,562	3,287	275	---
Congo, Brazzaville					
(688)	1950	675	566	109	---
(488)	1960	773	569	204	127
	1970	895	550	345	190
Congo, Dem. Rep.					
(782)	1950	11,390	10,540	850	312
(782)	1960	14,139	12,091	2,048	902
	1970	17,405	14,405	3,000	1,245
Gabon					
(168)	1950	418	390	28	---
(148)	1960	440	386	54	---
	1970	485	384	101	---
Sao Tome					
(008)	1950	60	52	8	---
(008)	1960	64	55	10	---
	1970	62	51	11	---
South West Africa					
(118)	1950	420	357	63	---
(008)	1960	526	403	123	---
	1970	625	415	210	---
Sp. Eq. Guinea					
(003)	1950	199	188	11	---
(003)	1960	246	223	23	---
	1970	292	247	45	---
Swaziland					
(268)	1950	205	205	---	---
(258)	1960	261	254	7	---
	1970	419	401	18	---
SOUTH AFRICA					
South Africa					
(112)	1950	12,458	7,582	4,876	2,945
(002)	1960	16,003	8,823	7,180	4,242
	1970	20,044	9,949	10,095	6,350

REGION AND COUNTRY		TOTAL	RURAL	URBAN	CITY
NORTHERN AMERICA					
	1950	165,563	59,920	105,643	71,660
	1960	198,688	60,131	138,557	98,966
	1970	228,766	56,889	171,877	131,344
Bermuda					
(008)	1950	37	---	37	---
(008)	1960	43	---	43	---
	1970	54	---	54	---
Canada					
(111)	1950	13,737	5,257	8,480	5,041
(111)	1960	17,909	5,633	12,276	7,710
	1970	21,673	5,489	16,184	10,684
Greenland					
(168)	1950	23	21	2	---
(008)	1960	33	30	3	---
	1970	49	43	6	---
St. Pierre and Miq.					
(118)	1950	5	5	---	---
(118)	1960	5	5	---	---
	1970	5	5	---	---
U.S.A.					
(002)	1950	151,761	54,637	97,124	66,619
(002)	1960	180,698	54,463	126,235	91,256
	1970	206,985	51,352	155,633	120,660
MIDDLE AMERICA					
	1950	34,670	21,089	13,581	4,730
	1960	46,917	25,233	21,684	8,111
	1970	67,404	31,689	35,715	13,511
British Honduras					
(228)	1950	67	42	25	---
(008)	1960	90	57	33	---
	1970	124	78	46	---
Canal Zone					
(002)	1950	53	36	17	---
(002)	1960	42	29	13	---
	1970	61	38	23	---

REGION AND COUNTRY		TOTAL	RURAL	URBAN	CITY
Costa Rica					
(008)	1950	805	537	268	140
(228)	1960	1,171	764	407	257
	1970	1,767	1,127	640	435
El Salvador					
(008)	1950	1,856	1,179	677	162
(118)	1960	2,454	1,518	936	239
	1970	3,499	2,107	1,392	475
Guatemala					
(002)	1950	2,791	2,095	696	294
(222)	1960	3,810	2,641	1,169	474
	1970	5,172	3,280	1,892	770
Honduras					
(061)	1950	1,445	1,189	256	---
(141)	1960	1,940	1,520	420	159
	1970	2,703	2,003	700	281
Mexico					
(002)	1950	25,791	14,808	10,983	3,897
(002)	1960	34,923	17,218	17,705	6,512
	1970	50,624	21,156	29,468	10,760
Nicaragua					
(008)	1950	1,057	688	369	109
(228)	1960	1,411	856	555	197
	1970	1,989	1,120	869	350
Panama					
(001)	1950	805	515	290	128
(001)	1960	1,076	630	446	273
	1970	1,465	780	685	440
CARIBBEAN					
	1950	16,261	10,535	5,726	2,337
	1960	20,252	12,465	7,788	3,514
	1970	25,752	14,818	10,934	5,315
Bahama Islands					
(228)	1950	79	49	30	---
(228)	1960	118	63	55	---
	1970	156	72	84	---

REGION AND COUNTRY		TOTAL	RURAL	URBAN	CITY
Barbados Islands					
(228)	1950	211	136	75	---
(008)	1960	232	138	94	---
	1970	253	139	114	---
Cayman Islands					
(338)	1950	7	7	---	---
(008)	1960	8	8	---	---
	1970	9	9	---	---
Cuba					
(220)	1950	5,516	2,397	3,119	1,332
(660)	1960	6,826	2,903	3,923	1,874
	1970	8,663	3,605	5,058	2,645
Dominican Republic					
(008)	1950	2,136	1,628	508	182
(008)	1960	3,033	2,115	918	367
	1970	4,324	2,723	1,601	760
Guadeloupe					
(228)	1950	206	176	30	---
(118)	1960	273	222	51	---
	1970	339	260	79	---
Haiti					
(008)	1950	3,097	2,720	377	134
(668)	1960	3,991	3,402	589	240
	1970	4,856	3,999	857	400
Jamaica					
(332)	1950	1,365	1,054	311	260
(002)	1960	1,629	1,153	476	377
	1970	2,020	1,293	727	560
Leeward Islands					
(224)	1950	115	88	26	---
(004)	1960	130	93	37	---
	1970	136	90	46	---
Martinique					
(222)	1950	222	157	65	---
(112)	1960	285	173	112	---
	1970	352	179	173	---

TABLE A (continued)

REGION AND COUNTRY		TOTAL	RURAL	URBAN	CITY
Neth. Antilles					
(338)	1950	162	96	66	---
(008)	1960	189	95	94	---
	1970	220	92	128	---
Puerto Rico					
(002)	1950	2,211	1,316	895	429
(002)	1960	2,350	1,313	1,037	656
	1970	2,855	1,494	1,361	950
Trinidad + Tobago					
(228)	1950	632	468	164	---
(008)	1960	828	500	328	---
	1970	1,106	517	589	---
Turks + Caicos Is.					
(338)	1950	6	6	---	---
(008)	1960	6	6	---	---
	1970	6	6	---	---
Virgin Islands (U.S.)					
(002)	1950	27	11	16	---
(002)	1960	32	14	18	---
	1970	71	27	44	---
Windward Islands					
(251)	1950	269	226	43	---
(061)	1960	323	267	56	---
	1970	386	313	73	---
TROPICAL SOUTH AMERICA					
	1950	83,646	53,679	29,967	13,816
	1960	113,490	62,763	50,727	27,001
	1970	149,910	70,365	79,545	48,162
Bolivia					
(002)	1950	3,019	2,403	616	300
(662)	1960	3,453	2,665	788	400
	1970	3,956	2,954	1,002	600
Brazil					
(008)	1950	52,022	33,239	18,783	9,094
(008)	1960	71,029	39,038	31,991	18,149
	1970	93,545	43,520	50,025	31,662

REGION AND COUNTRY		TOTAL	RURAL	URBAN	CITY
British Guiana					
(228)	1950	423	305	118	---
(008)	1960	560	398	162	148
	1970	737	516	221	200
Colombia					
(111)	1950	11,334	7,135	4,199	1,971
(221)	1960	15,416	8,273	7,143	3,732
	1970	21,168	9,520	11,648	7,465
Ecuador					
(008)	1950	3,203	2,289	914	469
(118)	1960	4,352	2,916	1,436	764
	1970	6,089	3,806	2,283	1,300
French Guiana					
(228)	1950	25	14	11	---
(118)	1960	33	16	17	---
	1970	41	18	23	---
Peru					
(368)	1950	8,319	5,366	2,953	947
(148)	1960	11,025	6,521	4,504	1,649
	1970	13,581	7,325	6,256	2,970
Surinam					
(008)	1950	209	137	71	---
(038)	1960	273	175	98	---
	1970	403	250	153	135
Venezuela					
(002)	1950	5,092	2,791	2,301	1,035
(112)	1960	7,349	2,761	4,588	2,159
	1970	10,390	2,456	7,934	3,830
TEMPERATE SOUTH AMERICA					
	1950	26,683	10,904	15,779	10,218
	1960	32,067	11,210	20,857	14,589
	1970	38,868	11,598	27,270	20,250
Argentina					
(222)	1950	17,070	6,270	10,800	7,784
(002)	1960	20,006	6,606	13,400	10,864
	1970	24,089	7,111	16,978	14,755

TABLE A (continued)

REGION AND COUNTRY		TOTAL	RURAL	URBAN	CITY
Chile					
(118)	1950	6,073	2,778	3,295	1,606
(008)	1960	7,772	2,744	5,028	2,452
	1970	9,510	2,503	7,007	3,520
Falkland Islands					
(228)	1950	2	2	---	---
(118)	1960	2	2	---	---
	1970	2	2	---	---
Paraguay					
(008)	1950	1,345	902	443	219
(118)	1960	1,751	1,149	602	311
	1970	2,378	1,526	852	445
Uruguay					
(668)	1950	2,193	952	1,241	609
(558)	1960	2,536	709	1,827	962
	1970	2,889	456	2,433	1,530
EAST ASIA					
	1950	601,392	528,627	72,765	48,287
	1960	721,281	591,335	129,946	85,500
	1970	817,575	610,593	206,982	131,380
China (Taiwan)					
(368)	1950	7,619	3,642	3,977	1,829
(258)	1960	10,612	4,400	6,212	3,181
	1970	14,402	5,130	9,272	5,420
China					
(558)	1950	560,000	498,310	61,690	40,555
(668)	1960	670,000	559,138	110,862	71,291
	1970	750,665	573,940	176,725	108,115
Hong Kong					
(338)	1950	1,950	389	1,561	1,561
(118)	1960	3,075	---	3,075	3,075
	1970	4,105	---	4,105	4,105
Korea, North					
(889)	1950	9,700	8,439	1,261	1,030
(889)	1960	10,600	8,600	2,000	1,690
	1970	13,685	10,685	3,000	2,380

REGION AND COUNTRY		TOTAL	RURAL	URBAN	CITY
Korea, South					
(114)	1950	20,513	16,763	3,750	3,124
(004)	1960	24,989	17,992	6,997	5,707
	1970	32,168	19,621	12,547	10,439
Macau					
(008)	1950	188	---	188	188
(008)	1960	169	---	169	169
	1970	280	---	280	280
Mongolia					
(338)	1950	732	587	145	---
(228)	1960	953	620	333	164
	1970	1,286	622	664	350
Ryukyu Islands					
(008)	1950	690	497	193	---
(008)	1960	883	585	298	223
	1970	984	595	389	291
JAPAN					
Japan					
(007)	1950	83,419	52,216	31,203	22,218
(007)	1960	93,419	34,086	59,333	39,180
	1970	102,795	17,286	85,509	56,560
SOUTHEAST ASIA					
	1950	170,967	147,688	23,279	12,188
	1960	218,317	182,007	36,310	21,189
	1970	284,951	227,758	57,193	34,507
Brunei					
(268)	1950	46	26	20	---
(008)	1960	84	47	36	---
	1970	118	66	52	---
Burma					
(664)	1950	18,766	16,341	2,425	977
(664)	1960	22,355	19,155	3,200	1,194
	1970	27,447	23,115	4,332	1,880
Cambodia					
(669)	1950	4,074	3,754	320	152
(449)	1960	5,440	4,890	550	337
	1970	6,850	5,905	878	700

REGION AND COUNTRY		TOTAL	RURAL	URBAN	CITY
Indonesia					
(368)	1950	76,000	66,663	9,337	4,637
(148)	1960	93,506	79,542	13,964	9,082
	1970	118,184	97,048	21,136	14,340
Laos					
(889)	1950	1,320	1,234	86	---
(889)	1960	2,330	2,130	200	114
	1970	2,986	2,586	400	210
West Malaysia					
(224)	1950	5,190	3,927	1,263	409
(224)	1960	6,909	4,499	2,410	774
	1970	9,376	5,085	4,291	1,600
Maldive Islands					
(258)	1950	82	73	9	---
(368)	1960	92	82	10	---
	1970	109	96	13	---
Philippines					
(112)	1950	20,275	16,246	4,029	2,526
(022)	1960	27,088	21,266	5,822	3,863
	1970	38,290	29,423	8,867	6,124
Portuguese Timor					
(008)	1950	442	398	44	---
(008)	1960	517	465	52	---
	1970	596	534	62	---
Sabah					
(113)	1950	330	286	44	---
(003)	1960	454	386	68	---
	1970	658	548	110	---
Sarawak					
(223)	1950	585	518	67	---
(003)	1960	750	638	112	---
	1970	990	802	188	---
Singapore					
(228)	1950	1,022	---	1,022	1,022
(228)	1960	1,634	---	1,634	1,634
	1970	2,113	---	2,113	2,113

REGION AND COUNTRY		TOTAL	RURAL	URBAN	CITY
Thailand					
(228)	1950	19,635	17,666	1,969	1,167
(008)	1960	26,258	23,254	3,004	1,705
	1970	35,898	31,239	4,659	2,825
Viet-Nam, North					
(689)	1950	12,000	11,069	931	448
(089)	1960	16,100	13,811	2,289	1,013
	1970	22,079	16,802	5,277	2,335
Viet-Nam, South					
(889)	1950	10,500	8,799	1,701	850
(889)	1960	14,100	11,156	2,944	1,473
	1970	18,380	13,584	4,796	2,380
West Irian					
(688)	1950	700	687	13	---
(678)	1960	700	686	14	---
	1970	877	858	19	---
SOUTHWEST ASIA					
	1950	61,669	46,740	14,929	6,484
	1960	80,381	56,644	23,737	12,176
	1970	103,235	66,584	36,651	22,422
Bahrain					
(008)	1950	110	32	78	---
(318)	1960	150	41	109	---
	1970	216	55	161	---
Cyprus					
(228)	1950	494	374	120	---
(008)	1960	574	368	206	---
	1970	631	329	302	112
Fed. of South Arabia (Southern Yemen)					
(788)	1950	696	565	131	107
(788)	1960	771	555	216	181
	1970	1,000	675	325	275
Gaza Strip					
(888)	1950	280	280	---	---
(778)	1960	377	377	---	---
	1970	514	514	---	---

REGION AND COUNTRY		TOTAL	RURAL	URBAN	CITY
Iran					
(664)	1950	16,276	11,929	4,347	2,301
(554)	1960	21,500	14,421	7,079	3,732
	1970	28,805	17,499	11,306	6,630
Iraq					
(228)	1950	5,180	3,373	1,807	780
(228)	1960	6,831	4,151	2,680	1,460
	1970	9,089	5,135	3,954	2,810
Israel					
(112)	1950	1,258	254	1,004	378
(112)	1960	2,114	477	1,637	833
	1970	2,908	543	2,365	1,605
Jordan					
(114)	1950	1,290	843	447	---
(114)	1960	1,695	1,028	667	225
	1970	2,421	1,357	1,064	475
Kuwait					
(334)	1950	170	72	98	---
(114)	1960	278	83	195	146
	1970	550	108	442	325
Lebanon					
(888)	1950	1,773	1,303	470	321
(888)	1960	2,110	1,412	698	565
	1970	2,600	1,566	1,034	850
Muscat and Oman					
(883)	1950	550	537	13	---
(883)	1960	565	545	20	---
	1970	565	535	30	---
Qatar					
(888)	1950	20	10	10	---
(888)	1960	45	18	27	---
	1970	95	30	65	---
Saudi Arabia					
(883)	1950	5,250	4,750	500	100
(883)	1960	6,200	5,200	1,000	476
	1970	7,357	5,500	1,857	995

REGION AND COUNTRY		TOTAL	RURAL	URBAN	CITY
Syria					
(668)	1950	3,442	2,226	1,216	775
(008)	1960	4,561	2,876	1,685	1,203
	1970	6,101	3,750	2,351	1,880
Trucial Oman					
(888)	1950	80	60	20	---
(888)	1960	100	60	40	---
	1970	158	71	87	---
Turkey					
(008)	1950	20,800	16,207	4,593	1,722
(008)	1960	27,510	20,202	7,308	3,355
	1970	35,225	24,218	11,007	6,465
Yemen					
(888)	1950	4,000	3,925	75	---
(888)	1960	5,000	4,830	170	---
	1970	5,000	4,699	301	---
SOUTH CENTRAL ASIA					
	1950	462,705	391,727	70,978	33,407
	1960	560,766	468,524	92,242	47,177
	1970	705,889	580,580	125,309	69,264
Afghanistan					
(889)	1950	12,000	11,306	694	218
(889)	1960	14,340	13,444	896	393
	1970	16,715	15,587	1,128	735
Bhutan					
(888)	1950	537	537	---	---
(888)	1960	681	681	---	---
	1970	833	833	---	---
Ceylon					
(228)	1950	7,678	6,529	1,149	722
(228)	1960	9,896	8,422	1,474	950
	1970	12,685	10,585	2,100	1,350
India					
(114)	1950	354,931	294,148	60,783	28,436
(114)	1960	429,016	351,975	77,041	38,593
	1970	544,621	442,188	102,433	54,492

TABLE A (continued)

REGION AND COUNTRY		TOTAL	RURAL	URBAN	CITY
Kashmir-Jammu					
(634)	1950	4,370	3,849	521	242
(414)	1960	4,797	4,124	673	393
	1970	5,507	4,606	901	500
Nepal					
(224)	1950	8,000	7,808	192	121
(114)	1960	9,180	8,924	256	205
	1970	11,143	10,591	552	440
Pakistan					
(114)	1950	75,053	67,417	7,636	3,668
(114)	1960	92,696	80,801	11,895	6,643
	1970	114,191	96,013	18,178	11,747
Sikkim					
(118)	1950	136	133	3	---
(148)	1960	160	153	7	---
	1970	194	177	17	---
NORTHERN EUROPE					
	1950	72,551	22,111	50,440	40,776
	1960	75,879	21,031	54,848	43,487
	1970	81,114	20,336	60,778	47,253
Channel Islands					
(118)	1950	104	62	42	---
(118)	1960	110	69	41	---
	1970	119	67	52	---
Denmark					
(000)	1950	4,281	1,399	2,882	1,433
(000)	1960	4,585	1,188	3,397	1,569
	1970	4,963	986	3,977	1,903
Faeroe Islands					
(008)	1950	32	26	6	---
(008)	1960	35	28	7	---
	1970	40	30	10	---
Finland					
(000)	1950	4,030	2,357	1,673	660
(000)	1960	4,446	1,959	2,487	897
	1970	4,768	1,509	3,259	1,160

REGION AND COUNTRY		TOTAL	RURAL	URBAN	CITY
Iceland					
(008)	1950	143	56	87	---
(008)	1960	176	59	117	---
	1970	212	60	152	---
Ireland					
(111)	1950	2,969	1,764	1,205	744
(111)	1960	2,834	1,538	1,296	776
	1970	2,936	1,448	1,488	905
Isle of Man					
(118)	1950	55	25	30	---
(118)	1960	48	21	27	---
	1970	52	22	30	---
Norway					
(062)	1950	3,279	1,895	1,384	649
(002)	1960	3,591	1,841	1,750	729
	1970	3,876	1,749	2,127	989
Sweden					
(062)	1950	7,042	3,138	3,904	1,504
(002)	1960	7,495	2,925	4,570	1,881
	1970	8,083	2,741	5,342	2,644
United Kingdom					
(118)	1950	50,616	11,389	39,227	35,786
(118)	1960	52,559	11,403	41,156	37,635
	1970	56,065	11,724	44,341	39,652
WESTERN EUROPE					
	1950	123,245	45,356	77,889	45,419
	1960	134,554	43,028	91,525	55,190
	1970	150,219	40,490	109,729	67,652
Austria					
(114)	1950	6,935	3,536	3,399	2,611
(114)	1960	7,048	3,522	3,526	2,651
	1970	7,449	3,647	3,802	2,705
Belgium					
(224)	1950	8,639	3,163	5,476	2,483
(114)	1960	9,153	3,096	6,057	2,601
	1970	9,801	3,053	6,748	2,768

REGION AND COUNTRY		TOTAL	RURAL	URBAN	CITY
France					
(222)	1950	41,736	19,138	22,598	10,946
(112)	1960	45,684	17,658	28,026	15,507
	1970	51,402	16,515	34,887	20,741
Germany, Fed. Rep.					
(002)	1950	50,774	13,958	36,816	24,553
(112)	1960	55,423	12,412	43,011	28,496
	1970	61,796	10,969	50,827	33,418
Liechtenstein					
(008)	1950	14	11	3	---
(008)	1960	17	13	4	---
	1970	22	17	5	---
Luxembourg					
(222)	1950	296	122	174	---
(002)	1960	315	119	196	---
	1970	343	118	225	---
Monaco					
(118)	1950	22	---	22	---
(118)	1960	23	---	23	---
	1970	26	---	26	---
The Netherlands					
(224)	1950	10,114	2,984	7,130	3,667
(004)	1960	11,462	3,720	7,742	4,356
	1970	13,110	3,648	9,462	5,924
Switzerland					
(004)	1950	4,715	2,444	2,271	1,159
(004)	1960	5,429	2,488	2,941	1,579
	1970	6,270	2,523	3,747	2,096
EASTERN EUROPE					
	1950	88,634	51,068	37,566	15,322
	1960	96,902	50,023	46,879	19,849
	1970	103,788	47,124	56,664	25,170
Bulgaria					
(228)	1950	7,251	5,264	1,987	658
(228)	1960	7,867	4,940	2,927	1,106
	1970	8,467	4,485	3,982	1,785

REGION AND COUNTRY		TOTAL	RURAL	URBAN	CITY
Czechoslovakia					
(022)	1950	12,338	7,147	5,191	1,722
(112)	1960	13,654	7,215	6,439	1,972
	1970	14,577	6,993	7,584	2,260
Germany, East					
(002)	1950	18,388	5,362	13,026	3,702
(662)	1960	17,241	3,804	13,437	3,677
	1970	16,999	2,685	14,314	3,834
Hungary					
(118)	1950	9,338	5,906	3,432	1,829
(008)	1960	9,961	6,003	3,958	2,193
	1970	11,064	6,343	4,721	2,700
Poland					
(008)	1950	25,008	15,249	9,759	5,771
(008)	1960	29,776	15,570	14,206	7,919
	1970	32,980	14,571	18,409	10,171
Romania					
(118)	1950	16,311	12,140	4,171	1,640
(338)	1960	18,403	12,491	5,912	2,982
	1970	19,701	12,047	7,654	4,420
SOUTHERN EUROPE					
	1950	108,661	64,704	43,957	21,567
	1960	117,694	64,080	53,614	28,323
	1970	128,366	63,312	65,054	38,018
Albania					
(000)	1950	1,219	969	250	---
(000)	1960	1,626	1,124	502	136
	1970	2,138	1,388	750	220
Andorra					
(558)	1950	6	6	---	---
(668)	1960	8	8	---	---
	1970	16	16	---	---
Gibraltar					
(118)	1950	23	---	23	---
(118)	1960	24	---	24	---
	1970	26	---	26	---

REGION AND COUNTRY		TOTAL	RURAL	URBAN	CITY
Greece					
(112)	1950	7,554	3,701	3,853	1,636
(112)	1960	8,327	3,581	4,746	2,285
	1970	8,876	3,324	5,552	3,005
Holy See					
(448)	1950	1	---	1	---
(668)	1960	1	---	1	---
	1970	1	---	1	---
Italy					
(118)	1950	46,769	26,213	20,556	9,460
(118)	1960	49,642	25,928	23,714	12,011
	1970	53,648	26,042	27,606	15,801
Malta + Gozo Is.					
(118)	1950	312	126	186	---
(118)	1960	329	119	210	---
	1970	312	101	211	---
Portugal					
(002)	1950	8,441	5,806	2,635	1,816
(002)	1960	8,889	5,879	3,010	2,081
	1970	9,723	6,174	3,549	2,350
San Marino					
(668)	1950	13	9	4	---
(448)	1960	15	11	4	---
	1970	19	15	4	---
Spain					
(006)	1950	27,977	14,339	13,638	6,740
(006)	1960	30,431	14,025	16,406	8,483
	1970	32,958	13,589	19,369	10,900
Yugoslavia					
(112)	1950	16,346	13,535	2,811	1,915
(112)	1960	18,402	13,405	4,997	3,327
	1970	20,649	12,663	7,986	5,742
AUSTRALIA-NEW ZEALAND					
	1950	10,165	3,049	7,116	5,019
	1960	12,760	2,844	9,916	6,810
	1970	15,280	2,403	12,877	9,343

REGION AND COUNTRY		TOTAL	RURAL	URBAN	CITY
Australia					
(221)	1950	8,257	2,300	5,957	4,392
(111)	1960	10,388	1,976	8,412	6,009
	1970	12,404	1,424	10,980	8,023
New Zealand					
(118)	1950	1,908	749	1,159	627
(118)	1960	2,372	868	1,504	801
	1970	2,876	979	1,897	1,320
OCEANIA					
	1950	2,344	2,228	116	---
	1960	3,062	2,877	185	---
	1970	3,913	3,608	305	---
American Samoa					
(008)	1950	19	17	2	---
(008)	1960	20	19	1	---
	1970	36	34	2	---
Christmas Island					
(228)	1950	1	1	---	---
(118)	1960	3	3	---	---
	1970	3	3	---	---
Cocos Islands					
(228)	1950	1	1	---	---
(118)	1960	1	1	---	---
	1970	1	1	---	---
Cook Islands					
(118)	1950	15	15	---	---
(118)	1960	18	18	---	---
	1970	21	21	---	---
Fiji					
(268)	1950	289	239	50	---
(258)	1960	394	321	72	---
	1970	540	434	106	---
French Polynesia					
(228)	1950	61	47	14	---
(118)	1960	80	61	19	---
	1970	106	80	26	---

REGION AND COUNTRY		TOTAL	RURAL	URBAN	CITY
Gilbert + Ellice Is.					
(228)	1950	38	38	---	---
(258)	1960	46	39	7	---
	1970	62	49	13	---
Guam					
(008)	1950	59	58	1	---
(008)	1960	67	62	5	---
	1970	100	80	20	---
Johnston Island					
(008)	1950	---	---	---	---
(008)	1960	---	---	---	---
	1970	---	---	---	---
Midway Island					
(008)	1950	---	---	---	---
(008)	1960	2	2	---	---
	1970	2	2	---	---
Nauru					
(128)	1950	3	3	---	---
(118)	1960	4	4	---	---
	1970	7	7	---	---
New Caledonia					
(328)	1950	63	48	15	---
(228)	1960	78	47	30	---
	1970	100	45	55	---
New Guinea					
(228)	1950	1,080	1,080	---	---
(118)	1960	1,402	1,402	---	---
	1970	1,663	1,663	---	---
New Hebrides					
(558)	1950	49	49	---	---
(668)	1960	60	60	---	---
	1970	90	90	---	---
Niue Island					
(118)	1950	5	5	---	---
(118)	1960	5	5	---	---
	1970	5	5	---	---

REGION AND COUNTRY		TOTAL	RURAL	URBAN	CITY
Norfolk Island					
(118)	1950	1	1	---	---
(118)	1960	1	1	---	---
	1970	1	1	---	---
Pacific Islands					
(338)	1950	57	57	---	---
(118)	1960	77	77	---	---
	1970	99	99	---	---
Papua					
(888)	1950	373	361	12	---
(888)	1960	503	489	14	---
	1970	685	656	29	---
Solomon Is. (UK)					
(888)	1950	100	98	2	---
(888)	1960	124	120	4	---
	1970	153	147	6	---
Tokelau Islands					
(118)	1950	2	2	---	---
(118)	1960	2	2	---	---
	1970	2	2	---	---
Tonga					
(388)	1950	48	40	8	---
(288)	1960	63	53	10	---
	1970	88	74	14	---
Wake Island					
(008)	1950	---	---	---	---
(008)	1960	1	1	---	---
	1970	1	1	---	---
Western Samoa					
(118)	1950	79	67	12	---
(118)	1960	111	90	21	---
	1970	148	114	34	---
U.S.S.R.					
U.S.S.R.					
(638)	1950	180,050	103,550	76,500	37,530
(418)	1960	214,400	106,982	107,418	53,311
	1970	244,125	92,125	152,000	74,982

TABLE B

EXPLANATION

The preceding table--Table A--gave for each country and
region the urban and city population as well as the rural and the
total population. The present table--Table B--omits all except
the urban population but divides it into four classes according
to size of place. For convenience, the classes are designated
with Roman numerals. Class I refers to urban places with fewer
than 100,000 inhabitants, and its column gives the population
living in such places at each of the three dates. These places
are referred to in our study as "towns" in order to distinguish
them from cities. We designate all places having 100,000 or more
inhabitants as "cities"; accordingly, the next three columns all
refer to "cities." Class II refers to cities of 100,000 to
499,999; Class III to cities of 500,000 to 1,000,000; and Class
IV to cities of 1,000,000 or more. In other words, the population figures shown in the last three columns of the present table
add up, horizontally, to the total "city" population, and the
population figures in all four columns add up to the total urban
population.

In addition to the population living in places classified
by size, the present table also gives, in parentheses, the number
of cities in each of the city size-classes. If the figures in
parentheses are summed horizontally, one has the total number of
cities in the given country at the date in question. The table
does not give the number of towns (Class I) because we do not
have this information. As explained in the introduction, we have
data for each individual place ("city") of 100,000 or over, but
we do not have data for each individual place under that size,
because the task of collecting and estimating the population of
each such place would be too formidable for us. Our figures for
the combined town population of each country and region are obtained by subtraction--that is, by subtracting the city population from the total urban population in each case--whereas our
data for the city population are obtained by summing the figures
for the individual cities.

The name and population of each city of 100,000 or more,
listed by region and country, are given in Table E below, and the
hundred largest of these at each of the three dates are re-listed,
by rank, in Table F.

Attention is again called to the fact that whenever possible our data for urban places of 100,000 or more are for
"urbanized areas," or "urban agglomerations," rather than for

"cities proper."   In Table E, below, the cities marked with an asterisk are UA's whereas those without an asterisk are CP's.

The reader should be warned against one possible misuse of the present table.   Each class is composed of all the urban places of that size <u>at the date in question</u>.   Consequently, the change in population of a given class from one date to the next is not an accurate measure of the growth of cities according to their size. For example, the cities in Class II--cities of 100,000-to-499,999 --in 1970 are not necessarily the same cities that were in that class in 1960, because during the decade some new cities may have entered that class and some old ones may have left it.   In order to judge the rate of growth of cities according to their size, one has to follow the <u>same</u> cities from one date to the next. This is done in the companion volume, which is devoted to the analysis of world urbanization.

Some countries have no urban population at all, and many have no cities or have none in one or more of the size-classes shown here.   A zero quantity is represented by three dashes (---).

TABLE B

URBAN POPULATION AND NUMBER OF CITIES,* BY SIZE-CLASS,
1950, 1960, AND (PROJECTED) 1970

REGION AND COUNTRY	CLASS I	CLASS II		CLASS III		CLASS IV	
NORTHERN AFRICA							
1950	5,109	(15)	2,351	(3)	1,793	(2)	3,539
1960	7,473	(24)	4,289	(3)	2,497	(2)	5,263
1970	11,483	(31)	6,557	(3)	2,238	(3)	9,123
Algeria							
1950	1,121	(3)	531	(1)	531		---
1960	1,596	(4)	886	(1)	844		---
1970	3,356	(4)	873	(1)	988		---
Ifni							
1950	8		---		---		---
1960	13		---		---		---
1970	17		---		---		---
Libya							
1950	98	(1)	114		---		---
1960	44	(2)	288		---		---
1970	38	(2)	483		---		---
Morocco							
1950	657	(5)	768	(1)	647		---
1960	1,187	(7)	1,235	(1)	965		---
1970	1,766	(8)	1,706	(1)	550	(1)	1,462
Sp. North Africa							
1950	142		---		---		---
1960	153		---		---		---
1970	163		---		---		---
Spanish Sahara							
1950	4		---		---		---
1960	10		---		---		---
1970	32		---		---		---
Sudan							
1950	338	(1)	230		---		---
1960	538	(1)	320		---		---
1970	853	(1)	450		---		---

*Population in thousands; number of cities in parentheses. Number of places in Class I (under 100,000) not available (see Explanation).

REGION AND COUNTRY	CLASS I	CLASS II		CLASS III		CLASS IV	
Tunisia							
1950	473		---	(1)	615		---
1960	891		---	(1)	648		---
1970	1,033	(3)	385	(1)	700		---
U.A.R							
1950	2,268	(5)	708		---	(2)	3,539
1960	3,041	(10)	1,560		---	(2)	5,263
1970	4,223	(13)	2,660		---	(2)	7,661
WESTERN AFRICA							
1950	4,549	(9)	1,664		---		---
1960	8,015	(19)	3,519	(1)	568		---
1970	13,761	(27)	5,354	(4)	2,910		---
Cape Verde Islands							
1950	10		---		---		---
1960	13		---		---		---
1970	23		---		---		---
Dahomey							
1950	135		---		---		---
1960	244		---		---		---
1970	263	(1)	175		---		---
Gambia							
1950	19		---		---		---
1960	25		---		---		---
1970	37		---		---		---
Ghana							
1950	516	(1)	173		---		---
1960	821	(3)	730		---		---
1970	1,417	(4)	823	(1)	750		---
Guinea							
1950	119		---		---		---
1960	128	(1)	112		---		---
1970	231	(1)	220		---		---
Ivory Coast							
1950	197		---		---		---
1960	331	(1)	180		---		---
1970	749	(2)	495		---		---

86

REGION AND COUNTRY	CLASS I	CLASS II		CLASS III		CLASS IV
Liberia						
1950	42	---		---		---
1960	128	---		---		---
1970	344	---		---		---
Mali						
1950	141	---		---		---
1960	117	(1)	130	---		---
1970	204	(1)	225	---		---
Mauritania						
1950	15	---		---		---
1960	22	---		---		---
1970	28	---		---		---
Niger						
1950	48	---		---		---
1960	76	---		---		---
1970	118	---		---		---
Nigeria						
1950	2,695	(7)	1,305	---		---
1960	5,229	(11)	1,903	(1)	568	---
1970	9,205	(17)	3,061	(2)	1,560	---
Portuguese Guinea						
1950	51	---		---		---
1960	71	---		---		---
1970	96	---		---		---
Saint Helena						
1950	---	---		---		---
1960	---	---		---		---
1970	---	---		---		---
Senegal						
1950	229	(1)	186	---		---
1960	372	(1)	358	---		---
1970	481	---		(1)	600	---
Sierra Leone						
1950	175	---		---		---
1960	144	(1)	106	---		---
1970	187	(1)	175	---		---

REGION AND COUNTRY	CLASS I	CLASS II		CLASS III		CLASS IV
Toga						
1950	59		---		---	---
1960	139		---		---	---
1970	125	(1)	180		---	---
Upper Volta						
1950	98		---		---	---
1960	154		---		---	---
1970	253		---		---	---
EASTERN AFRICA						
1950	2,514	(4)	812		---	---
1960	3,579	(10)	2,114		---	---
1970	4,871	(14)	3,578	(2)	1,131	---
Burundi						
1950	18		---		---	---
1960	47		---		---	---
1970	93		---		---	---
Comoro Islands						
1950	6		---		---	---
1960	10		---		---	---
1970	21		---		---	---
Ethiopia						
1950	558	(1)	392		---	---
1960	749	(2)	551		---	---
1970	857	(1)	155	(1)	631	---
French Somaliland						
1950	19		---		---	---
1960	37		---		---	---
1970	66		---		---	---
Kenya						
1950	177	(1)	135		---	---
1960	172	(2)	434		---	---
1970	221	(1)	279	(1)	500	---
Madagascar						
1950	202	(1)	177		---	---
1960	333	(1)	250		---	---
1970	459	(1)	432		---	---

REGION AND COUNTRY	CLASS I	CLASS II		CLASS III	CLASS IV
Malawi					
1950	34		---	---	---
1960	91		---	---	---
1970	66	(1)	174	---	---
Mauritius					
1950	142		---	---	---
1960	281		---	---	---
1970	323	(1)	146	---	---
Mozambique					
1950	126		---	---	---
1960	62	(1)	178	---	---
1970	114	(1)	325	---	---
Reunion					
1950	59		---	---	---
1960	107		---	---	---
1970	181		---	---	---
Rwanda					
1950	2		---	---	---
1960	5		---	---	---
1970	10		---	---	---
Seychelles					
1950	10		---	---	---
1960	10		---	---	---
1970	16		---	---	---
Somalia					
1950	301		---	---	---
1960	400		---	---	---
1970	513	(1)	200	---	---
Southern Rhodesia					
1950	148	(1)	108	---	---
1960	174	(2)	418	---	---
1970	303	(2)	697	---	---
Tanganyika					
1950	235		---	---	---
1960	286	(1)	148	---	---
1970	569	(1)	350	---	---

REGION AND COUNTRY	CLASS I	CLASS II		CLASS III		CLASS IV
Uganda						
1950	102		---		---	---
1960	119	(1)	135		---	---
1970	287	(1)	325		---	---
Zambia						
1950	317		---		---	---
1960	610		---		---	---
1970	642	(3)	495		---	---
Zanzibar						
1950	58		---		---	---
1960	86		---		---	---
1970	130		---		---	---
MIDDLE AND SOUTHERN AFRICA						
1950	1,290	(3)	454		---	---
1960	2,248	(7)	1,407		---	---
1970	3,592	(9)	1,713	(1)	580	---
Angola						
1950	105	(1)	142		---	---
1960	167	(1)	225		---	---
1970	263	(1)	335		---	---
Basutoland (Lesotho)						
1950	4		---		---	---
1960	8		---		---	---
1970	16		---		---	---
Bechuanaland (Botswana)						
1950	75		---		---	---
1960	101		---		---	---
1970	140		---		---	---
Cameroon						
1950	216		---		---	---
1960	235	(1)	153		---	---
1970	405	(2)	343		---	---
Central African Rep.						
1950	77		---		---	---
1960	168		---		---	---
1970	198	(1)	180		---	---

REGION AND COUNTRY	CLASS I	CLASS II		CLASS III		CLASS IV	
Chad							
1950	57		---		---		---
1960	129		---		---		---
1970	275		---		---		---
Congo, Brazzaville							
1950	109		---		---		---
1960	77	(1)	127		---		---
1970	155	(1)	190		---		---
Congo, Dem. Rep.							
1950	538	(2)	312		---		---
1960	1,146	(4)	902		---		---
1970	1,755	(4)	665	(1)	580		---
Gabon							
1950	28		---		---		---
1960	54		---		---		---
1970	101		---		---		---
Sao Tome							
1950	8		---		---		---
1960	10		---		---		---
1970	11		---		---		---
South West Africa							
1950	63		---		---		---
1960	123		---		---		---
1970	210		---		---		---
Sp. Eq. Guinea							
1950	11		---		---		---
1960	23		---		---		---
1970	45		---		---		---
Swaziland							
1950	---		---		---		---
1960	7		---		---		---
1970	18		---		---		---
SOUTH AFRICA							
1950	1,931	(8)	1,522	(2)	1,423		---
1960	2,938	(8)	1,601	(2)	1,488	(1)	1,153
1970	3,745	(12)	2,150	(2)	1,700	(2)	2,500

TABLE B (continued)

REGION AND COUNTRY	CLASS I	CLASS II		CLASS III		CLASS IV	
NORTHERN AMERICA							
1950	33,983	(104)	21,486	(15)	9,820	(14)	40,354
1960	39,591	(128)	27,330	(23)	16,131	(18)	55,505
1970	40,533	(141)	30,623	(27)	18,050	(28)	82,671
Bermuda							
1950	37		---		---		---
1960	43		---		---		---
1970	54		---		---		---
Canada							
1950	3,439	(11)	2,069	(1)	543	(2)	2,429
1960	4,566	(13)	3,226	(1)	763	(2)	3,721
1970	5,500	(13)	3,143	(4)	2,593	(2)	4,948
Greenland							
1950	2		---		---		---
1960	3		---		---		---
1970	6		---		---		---
St. Pierre and Miq.							
1950	---		---		---		---
1960	---		---		---		---
1970	---		---		---		---
U.S.A.							
1950	30,505	(93)	19,417	(14)	9,277	(12)	37,925
1960	34,979	(115)	24,104	(22)	15,368	(16)	51,784
1970	34,973	(128)	27,480	(23)	15,457	(26)	77,723
MIDDLE AMERICA							
1950	8,851	(14)	2,496		---	(1)	2,234
1960	13,573	(20)	3,945	(2)	1,334	(1)	2,832
1970	22,204	(25)	6,295	(2)	1,302	(3)	5,914
British Honduras							
1950	25		---		---		---
1960	33		---		---		---
1970	46		---		---		---
Canal Zone							
1950	17		---		---		---
1960	13		---		---		---
1970	23		---		---		---

REGION AND COUNTRY	CLASS I	CLASS II		CLASS III		CLASS IV	
Costa Rica							
1950	128	(1)	140		---		---
1960	150	(1)	257		---		---
1970	205	(1)	435		---		---
El Salvador							
1950	515	(1)	162		---		---
1960	697	(1)	239		---		---
1970	917	(2)	475		---		---
Guatemala							
1950	402	(1)	294		---		---
1960	695	(1)	474		---		---
1970	1,122		---	(1)	770		---
Honduras							
1950	256		---		---		---
1960	261	(1)	159		---		---
1970	419	(1)	281		---		---
Mexico							
1950	7,086	(9)	1,663		---	(1)	2,234
1960	11,193	(14)	2,346	(2)	1,334	(1)	2,832
1970	18,708	(19)	4,314	(1)	532	(3)	5,914
Nicaragua							
1950	260	(1)	109		---		---
1960	358	(1)	197		---		---
1970	519	(1)	350		---		---
Panama							
1950	162	(1)	128		---		---
1960	173	(1)	273		---		---
1970	245	(1)	440		---		---
CARIBBEAN							
1950	3,389	(6)	1,256		---	(1)	1,081
1960	4,274	(6)	1,423	(1)	542	(1)	1,549
1970	5,619	(8)	1,586	(3)	2,029	(1)	1,700
Bahama Islands							
1950	30		---		---		---
1960	55		---		---		---
1970	84		---		---		---

REGION AND COUNTRY	CLASS I	CLASS II		CLASS III		CLASS IV	
Barbados Islands							
1950	75		---		---		---
1960	94		---		---		---
1970	114		---		---		---
Cayman Islands							
1950	---		---		---		---
1960	---		---		---		---
1970	---		---		---		---
Cuba							
1950	1,787	(2)	251		---	(1)	1,081
1960	2,049	(2)	325		---	(1)	1,549
1970	2,413	(5)	945		---	(1)	1,700
Dominican Republic							
1950	326	(1)	182		---		---
1960	551	(1)	367		---		---
1970	841	(1)	110	(1)	650		---
Guadeloupe							
1950	30		---		---		---
1960	51		---		---		---
1970	79		---		---		---
Haiti							
1950	243	(1)	134		---		---
1960	349	(1)	240		---		---
1970	457	(1)	400		---		---
Jamaica							
1950	51	(1)	260		---		---
1960	99	(1)	377		---		---
1970	167		---	(1)	560		---
Leeward Islands							
1950	26		---		---		---
1960	37		---		---		---
1970	46		---		---		---
Martinique							
1950	65		---		---		---
1960	112		---		---		---
1970	173		---		---		---

REGION AND COUNTRY	CLASS I	CLASS II		CLASS III		CLASS IV	
Neth. Antilles							
1950	66	---		---		---	
1960	94	---		---		---	
1970	128	---		---		---	
Puerto Rico							
1950	466	(1)	429	---		---	
1960	381	(1)	114	(1)	542	---	
1970	411	(1)	131	(1)	819	---	
Trinidad + Tobago							
1950	164	---		---		---	
1960	328	---		---		---	
1970	589	---		---		---	
Turks + Caicos Is.							
1950	---	---		---		---	
1960	---	---		---		---	
1970	---	---		---		---	
Virgin Islands							
1950	16	---		---		---	
1960	18	---		---		---	
1970	44	---		---		---	
Windward Islands							
1950	43	---		---		---	
1960	56	---		---		---	
1970	73	---		---		---	
TROPICAL SOUTH AMERICA							
1950	16,151	(25)	5,374	(4)	2,941	(2)	5,501
1960	23,726	(44)	9,192	(5)	3,425	(6)	14,384
1970	31,383	(47)	10,351	(11)	7,560	(10)	30,251
Bolivia							
1950	316	(1)	300	---		---	
1960	388	(1)	400	---		---	
1970	402	(1)	100	(1)	500	---	
Brazil							
1950	9,689	(13)	2,900	(1)	693	(2)	5,501
1960	13,842	(26)	4,959	(4)	2,846	(3)	10,344
1970	18,363	(25)	6,130	(5)	3,518	(6)	22,014

REGION AND COUNTRY	CLASS I	CLASS II		CLASS III		CLASS IV	
British Guiana							
1950	118		---		---		---
1960	14	(1)	148		---		---
1970	21	(1)	200		---		---
Colombia							
1950	2,228	(7)	1,364	(1)	607		---
1960	3,411	(9)	1,912	(1)	579	(1)	1,241
1970	4,183	(11)	2,315	(2)	1,560	(2)	3,590
Ecuador							
1950	445	(2)	469		---		---
1960	672	(2)	764		---		---
1970	983		---	(2)	1,300		---
French Guiana							
1950	11		---		---		---
1960	17		---		---		---
1970	23		---		---		---
Peru							
1950	2,006		---	(1)	947		---
1960	2,855	(1)	130		---	(1)	1,519
1970	3,286	(3)	470		---	(1)	2,500
Surinam							
1950	71		---		---		---
1960	98		---		---		---
1970	18	(1)	135		---		---
Venezuela							
1950	1,266	(2)	341	(1)	694		---
1960	2,429	(4)	879		---	(1)	1,280
1970	4,104	(5)	1,001	(1)	682	(1)	2,147
TEMPERATE SOUTH AMERICA							
1950	5,561	(12)	2,561	(2)	1,169	(2)	6,488
1960	6,268	(16)	3,459	(3)	2,223	(2)	8,907
1970	7,020	(17)	3,861	(4)	2,859	(3)	13,530
Argentina							
1950	3,016	(9)	2,011	(1)	560	(1)	5,213
1960	2,536	(12)	2,603	(2)	1,261	(1)	7,000
1970	2,223	(11)	2,496	(4)	2,859	(1)	9,400

REGION AND COUNTRY	CLASS I	CLASS II		CLASS III		CLASS IV	
Chile							
1950	1,689	(2)	331		---	(1)	1,275
1960	2,576	(3)	545		---	(1)	1,907
1970	3,487	(5)	920		---	(1)	2,600
Falkland Islands							
1950	---		---		---		---
1960	---		---		---		---
1970	---		---		---		---
Paraguay							
1950	224	(1)	219		---		---
1960	291	(1)	311		---		---
1970	407	(1)	445		---		---
Uruguay							
1950	632		---	(1)	609		---
1960	865		---	(1)	962		---
1970	903		---		---	(1)	1,530
EAST ASIA							
1950	24,478	(92)	17,086	(18)	11,723	(10)	19,478
1960	44,446	(110)	21,906	(21)	15,431	(22)	48,163
1970	75,602	(129)	29,872	(17)	12,475	(35)	89,033
China (Taiwan)							
1950	2,148	(6)	1,079	(1)	750		---
1960	3,031	(8)	1,852		---	(1)	1,329
1970	3,852	(10)	2,535	(1)	735	(1)	2,150
China							
1950	21,135	(76)	14,190	(15)	9,915	(8)	16,450
1960	39,571	(87)	17,040	(19)	14,101	(18)	40,150
1970	68,610	(96)	22,790	(12)	8,800	(31)	76,525
Hong Kong							
1950	---		---		---	(1)	1,561
1960	---		---		---	(1)	3,075
1970	---		---		---	(1)	4,105
Korea, North							
1950	231	(3)	514	(1)	516		---
1960	310	(6)	1,037	(1)	653		---
1970	620	(8)	1,580	(1)	800		---

REGION AND COUNTRY	CLASS I	CLASS II		CLASS III		CLASS IV	
Korea, South							
1950	626	(6)	1,115	(1)	542	(1)	1,467
1960	1,290	(6)	1,421	(1)	677	(2)	3,609
1970	2,108	(12)	2,046	(3)	2,140	(2)	6,253
Macau							
1950	---	(1)	188	---		---	
1960	---	(1)	169	---		---	
1970	---	(1)	280	---		---	
Mongolia							
1950	145		---	---		---	
1960	169	(1)	164	---		---	
1970	314	(1)	350	---		---	
Ryukyu Islands							
1950	193		---	---		---	
1960	75	(1)	223	---		---	
1970	98	(1)	291	---		---	
<u>JAPAN</u>							
Japan							
1950	8,985	(58)	10,136	(2)	1,716	(4)	10,366
1960	20,153	(104)	19,313	(3)	1,804	(6)	18,063
1970	28,949	(119)	26,881	(5)	3,261	(9)	26,418
<u>SOUTHEAST ASIA</u>							
1950	11,091	(22)	4,306	(5)	3,627	(3)	4,255
1960	15,121	(36)	7,835	(3)	2,482	(6)	10,872
1970	22,686	(44)	8,469	(9)	5,975	(9)	20,063
Brunei							
1950	20		---	---		---	
1960	36		---	---		---	
1970	52		---	---		---	
Burma							
1950	1,448	(2)	281	(1)	696	---	
1960	2,006	(2)	310	(1)	884	---	
1970	2,452	(4)	680	---		(1)	1,200

REGION AND COUNTRY	CLASS I	CLASS II		CLASS III		CLASS IV	
Cambodia							
1950	168	(1)	152		---		---
1960	213	(1)	337		---		---
1970	178		---	(1)	700		---
Indonesia							
1950	4,700	(8)	1,995	(2)	1,190	(1)	1,452
1960	4,882	(18)	4,188	(1)	954	(2)	3,940
1970	6,796	(17)	3,540	(5)	3,400	(3)	7,400
Laos							
1950	86		---		---		---
1960	86	(1)	114		---		---
1970	190	(1)	210		---		---
West Malaysia							
1950	854	(2)	409		---		---
1960	1,636	(3)	774		---		---
1970	2,691	(5)	950	(1)	650		---
Maldive Islands							
1950	9		---		---		---
1960	10		---		---		---
1970	13		---		---		---
Philippines							
1950	1,503	(6)	745		---	(1)	1,781
1960	1,959	(7)	1,159		---	(1)	2,704
1970	2,743	(10)	2,024		---	(1)	4,100
Portuguese Timor							
1950	44		---		---		---
1960	52		---		---		---
1970	62		---		---		---
Sabah							
1950	44		---		---		---
1960	68		---		---		---
1970	110		---		---		---
Sarawak							
1950	67		---		---		---
1960	112		---		---		---
1970	188		---		---		---

TABLE B (continued)

REGION AND COUNTRY	CLASS I	CLASS II		CLASS III		CLASS IV	
Singapore							
1950	---		---		---	(1)	1,022
1960	---		---		---	(1)	1,634
1970	---		---		---	(1)	2,113
Thailand							
1950	802	(1)	276	(1)	891		---
1960	1,299	(1)	375		---	(1)	1,330
1970	1,834	(1)	100	(1)	625	(1)	2,100
Viet-Nam, North							
1950	483	(2)	448		---		---
1960	1,276	(1)	369	(1)	644		---
1970	2,942	(3)	335	(1)	600	(1)	1,400
Viet-Nam, South							
1950	851		---	(1)	850		---
1960	1,471	(2)	209		---	(1)	1,264
1970	2,416	(3)	630		---	(1)	1,750
West Irian							
1950	13		---		---		---
1960	14		---		---		---
1970	19		---		---		---
SOUTHWEST ASIA							
1950	8,445	(21)	3,888	(2)	1,523	(1)	1,073
1960	11,561	(36)	6,875	(3)	1,995	(2)	3,306
1970	14,229	(47)	9,462	(7)	4,610	(4)	8,350
Bahrain							
1950	78		---		---		---
1960	109		---		---		---
1970	161		---		---		---
Cyprus							
1950	120		---		---		---
1960	206		---		---		---
1970	190	(1)	112		---		---
Fed. of South Arabia (Southern Yemen)							
1950	24	(1)	107		---		---
1960	35	(1)	181		---		---
1970	50	(1)	275		---		---

REGION AND COUNTRY	CLASS I	CLASS II		CLASS III		CLASS IV	
Gaza Strip							
1950	---		---		---		---
1960	---		---		---		---
1970	---		---		---		---
Iran							
1950	2,046	(7)	1,228		---	(1)	1,073
1960	3,347	(10)	1,893		---	(1)	1,839
1970	4,676	(11)	2,370	(2)	1,010	(1)	3,250
Iraq							
1950	1,027	(2)	240	(1)	540		---
1960	1,220	(4)	645	(1)	815		---
1970	1,144	(8)	1,560		---	(1)	1,250
Israel							
1950	626	(2)	378		---		---
1960	804	(4)	833		---		---
1970	760	(2)	705	(1)	900		---
Jordan							
1950	447		---		---		---
1960	442	(1)	225		---		---
1970	589	(2)	475		---		---
Kuwait							
1950	98		---		---		---
1960	49	(1)	146		---		---
1970	117	(1)	325		---		---
Lebanon							
1950	149	(1)	321		---		---
1960	133	(2)	565		---		---
1970	184	(2)	250	(1)	600		---
Muscat and Oman							
1950	13		---		---		---
1960	20		---		---		---
1970	30		---		---		---
Qatar							
1950	10		---		---		---
1960	27		---		---		---
1970	65		---		---		---

TABLE B (continued)

REGION AND COUNTRY	CLASS I	CLASS II		CLASS III		CLASS IV	
Saudi Arabia							
1950	400	(1)	100	---		---	
1960	524	(3)	476	---		---	
1970	862	(5)	995	---		---	
Syria							
1950	441	(3)	775	---		---	
1960	482	(3)	673	(1)	530	---	
1970	471	(3)	530	(2)	1,350	---	
Trucial Oman							
1950	20	---		---		---	
1960	40	---		---		---	
1970	87	---		---		---	
Turkey							
1950	2,871	(4)	739	(1)	983	---	
1960	3,953	(7)	1,238	(1)	650	(1)	1,467
1970	4,542	(11)	1,865	(1)	750	(2)	3,850
Yemen							
1950	75	---		---		---	
1960	170	---		---		---	
1970	301	---		---		---	
SOUTH CENTRAL ASIA							
1950	37,571	(81)	14,674	(6)	4,648	(6)	14,085
1960	45,065	(105)	21,336	(6)	4,465	(9)	21,376
1970	56,955	(125)	26,829	(17)	10,932	(12)	31,503
Afghanistan							
1950	476	(1)	218	---		---	
1960	503	(2)	393	---		---	
1970	393	(2)	235	(1)	500	---	
Bhutan							
1950	---	---		---		---	
1960	---	---		---		---	
1970	---	---		---		---	
Ceylon							
1950	427	---		(1)	722	---	
1960	524	---		(1)	950	---	
1970	750	(1)	100	---		(1)	1,250

TABLE B (continued)

REGION AND COUNTRY	CLASS I		CLASS II		CLASS III		CLASS IV
India							
1950	32,347	(69)	12,337	(4)	3,100	(5)	12,999
1960	38,448	(87)	17,379	(4)	2,984	(7)	18,230
1970	47,941	(105)	22,117	(12)	7,270	(9)	25,105
Kashmir-Jammu							
1950	279	(1)	242		---		---
1960	280	(2)	393		---		---
1970	401	(2)	500		---		---
Nepal							
1950	71	(1)	121		---		---
1960	51	(1)	205		---		---
1970	112	(1)	440		---		---
Pakistan							
1950	3,968	(9)	1,756	(1)	826	(1)	1,086
1960	5,247	(13)	2,966	(1)	531	(2)	3,146
1970	6,431	(14)	3,437	(4)	3,162	(2)	5,148
Sikkim							
1950	3		---		---		---
1960	7		---		---		---
1970	17		---		---		---
NORTHERN EUROPE							
1950	9,664	(52)	11,230	(10)	6,285	(8)	23,261
1960	11,361	(50)	11,235	(11)	6,802	(9)	25,450
1970	13,525	(53)	11,788	(13)	8,600	(9)	26,865
Channel Islands							
1950	42		---		---		---
1960	41		---		---		---
1970	52		---		---		---
Denmark							
1950	1,449	(2)	265		---	(1)	1,168
1960	1,828	(2)	307		---	(1)	1,262
1970	2,074	(3)	423		---	(1)	1,480
Faeroe Islands							
1950	6		---		---		---
1960	7		---		---		---
1970	10		---		---		---

REGION AND COUNTRY	CLASS I	CLASS II		CLASS III		CLASS IV	
Finland							
1950	1,013	(3)	660		---		---
1960	1,590	(2)	331	(1)	566		---
1970	2,099	(2)	403	(1)	757		---
Iceland							
1950	87		---		---		---
1960	117		---		---		---
1970	152		---		---		---
Ireland							
1950	461	(1)	112	(1)	632		---
1960	520	(1)	115	(1)	661		---
1970	583	(1)	130	(1)	775		---
Isle of Man							
1950	30		---		---		---
1960	27		---		---		---
1970	30		---		---		---
Norway							
1950	735	(1)	144	(1)	505		---
1960	1,021	(1)	149	(1)	580		---
1970	1,138	(3)	399	(1)	590		---
Sweden							
1950	2,400	(2)	576	(1)	928		---
1960	2,689	(2)	732		---	(1)	1,149
1970	2,698	(3)	644	(1)	650	(1)	1,350
United Kingdom							
1950	3,441	(43)	9,473	(7)	4,220	(7)	22,093
1960	3,521	(42)	9,601	(8)	4,995	(7)	23,039
1970	4,689	(41)	9,789	(9)	5,828	(7)	24,035
WESTERN EUROPE							
1950	32,470	(67)	13,865	(13)	9,245	(10)	22,309
1960	36,335	(83)	17,096	(15)	11,104	(11)	26,990
1970	42,077	(86)	20,418	(13)	8,891	(17)	38,343
Austria							
1950	788	(4)	750		---	(1)	1,861
1960	875	(4)	777		---	(1)	1,874
1970	1,097	(4)	815		---	(1)	1,890

REGION AND COUNTRY	CLASS I	CLASS II		CLASS III		CLASS IV	
Belgium							
1950	2,993	(3)	921	(2)	1,562		---
1960	3,456	(3)	951	(1)	637	(1)	1,013
1970	3,980	(3)	990	(1)	674	(1)	1,104
France							
1950	11,652	(20)	3,691	(2)	1,257	(1)	5,998
1960	12,519	(34)	6,631	(2)	1,589	(1)	7,287
1970	14,146	(37)	8,699	(2)	1,041	(3)	11,001
Germany, Fed. Rep.							
1950	12,263	(26)	5,998	(6)	4,105	(8)	14,450
1960	14,515	(24)	5,769	(8)	5,911	(8)	16,816
1970	17,409	(23)	5,700	(8)	5,731	(10)	21,987
Liechtenstein							
1950	3		---		---		---
1960	4		---		---		---
1970	5		---		---		---
Luxembourg							
1950	174		---		---		---
1960	196		---		---		---
1970	225		---		---		---
Monaco							
1950	22		---		---		---
1960	23		---		---		---
1970	26		---		---		---
The Netherlands							
1950	3,463	(9)	1,346	(3)	2,321		---
1960	3,386	(13)	1,926	(3)	2,430		---
1970	3,538	(13)	2,785	(1)	778	(2)	2,361
Switzerland							
1950	1,112	(5)	1,159		---		---
1960	1,362	(5)	1,042	(1)	537		---
1970	1,651	(6)	1,429	(1)	667		---
EASTERN EUROPE							
1950	22,244	(28)	5,610	(4)	2,837	(5)	6,875
1960	27,030	(42)	8,606	(4)	3,162	(5)	8,081
1970	31,494	(45)	9,338	(6)	3,803	(7)	12,029

REGION AND COUNTRY	CLASS I	CLASS II		CLASS III		CLASS IV	
Bulgaria							
1950	1,329	(1)	138	(1)	520		---
1960	1,821	(3)	419	(1)	687		---
1970	2,197	(5)	865	(1)	920		---
Czechoslovakia							
1950	3,469	(4)	791	(1)	931		---
1960	4,467	(4)	974	(1)	998		---
1970	5,324	(5)	1,210		---	(1)	1,050
Germany, East							
1950	9,324	(8)	1,895	(1)	618	(1)	1,189
1960	9,760	(9)	2,010	(1)	590	(1)	1,077
1970	10,480	(8)	1,607	(2)	1,127	(1)	1,100
Hungary							
1950	1,603	(2)	229		---	(1)	1,600
1960	1,765	(3)	389		---	(1)	1,804
1970	2,021	(4)	640		---	(1)	2,060
Poland							
1950	3,988	(9)	2,028	(1)	768	(2)	2,975
1960	6,287	(12)	3,181	(1)	887	(2)	3,851
1970	8,238	(10)	2,296	(3)	1,756	(3)	6,119
Romania							
1950	2,531	(4)	529		---	(1)	1,111
1960	2,930	(11)	1,633		---	(1)	1,349
1970	3,234	(13)	2,720		---	(1)	1,700
SOUTHERN EUROPE							
1950	22,390	(49)	8,692	(7)	4,613	(6)	8,262
1960	25,291	(62)	11,503	(7)	5,184	(7)	11,636
1970	27,036	(82)	16,267	(5)	3,498	(10)	18,253
Albania							
1950	250		---		---		---
1960	366	(1)	136		---		---
1970	530	(1)	220		---		---
Andorra							
1950	---		---		---		---
1960	---		---		---		---
1970	---		---		---		---

REGION AND COUNTRY	CLASS I	CLASS II		CLASS III		CLASS IV	
Gibraltar							
1950	23		---		---		---
1960	24		---		---		---
1970	26		---		---		---
Greece							
1950	2,217	(1)	291		---	(1)	1,345
1960	2,461	(2)	473		---	(1)	1,812
1970	2,547	(2)	580		---	(1)	2,425
Holy See							
1950	1		---		---		---
1960	1		---		---		---
1970	1		---		---		---
Italy							
1950	11,096	(21)	4,251	(3)	2,352	(2)	2,857
1960	11,703	(25)	5,017	(3)	2,323	(3)	4,671
1970	11,805	(34)	6,518	(3)	2,138	(4)	7,145
Malta + Gozo Is.							
1950	186		---		---		---
1960	210		---		---		---
1970	211		---		---		---
Portugal							
1950	819		---	(1)	655	(1)	1,161
1960	929		---	(1)	746	(1)	1,335
1970	1,199		---	(1)	850	(1)	1,500
San Marino							
1950	4		---		---		---
1960	4		---		---		---
1970	4		---		---		---
Spain							
1950	6,898	(21)	3,332	(1)	509	(2)	2,899
1960	7,923	(23)	4,160	(1)	505	(2)	3,818
1970	8,469	(28)	5,550	(1)	510	(2)	4,840
Yugoslavia							
1950	896	(6)	818	(2)	1,097		---
1960	1,670	(11)	1,717	(2)	1,610		---
1970	2,244	(17)	3,399		---	(2)	2,343

REGION AND COUNTRY	CLASS I	CLASS II		CLASS III		CLASS IV	
AUSTRALIA-NEW ZEALAND							
1950	2,097	(7)	1,979		---	(2)	3,040
1960	3,106	(7)	1,652	(2)	1,174	(2)	3,984
1970	3,534	(9)	1,508	(4)	2,915	(2)	4,920
Australia							
1950	1,565	(4)	1,352		---	(2)	3,040
1960	2,403	(4)	851	(2)	1,174	(2)	3,984
1970	2,957	(5)	823	(3)	2,280	(2)	4,920
New Zealand							
1950	532	(3)	627		---		---
1960	703	(3)	801		---		---
1970	577	(4)	685	(1)	635		---
OCEANIA							
1950	116		---		---		---
1960	185		---		---		---
1970	305		---		---		---
American Samoa							
1950	2		---		---		---
1960	1		---		---		---
1970	2		---		---		---
Christmas Island							
1950	---		---		---		---
1960	---		---		---		---
1970	---		---		---		---
Cocos Islands							
1950	---		---		---		---
1960	---		---		---		---
1970	---		---		---		---
Cook Islands							
1950	---		---		---		---
1960	---		---		---		---
1970	---		---		---		---
Fiji							
1950	50		---		---		---
1960	72		---		---		---
1970	106		---		---		---

REGION AND COUNTRY	CLASS I	CLASS II	CLASS III	CLASS IV
French Polynesia				
1950	14	---	---	---
1960	19	---	---	---
1970	26	---	---	---
Gilbert + Ellice Is.				
1950	---	---	---	---
1960	7	---	---	---
1970	13	---	---	---
Guam				
1950	1	---	---	---
1960	5	---	---	---
1970	20	---	---	---
Johnston Island				
1950	---	---	---	---
1960	---	---	---	---
1970	---	---	---	---
Midway Islands				
1950	---	---	---	---
1960	---	---	---	---
1970	---	---	---	---
Nauru				
1950	---	---	---	---
1960	---	---	---	---
1970	---	---	---	---
New Caledonia				
1950	15	---	---	---
1960	30	---	---	---
1970	55	---	---	---
New Guinea				
1950	---	---	---	---
1960	---	---	---	---
1970	---	---	---	---
New Hebrides				
1950	---	---	---	---
1960	---	---	---	---
1970	---	---	---	---

TABLE B (continued)

REGION AND COUNTRY	CLASS I	CLASS II	CLASS III	CLASS IV
Niue Island				
1950	---	---	---	---
1960	---	---	---	---
1970	---	---	---	---
Norfolk Island				
1950	---	---	---	---
1960	---	---	---	---
1970	---	---	---	---
Pacific Islands				
1950	---	---	---	---
1960	---	---	---	---
1970	---	---	---	---
Papua				
1950	12	---	---	---
1960	14	---	---	---
1970	29	---	---	---
Solomon Is. (UK)				
1950	2	---	---	---
1960	4	---	---	---
1970	6	---	---	---
Tokelau Islands				
1950	---	---	---	---
1960	---	---	---	---
1970	---	---	---	---
Tonga				
1950	8	---	---	---
1960	10	---	---	---
1970	14	---	---	---
Wake Island				
1950	---	---	---	---
1960	---	---	---	---
1970	---	---	---	---
Western Samoa				
1950	12	---	---	---
1960	21	---	---	---
1970	34	---	---	---

REGION AND COUNTRY	CLASS I	CLASS II	CLASS III	CLASS IV
U.S.S.R.				
U.S.S.R.				
1950	38,970	(98) 19,918	(14) 9,134	(2) 8,478
1960	54,107	(134) 26,600	(21) 15,056	(4) 11,655
1970	77,018	(166) 35,776	(25) 18,646	(10) 20,560

TABLE C

EXPLANATION

The two preceding tables gave the absolute population figures. They showed the total population of each country, the
urban population, and the urban population subdivided into four
classes according to size. The present table converts these
data into proportions. It shows, for each country and region,
the percentage of the total population residing in places classified by size. It uses the same size-categories as were used
in the previous tables.

In the present study the term "rural" designates a residual
category. It is the non-urban population. As such it includes
people residing in all types of non-urban settlements, from
scattered farmsteads and dispersed dwellings to hamlets and
villages. The exact meaning of "rural" depends on how "urban"
is defined in each country (see the Explanation of Table A).
Similarly, the first class of the urban population--the "town"
class--is residual. It is the remainder when the city population (i.e. in places of 100,000 and over) is subtracted from the
total urban population. The size of the town class, like the
size of the rural, depends in part on how the lower limit of
"urban" is defined.

To avoid cumbersome column headings, we have given the
urban classes Roman numerals. Although the meaning of these
divisions was explained in connection with Table B, the explanation is repeated here for convenience.

Class I.   Places defined as urban but having fewer than
           100,000 inhabitants. These are referred to as
           "towns" in our study, and their population is
           called the "town population."

Class II. Cities of 100,000 to 499,999 inhabitants.

Class III. Cities of 500,000 to 999,999 inhabitants.

Class IV. Cities of 1,000,000 or more inhabitants.

Except for slight discrepancies due to rounding, all five
columns in the present table add horizontally to 100.0 per cent.
In other words, the classes shown make up the total population
of each country or region. Since the percentages are derived
from the absolute figures given in Tables A and B, the explana-
tory notes to those two tables should be consulted for further
details.

TABLE C

PER CENT OF POPULATION IN RURAL AREAS AND
IN FOUR URBAN SIZE-CLASSES, 1950, 1960, AND 1970

REGION AND COUNTRY	RURAL	URBAN CLASS			
		I	II	III	IV
NORTHERN AFRICA					
1950	75.4	9.8	4.5	3.4	6.8
1960	70.4	11.3	6.5	3.8	8.0
1970	65.4	13.5	7.7	2.6	10.7
Algeria					
1950	75.5	12.6	6.0	6.0	---
1960	68.8	14.8	8.2	8.2	---
1970	61.8	24.6	6.4	7.2	---
Ifni					
1950	79.1	20.9	---	---	---
1960	74.3	25.7	---	---	---
1970	68.5	31.5	---	---	---
Libya					
1950	78.8	9.8	11.4	---	---
1960	75.4	3.3	21.3	---	---
1970	71.8	2.05	26.1	---	---
Morocco					
1950	76.9	7.3	8.6	7.2	---
1960	70.9	10.2	10.6	8.3	---
1970	64.7	11.4	11.0	3.5	9.4
Sp. North Africa					
1950	---	100.0	---	---	---
1960	---	100.0	---	---	---
1970	---	100.0	---	---	---
Spanish Sahara					
1950	81.0	19.0	---	---	---
1960	58.0	42.0	---	---	---
1970	33.3	66.7	---	---	---
Sudan					
1950	93.7	3.8	2.6	---	---
1960	92.7	4.6	2.7	---	---
1970	91.7	5.5	2.9	---	---
Tunisia					
1950	69.4	13.3	---	17.3	---
1960	63.0	21.4	---	15.6	---
1970	56.6	21.2	7.9	14.3	---

TABLE C (continued)

REGION AND COUNTRY	RURAL	URBAN CLASS			
		I	II	III	IV
U.A.R.					
1950	68.2	11.1	3.5	---	17.3
1960	62.2	11.7	6.0	---	20.2
1970	56.3	12.7	8.0	---	23.0
WESTERN AFRICA					
1950	89.4	7.8	2.8	---	---
1960	85.3	9.8	4.3	.7	---
1970	80.3	12.3	4.8	2.6	---
Cape Verde Islands					
1950	93.2	6.8	---	---	---
1960	93.4	6.5	---	---	---
1970	90.6	9.4	---	---	---
Dahomey					
1950	91.4	8.6	---	---	---
1960	88.1	11.9	---	---	---
1970	84.0	9.6	6.4	---	---
Gambia					
1950	92.9	7.1	---	---	---
1960	91.4	8.6	---	---	---
1970	89.8	10.2	---	---	---
Ghana					
1950	85.8	10.7	3.6	---	---
1960	76.9	12.2	10.9	---	---
1970	66.1	16.1	9.3	8.5	---
Guinea					
1950	94.7	5.3	---	---	---
1960	92.2	4.2	3.6	---	---
1970	88.8	5.8	5.5	---	---
Ivory Coast					
1950	92.4	7.6	---	---	---
1960	84.2	10.2	5.6	---	---
1970	71.0	17.5	11.5	---	---
Liberia					
1950	95.1	4.9	---	---	---
1960	87.0	13.0	---	---	---
1970	70.5	29.5	---	---	---

TABLE C (continued)

REGION AND COUNTRY	RURAL	URBAN CLASS			
		I	II	III	IV
Mali					
1950	95.9	4.1	---	---	---
1960	94.0	2.8	3.1	---	---
1970	91.4	4.1	4.5	---	---
Mauritania					
1950	97.9	2.1	---	---	---
1960	97.7	2.3	---	---	---
1970	97.6	2.4	---	---	---
Niger					
1950	97.7	2.3	---	---	---
1960	97.4	2.6	---	---	---
1970	96.9	3.1	---	---	---
Nigeria					
1950	86.9	8.8	4.3	---	---
1960	83.2	11.4	4.1	1.2	---
1970	79.1	13.9	4.6	2.4	---
Portuguese Guinea					
1950	90.0	10.0	---	---	---
1960	86.3	13.7	---	---	---
1970	81.9	18.1	---	---	---
Saint Helena					
1950	100.0	---	---	---	---
1960	100.0	---	---	---	---
1970	100.0	---	---	---	---
Senegal					
1950	80.2	10.9	8.9	---	---
1960	76.5	12.0	11.5	---	---
1970	72.7	12.2	---	15.2	---
Sierra Leone					
1950	91.3	8.7	---	---	---
1960	88.8	6.5	4.8	---	---
1970	85.8	7.3	6.9	---	---
Togo					
1950	94.7	5.3	---	---	---
1960	90.3	9.7	---	---	---
1970	83.5	6.8	9.7	---	---

TABLE C (continued)

| REGION AND | RURAL | URBAN CLASS | | | |
COUNTRY		I	II	III	IV
Upper Volta					
1950	97.3	2.7	---	---	---
1960	96.4	3.6	---	---	---
1970	95.3	4.7	---	---	---
EASTERN AFRICA					
1950	94.4	4.2	1.4	---	---
1960	92.5	4.7	2.8	---	---
1970	90.1	5.0	3.7	1.2	---
Burundi					
1950	99.0	1.0	---	---	---
1960	98.4	1.6	---	---	---
1970	97.4	2.6	---	---	---
Comoro Islands					
1950	96.2	3.8	---	---	---
1960	94.8	5.2	---	---	---
1970	92.7	7.3	---	---	---
Ethiopia					
1950	94.1	3.5	2.4	---	---
1960	93.7	3.6	2.7	---	---
1970	93.4	3.5	.6	2.5	---
French Somaliland					
1950	66.7	33.3	---	---	---
1960	54.7	45.3	---	---	---
1970	43.1	56.9	---	---	---
Kenya					
1950	94.8	2.9	2.2	---	---
1960	92.5	2.1	5.3	---	---
1970	90.8	2.0	2.6	4.6	---
Madagascar					
1950	91.1	4.7	4.2	---	---
1960	89.2	6.2	4.6	---	---
1970	87.0	6.7	6.3	---	---
Malawi					
1950	98.8	1.2	---	---	---
1960	97.4	2.6	---	---	---
1970	94.6	1.5	3.9	---	---

TABLE C (continued)

REGION AND COUNTRY	RURAL	URBAN CLASS			
		I	II	III	IV
Mauritius					
1950	70.4	29.6	---	---	---
1960	57.6	42.4	---	---	---
1970	45.3	37.7	17.0	---	---
Mozambique					
1950	97.8	2.2	---	---	---
1960	96.4	.9	2.7	---	---
1970	94.0	1.5	4.4	---	---
Reunion					
1950	75.9	24.1	---	---	---
1960	68.2	31.8	---	---	---
1970	60.4	39.6	---	---	---
Rwanda					
1950	99.9	.1	---	---	---
1960	99.8	.2	---	---	---
1970	99.7	.3	---	---	---
Seychelles					
1950	73.1	26.9	---	---	---
1960	75.0	25.0	---	---	---
1970	68.0	32.0	---	---	---
Somalia					
1950	84.0	16.0	---	---	---
1960	80.1	19.9	---	---	---
1970	75.8	17.4	6.8	---	---
Southern Rhodesia					
1950	90.3	5.6	4.1	---	---
1960	83.7	4.8	11.5	---	---
1970	79.9	6.1	14.0	---	---
Tanganyika					
1950	97.0	3.0	---	---	---
1960	95.3	3.1	1.6	---	---
1970	92.9	4.4	2.7	---	---
Uganda					
1950	98.0	2.0	---	---	---
1960	96.2	1.8	2.0	---	---
1970	92.8	3.4	3.8	---	---

TABLE C (continued)

REGION AND COUNTRY	RURAL	URBAN CLASS			
		I	II	III	IV
Zambia					
1950	87.0	13.0	---	---	---
1960	81.0	19.0	---	---	---
1970	73.7	14.8	11.4	---	---
Zanzibar					
1950	78.7	21.3	---	---	---
1960	72.2	27.8	---	---	---
1970	65.2	34.8	---	---	---
MIDDLE AND SOUTHERN AFRICA					
1950	93.4	4.9	1.7	---	---
1960	88.4	7.1	4.5	---	---
1970	84.6	9.4	4.5	1.5	---
Angola					
1950	94.0	2.5	3.4	---	---
1960	91.9	3.5	4.7	---	---
1970	89.2	4.8	6.1	---	---
Basutoland (Lesotho)					
1950	99.4	.6	---	---	---
1960	99.0	1.0	---	---	---
1970	98.3	1.7	---	---	---
Bechuanaland (Botswana)					
1950	79.7	20.3	---	---	---
1960	79.1	20.9	---	---	---
1970	78.4	21.6	---	---	---
Cameroon					
1950	94.9	5.1	---	---	---
1960	91.7	5.0	3.3	---	---
1970	87.2	6.9	5.9	---	---
Central African Rep.					
1950	92.8	7.2	---	---	---
1960	86.3	13.7	---	---	---
1970	76.2	12.5	11.4	---	---
Chad					
1950	97.8	2.2	---	---	---
1960	95.8	4.2	---	---	---
1970	92.3	7.7	---	---	---

TABLE C (continued)

REGION AND COUNTRY	RURAL	URBAN CLASS			
		I	II	III	IV
Congo, Brazzaville					
1950	83.9	16.1	---	---	---
1960	73.6	10.0	16.4	---	---
1970	61.5	17.3	21.2	---	---
Congo, Dem. Rep.					
1950	92.5	4.7	2.7	---	---
1960	85.5	8.1	6.4	---	---
1970	82.8	10.1	3.8	3.3	---
Gabon					
1950	93.3	6.7	---	---	---
1960	87.7	12.3	---	---	---
1970	79.2	20.8	---	---	---
Sao Tome					
1950	87.0	13.0	---	---	---
1960	84.9	15.1	---	---	---
1970	82.1	17.9	---	---	---
South West Africa					
1950	85.1	14.9	---	---	---
1960	76.6	23.4	---	---	---
1970	66.4	33.6	---	---	---
Sp. Eq. Guinea					
1950	94.4	5.6	---	---	---
1960	90.5	9.5	---	---	---
1970	84.6	15.4	---	---	---
Swaziland					
1950	100.0	---	---	---	---
1960	97.2	2.8	---	---	---
1970	95.7	4.3	---	---	---
SOUTH AFRICA					
South Africa					
1950	60.9	15.5	12.2	11.4	---
1960	55.1	18.4	10.0	9.3	7.2
1970	49.6	18.7	10.7	8.5	12.5
NORTHERN AMERICA					
1950	36.2	20.5	13.0	5.9	24.4
1960	30.3	19.9	13.8	8.1	27.9
1970	24.9	17.7	13.4	7.9	36.1

TABLE C (continued)

REGION AND COUNTRY	RURAL	URBAN CLASS			
		I	II	III	IV
Bermuda					
1950	---	100.0	---	---	---
1960	---	100.0	---	---	---
1970	---	100.0	---	---	---
Canada					
1950	38.3	25.0	15.1	4.0	17.7
1960	31.5	25.5	18.0	4.3	20.8
1970	25.3	25.4	14.5	12.0	22.8
Greenland					
1950	91.7	8.3	---	---	---
1960	90.3	9.7	---	---	---
1970	87.8	12.2	---	---	---
St. Pierre and Miq.					
1950	100.0	---	---	---	---
1960	100.0	---	---	---	---
1970	100.0	---	---	---	---
U.S.A.					
1950	36.0	20.1	12.8	6.1	25.0
1960	30.1	19.4	13.3	8.5	28.7
1970	24.8	16.9	13.3	7.5	37.6
MIDDLE AMERICA					
1950	60.8	25.5	7.2	---	6.4
1960	53.8	28.9	8.4	2.8	6.0
1970	47.0	32.9	9.3	1.9	8.8
British Honduras					
1950	63.3	36.7	---	---	---
1960	63.3	36.7	---	---	---
1970	62.9	37.1	---	---	---
Canal Zone					
1950	67.4	32.6	---	---	---
1960	68.2	31.8	---	---	---
1970	62.3	37.7	---	---	---
Costa Rica					
1950	66.7	15.9	17.4	---	---
1960	65.2	12.8	21.9	---	---
1970	63.8	11.6	24.6	---	---

TABLE C (continued)

REGION AND COUNTRY	RURAL	URBAN CLASS			
		I	II	III	IV
El Salvador					
1950	63.5	27.7	8.7	---	---
1960	61.9	28.4	9.7	---	---
1970	60.2	26.2	13.6	---	---
Guatemala					
1950	75.1	14.4	10.5	---	---
1960	69.3	18.2	12.4	---	---
1970	63.4	21.7	---	14.9	---
Honduras					
1950	82.3	17.7	---	---	---
1960	78.4	13.5	8.2	---	---
1970	74.1	15.5	10.4	---	---
Mexico					
1950	57.4	27.5	6.4	---	8.7
1960	49.3	32.1	6.7	3.8	8.1
1970	41.8	37.0	8.5	1.1	11.7
Nicaragua					
1950	65.1	24.6	10.3	---	---
1960	60.7	25.4	14.0	---	---
1970	56.3	26.1	17.6	---	---
Panama					
1950	64.0	20.1	15.9	---	---
1960	58.6	16.1	25.4	---	---
1970	53.2	16.7	30.0	---	---
CARIBBEAN					
1950	64.8	20.8	7.7	---	6.6
1960	61.5	21.1	7.0	2.7	7.6
1970	57.5	21.8	6.2	7.9	6.6
Bahama Islands					
1950	61.5	38.5	---	---	---
1960	53.7	46.3	---	---	---
1970	46.2	53.8	---	---	---
Barbados Islands					
1950	64.3	35.7	---	---	---
1960	59.6	40.4	---	---	---
1970	54.9	45.1	---	---	---

TABLE C (continued)

REGION AND COUNTRY	RURAL	URBAN CLASS			
		I	II	III	IV
Cayman Islands					
1950	100.0	---	---	---	---
1960	100.0	---	---	---	---
1970	100.0	---	---	---	---
Cuba					
1950	43.5	32.4	4.6	---	19.6
1960	42.5	30.0	4.8	---	22.7
1970	41.6	27.9	10.9	---	19.6
Dominican Republic					
1950	76.2	15.3	8.5	---	---
1960	69.7	18.2	12.1	---	---
1970	63.0	19.4	2.5	15.0	---
Guadeloupe					
1950	85.4	14.6	---	---	---
1960	81.3	18.7	---	---	---
1970	76.7	23.3	---	---	---
Haiti					
1950	87.8	7.8	4.3	---	---
1960	85.2	8.7	6.0	---	---
1970	82.4	9.4	8.2	---	---
Jamaica					
1950	77.2	3.7	19.0	---	---
1960	70.8	6.1	23.1	---	---
1970	64.0	8.3	---	27.7	---
Leeward Islands					
1950	77.0	23.0	---	---	---
1960	71.5	28.5	---	---	---
1970	66.2	33.8	---	---	---
Martinique					
1950	70.8	29.2	---	---	---
1960	60.7	39.3	---	---	---
1970	50.9	49.1	---	---	---
Neth. Antilles					
1950	59.3	40.7	---	---	---
1960	50.2	49.8	---	---	---
1970	41.8	58.2	---	---	---

TABLE C (continued)

REGION AND COUNTRY	RURAL	URBAN CLASS			
		I	II	III	IV
Puerto Rico					
1950	59.5	21.1	19.4	---	---
1960	55.9	16.2	4.9	23.1	---
1970	52.3	14.4	4.6	28.7	---
Trinidad and Tobago					
1950	74.1	25.9	---	---	---
1960	60.4	39.6	---	---	---
1970	46.7	53.3	---	---	---
Turks and Caicos Is.					
1950	100.0	---	---	---	---
1960	100.0	---	---	---	---
1970	100.0	---	---	---	---
Virgin Islands (U.S.)					
1950	41.6	58.4	---	---	---
1960	43.9	56.1	---	---	---
1970	38.0	62.0	---	---	---
Windward Islands					
1950	83.9	16.1	---	---	---
1960	82.6	17.4	---	---	---
1970	81.1	18.9	---	---	---
TROPICAL SOUTH AMERICA					
1950	64.2	19.3	6.4	3.5	6.6
1960	55.3	20.9	8.1	3.0	12.7
1970	46.9	20.9	6.9	5.0	20.2
Bolivia					
1950	79.6	10.5	9.9	---	---
1960	77.2	11.2	11.6	---	---
1970	74.7	10.2	2.5	12.6	---
Brazil					
1950	63.9	18.6	5.6	1.3	10.6
1960	55.0	19.5	7.0	4.0	14.6
1970	46.5	19.6	6.6	3.8	23.5
British Guiana					
1950	72.1	27.9	---	---	---
1960	71.1	2.5	26.4	---	---
1970	70.0	2.8	27.1	---	---

TABLE C (continued)

REGION AND COUNTRY	RURAL	URBAN CLASS			
		I	II	III	IV
Colombia					
1950	63.0	19.7	12.0	5.4	---
1960	53.7	22.1	12.4	3.8	8.1
1970	45.0	19.8	10.9	7.4	17.0
Ecuador					
1950	71.5	13.9	14.6	---	---
1960	67.0	15.4	17.6	---	---
1970	62.5	16.1	---	21.3	---
French Guiana					
1950	55.2	44.8	---	---	---
1960	49.4	50.6	---	---	---
1970	43.9	56.1	---	---	---
Peru					
1950	64.5	24.1	---	11.4	---
1960	59.1	25.9	1.2	---	13.8
1970	53.9	24.2	3.5	---	18.4
Surinam					
1950	65.8	34.2	---	---	---
1960	64.0	36.0	---	---	---
1970	62.0	4.5	33.5	---	---
Venezuela					
1950	54.8	24.9	6.7	13.6	---
1960	37.6	33.1	12.0	---	17.4
1970	23.6	39.5	9.6	6.6	20.7
TEMPERATE SOUTH AMERICA					
1950	40.9	20.8	9.6	4.4	24.3
1960	35.0	19.5	10.8	6.9	27.8
1970	29.8	18.1	9.9	7.4	34.8
Argentina					
1950	36.7	17.7	11.8	3.3	30.5
1960	33.0	12.7	13.0	6.3	35.0
1970	29.5	9.2	10.4	11.9	39.0
Chile					
1950	45.7	27.8	5.5	---	21.0
1960	35.3	33.1	7.0	---	24.5
1970	26.3	36.7	9.7	---	27.3

TABLE C (continued)

REGION AND COUNTRY	RURAL	URBAN CLASS			
		I	II	III	IV
Falkland Islands					
1950	100.0	---	---	---	---
1960	100.0	---	---	---	---
1970	100.0	---	---	---	---
Paraguay					
1950	67.1	16.7	16.3	---	---
1960	65.6	16.6	17.8	---	---
1970	64.2	17.1	18.7	---	---
Uruguay					
1950	43.4	28.8	---	27.8	---
1960	28.0	34.1	---	37.9	---
1970	15.8	31.3	---	---	53.0
EAST ASIA					
1950	87.9	4.1	2.8	1.9	3.2
1960	82.0	6.2	3.0	2.1	6.7
1970	74.7	9.2	3.7	1.5	10.9
China (Taiwan)					
1950	47.8	28.2	14.2	9.8	---
1960	41.5	28.6	17.5	---	12.5
1970	35.6	26.7	17.6	5.1	14.9
China					
1950	89.0	3.8	2.5	1.8	2.9
1960	83.5	5.9	2.5	2.1	6.0
1970	76.5	9.1	3.0	1.2	10.2
Hong Kong					
1950	19.9	---	---	---	80.1
1960	---	---	---	---	100.0
1970	---	---	---	---	100.0
Korea, North					
1950	87.0	2.4	5.3	5.3	---
1960	81.1	2.9	9.8	6.2	---
1970	78.1	4.5	11.5	5.8	---
Korea, South					
1950	81.7	3.1	5.4	2.6	7.2
1960	72.0	5.2	5.7	2.7	14.4
1970	61.0	6.6	6.4	6.7	19.4

TABLE C (continued)

REGION AND COUNTRY	RURAL	URBAN CLASS			
		I	II	III	IV
Macau					
1950	---	---	100.0	---	---
1960	---	---	100.0	---	---
1970	---	---	100.0	---	---
Mongolia					
1950	80.2	19.8	---	---	---
1960	65.1	17.7	17.2	---	---
1970	48.4	24.4	27.2	---	---
Ryukyu Islands					
1950	72.0	28.0	---	---	---
1960	66.3	8.5	25.3	---	---
1970	60.5	10.0	29.6	---	---
JAPAN					
Japan					
1950	62.6	10.8	12.2	2.1	12.4
1960	36.5	21.6	20.7	1.9	19.3
1970	16.8	28.2	26.2	3.2	25.7
SOUTHEAST ASIA					
1950	86.4	6.5	2.5	2.1	2.5
1960	83.4	6.9	3.6	1.1	5.0
1970	79.9	8.0	3.0	2.1	7.0
Brunei					
1950	57.0	43.0	---	---	---
1960	56.5	43.5	---	---	---
1970	55.9	44.1	---	---	---
Burma					
1950	87.1	7.7	1.5	3.7	---
1960	85.7	9.0	1.4	4.0	---
1970	84.2	8.9	2.5	---	4.4
Cambodia					
1950	92.1	4.1	3.7	---	---
1960	89.9	3.9	6.2	---	---
1970	87.2	2.6	---	10.2	---
Indonesia					
1950	87.7	6.2	2.6	1.6	1.9
1960	85.1	5.2	4.5	1.0	4.2
1970	82.1	5.8	3.0	2.9	6.3

TABLE C (continued)

REGION AND COUNTRY	RURAL	URBAN CLASS			
		I	II	III	IV
Laos					
1950	93.5	6.5	---	---	---
1960	91.4	3.7	4.9	---	---
1970	86.6	6.4	7.0	---	---
West Malaysia					
1950	75.7	16.5	7.9	---	---
1960	65.1	23.7	11.2	---	---
1970	54.2	28.7	10.1	6.9	---
Maldive Islands					
1950	89.0	11.0	---	---	---
1960	88.7	11.3	---	---	---
1970	88.1	11.9	---	---	---
Philippines					
1950	80.1	7.4	3.7	---	8.8
1960	78.5	7.2	4.3	---	10.0
1970	76.8	7.2	5.3	---	10.7
Portuguese Timor					
1950	90.1	9.9	---	---	---
1960	89.9	10.1	---	---	---
1970	89.6	10.4	---	---	---
Sabah					
1950	86.8	13.2	---	---	---
1960	85.1	14.9	---	---	---
1970	83.3	16.7	---	---	---
Sarawak					
1950	88.5	11.5	---	---	---
1960	85.1	14.9	---	---	---
1970	81.0	19.0	---	---	---
Singapore					
1950	---	---	---	---	100.0
1960	---	---	---	---	100.0
1970	---	---	---	---	100.0
Thailand					
1950	90.0	4.1	1.4	4.5	---
1960	88.6	4.9	1.4	---	5.1
1970	87.0	5.1	.3	1.7	5.8

TABLE C (continued)

REGION AND COUNTRY	RURAL	URBAN CLASS			
		I	II	III	IV
Viet-Nam, North					
1950	92.2	4.0	3.7	---	---
1960	85.8	7.9	2.3	4.0	---
1970	76.1	13.3	1.5	2.7	6.3
Viet-Nam, South					
1950	83.8	8.1	---	8.1	---
1960	79.1	10.4	1.5	---	9.0
1970	73.9	13.1	3.4	---	9.5
West Irian					
1950	98.1	1.9	---	---	---
1960	98.0	2.0	---	---	---
1970	97.8	2.2	---	---	---
SOUTHWEST ASIA					
1950	75.8	13.7	6.3	2.5	1.7
1960	70.5	14.4	8.6	2.5	4.1
1970	64.5	13.8	9.2	4.5	8.1
Bahrain					
1950	29.3	70.7	---	---	---
1960	27.3	72.7	---	---	---
1970	25.5	74.5	---	---	---
Cyprus					
1950	75.7	24.3	---	---	---
1960	64.1	35.9	---	---	---
1970	52.1	30.1	17.7	---	---
Fed. of South Arabia (Southern Yemen)					
1950	81.2	3.4	15.4	---	---
1960	72.0	4.5	23.5	---	---
1970	67.5	5.0	27.5	---	---
Gaza Strip					
1950	100.0	---	---	---	---
1960	100.0	---	---	---	---
1970	100.0	---	---	---	---
Iran					
1950	73.3	12.6	7.5	---	6.6
1960	67.1	15.6	8.8	---	8.6
1970	60.7	16.2	8.2	3.5	11.3

TABLE C (continued)

REGION AND COUNTRY	RURAL	URBAN CLASS			
		I	II	III	IV
Iraq					
1950	65.1	19.8	4.6	10.4	---
1960	60.8	17.9	9.4	11.9	---
1970	56.5	12.6	17.2	---	13.8
Israel					
1950	20.2	49.8	30.0	---	---
1960	22.6	38.0	39.4	---	---
1970	18.7	26.1	24.2	30.9	---
Jordan					
1950	65.3	34.7	---	---	---
1960	60.6	26.1	13.3	---	---
1970	56.1	24.3	19.6	---	---
Kuwait					
1950	42.4	57.6	---	---	---
1960	29.9	17.6	52.5	---	---
1970	19.6	21.3	59.1	---	---
Lebanon					
1950	73.5	8.4	18.1	---	---
1960	66.9	6.3	26.8	---	---
1970	60.2	7.1	9.6	23.1	---
Muscat and Oman					
1950	97.6	2.4	---	---	---
1960	96.5	3.5	---	---	---
1970	94.7	5.3	---	---	---
Qatar					
1950	50.0	50.0	---	---	---
1960	40.0	60.0	---	---	---
1970	31.6	68.4	---	---	---
Saudi Arabia					
1950	90.5	7.6	1.9	---	---
1960	83.9	8.5	7.7	---	---
1970	74.8	11.7	13.5	---	---
Syria					
1950	64.7	12.8	22.5	---	---
1960	63.1	10.6	14.8	11.6	---
1970	61.5	7.7	8.7	22.1	---

TABLE C (continued)

REGION AND COUNTRY	RURAL	URBAN CLASS			
		I	II	III	IV
Trucial Oman					
1950	75.0	25.0	---	---	---
1960	60.0	40.0	---	---	---
1970	44.9	55.1	---	---	---
Turkey					
1950	77.9	13.8	3.6	4.7	---
1960	73.4	14.4	4.5	2.4	5.3
1970	68.8	12.9	5.3	2.1	10.9
Yemen					
1950	98.1	1.9	---	---	---
1960	96.6	3.4	---	---	---
1970	94.0	6.0	---	---	---
SOUTH CENTRAL ASIA					
1950	84.8	8.0	3.2	1.0	3.0
1960	83.6	8.0	3.8	.8	3.8
1970	82.2	8.0	3.8	1.5	4.5
Afghanistan					
1950	94.2	4.0	1.8	---	---
1960	93.8	3.5	2.7	---	---
1970	93.3	2.4	1.4	3.0	---
Bhutan					
1950	100.0	---	---	---	---
1960	100.0	---	---	---	---
1970	100.0	---	---	---	---
Ceylon					
1950	85.0	5.6	---	9.4	---
1960	85.1	5.3	---	9.6	---
1970	83.4	6.0	.8	---	9.9
India					
1950	82.9	9.1	3.5	.9	3.7
1960	82.0	9.0	4.1	.7	4.2
1970	81.2	8.8	4.1	1.3	4.6
Kashmir-Jammu					
1950	88.1	6.4	5.5	---	---
1960	86.0	5.8	8.2	---	---
1970	83.6	7.3	9.1	---	---

TABLE C (continued)

REGION AND COUNTRY	RURAL	URBAN CLASS			
		I	II	III	IV
Nepal					
1950	97.6	.9	1.5	---	---
1960	97.2	.6	2.2	---	---
1970	95.0	1.0	3.9	---	---
Pakistan					
1950	90.6	4.5	2.3	1.1	1.4
1960	87.2	5.7	3.2	.6	3.4
1970	84.1	5.6	3.0	2.8	4.5
Sikkim					
1950	98.0	2.0	---	---	---
1960	95.7	4.2	---	---	---
1970	91.2	8.8	---	---	---
NORTHERN EUROPE					
1950	30.5	13.3	15.5	8.7	32.1
1960	27.7	15.0	14.8	9.0	33.5
1970	25.1	16.7	14.5	10.6	33.1
Channel Islands					
1950	59.8	40.2	---	---	---
1960	62.9	37.1	---	---	---
1970	56.3	43.7	---	---	---
Denmark					
1950	32.7	33.8	6.2	---	27.3
1960	25.9	39.9	6.7	---	27.5
1970	19.9	41.8	8.5	---	29.8
Faeroe Islands					
1950	82.5	17.5	---	---	---
1960	78.9	21.1	---	---	---
1970	75.0	25.0	---	---	---
Finland					
1950	58.5	25.1	16.4	---	---
1960	44.1	35.8	7.4	12.7	---
1970	31.6	44.0	8.5	15.9	---
Iceland					
1950	39.0	61.0	---	---	---
1960	33.5	66.5	---	---	---
1970	28.3	71.7	---	---	---

TABLE C (continued)

REGION AND COUNTRY	RURAL	URBAN CLASS			
		I	II	III	IV
Ireland					
1950	59.4	15.5	3.8	21.3	---
1960	54.3	18.3	4.1	23.3	---
1970	49.3	19.9	4.4	26.4	---
Isle of Man					
1950	45.5	54.5	---	---	---
1960	43.7	56.2	---	---	---
1970	42.3	57.7	---	---	---
Norway					
1950	57.8	22.4	4.4	15.4	---
1960	51.3	28.4	4.1	16.2	---
1970	45.1	29.4	10.3	15.2	---
Sweden					
1950	44.6	34.1	8.2	13.2	---
1960	39.0	35.9	9.8	---	15.3
1970	33.9	33.4	8.0	8.0	16.7
United Kingdom					
1950	22.5	6.8	18.7	8.3	43.6
1960	21.7	6.7	18.3	9.5	43.8
1970	20.9	8.4	17.5	10.4	42.9
WESTERN EUROPE					
1950	36.8	26.3	11.2	7.5	18.1
1960	32.0	27.0	12.7	8.3	20.1
1970	27.0	28.0	13.5	5.9	25.5
Austria					
1950	51.0	11.4	10.8	---	26.8
1960	50.0	12.4	11.0	---	26.6
1970	49.0	14.7	10.9	---	25.4
Belgium					
1950	36.6	34.6	10.7	18.1	---
1960	33.8	37.8	10.4	7.0	11.1
1970	31.1	40.6	10.1	6.9	11.3
France					
1950	45.9	27.9	8.8	3.0	14.4
1960	38.7	27.4	14.5	3.5	16.0
1970	32.1	27.5	16.9	2.0	21.4

TABLE C (continued)

REGION AND COUNTRY	RURAL	URBAN CLASS			
		I	II	III	IV
Germany, Fed. Rep.					
1950	27.5	24.2	11.8	8.1	28.5
1960	22.4	26.2	10.5	10.7	30.3
1970	17.8	28.2	9.2	9.3	35.6
Liechtenstein					
1950	80.7	19.3	---	---	---
1960	79.4	20.6	---	---	---
1970	77.3	22.7	---	---	---
Luxembourg					
1950	41.2	58.8	---	---	---
1960	37.8	62.2	---	---	---
1970	34.4	65.6	---	---	---
Monaco					
1950	---	100.0	---	---	---
1960	---	100.0	---	---	---
1970	---	100.0	---	---	---
The Netherlands					
1950	29.5	34.2	13.3	22.9	---
1960	32.5	29.5	16.8	21.2	---
1970	27.8	27.0	21.2	5.9	18.0
Switzerland					
1950	51.8	23.6	24.6	---	---
1960	45.8	25.1	19.2	9.9	---
1970	40.2	26.3	22.8	10.6	---
EASTERN EUROPE					
1950	57.6	25.1	6.3	3.2	7.8
1960	51.6	27.9	8.9	3.3	8.3
1970	45.4	30.3	9.0	3.7	11.6
Bulgaria					
1950	72.6	18.3	1.9	7.2	---
1960	62.8	23.1	5.3	8.7	---
1970	53.0	25.9	10.2	10.9	---
Czechoslovakia					
1950	57.9	28.1	6.4	7.5	---
1960	52.8	32.7	7.1	7.3	---
1970	48.0	36.5	8.3	---	7.2

TABLE C (continued)

REGION AND COUNTRY	RURAL	URBAN CLASS			
		I	II	III	IV
Germany, East					
1950	29.2	50.7	10.3	3.4	6.5
1960	22.1	56.6	11.7	3.4	6.2
1970	15.8	61.7	9.5	6.6	6.5
Hungary					
1950	63.2	17.2	2.5	---	17.1
1960	60.3	17.7	3.9	---	18.1
1970	57.3	18.3	5.8	---	18.6
Poland					
1950	61.0	15.9	8.1	3.1	11.9
1960	52.3	21.1	10.7	3.0	12.9
1970	44.2	25.0	7.0	5.3	18.6
Romania					
1950	74.4	15.5	3.2	---	6.8
1960	67.9	15.9	8.9	---	7.3
1970	61.1	16.4	13.8	---	8.6
SOUTHERN EUROPE					
1950	59.5	20.6	8.0	4.2	7.6
1960	54.4	21.5	9.8	4.4	9.9
1970	49.3	21.1	12.7	2.7	14.2
Albania					
1950	79.5	20.5	---	---	---
1960	69.1	22.5	8.4	---	---
1970	64.9	24.8	10.3	---	---
Andorra					
1950	100.0	---	---	---	---
1960	100.0	---	---	---	---
1970	100.0	---	---	---	---
Gibraltar					
1950	---	100.0	---	---	---
1960	---	100.0	---	---	---
1970	---	100.0	---	---	---
Greece					
1950	49.0	29.3	3.9	---	17.8
1960	43.0	29.6	5.7	---	21.8
1970	37.4	28.7	6.5	---	27.3

TABLE C (continued)

REGION AND COUNTRY	RURAL	URBAN CLASS			
		I	II	III	IV
Holy See					
1950	---	100.0	---	---	---
1960	---	100.0	---	---	---
1970	---	100.0	---	---	---
Italy					
1950	56.0	23.7	9.1	5.0	6.1
1960	52.2	23.6	10.1	4.7	9.4
1970	48.5	22.0	12.1	4.0	13.3
Malta and Gozo Is.					
1950	40.4	59.6	---	---	---
1960	36.2	63.8	---	---	---
1970	32.4	67.6	---	---	---
Portugal					
1950	68.8	9.7	---	7.8	13.8
1960	66.1	10.5	---	8.4	15.0
1970	63.5	12.3	---	8.7	15.4
San Marino					
1950	70.8	29.2	---	---	---
1960	74.7	25.3	---	---	---
1970	78.9	21.1	---	---	---
Spain					
1950	51.3	24.7	11.9	1.8	10.4
1960	46.1	26.0	13.7	1.7	12.5
1970	41.2	25.7	16.8	1.5	14.7
Yugoslavia					
1950	82.8	5.5	5.0	6.7	---
1960	72.8	9.1	9.3	8.7	---
1970	61.3	10.9	16.5	---	11.3
AUSTRALIA-NEW ZEALAND					
1950	30.0	20.6	19.5	---	29.9
1960	22.3	24.3	12.9	9.2	31.2
1970	15.7	23.1	9.9	19.1	32.2
Australia					
1950	27.9	19.0	16.4	---	36.8
1960	19.0	23.1	8.2	11.3	38.4
1970	11.5	23.8	6.6	18.4	39.7

TABLE C (continued)

REGION AND COUNTRY	RURAL	URBAN CLASS			
		I	II	III	IV
New Zealand					
1950	39.3	27.9	32.9	---	---
1960	36.6	29.6	33.8	---	---
1970	34.0	20.1	23.8	22.1	---
OCEANIA					
1950	95.1	4.9	---	---	---
1960	94.0	6.0	---	---	---
1970	91.5	8.5	---	---	---
American Samoa					
1950	91.5	8.5	---	---	---
1960	93.5	6.5	---	---	---
1970	94.4	5.6	---	---	---
Christmas Island					
1950	100.0	---	---	---	---
1960	100.0	---	---	---	---
1970	100.0	---	---	---	---
Cocos Islands					
1950	100.0	---	---	---	---
1960	100.0	---	---	---	---
1970	100.0	---	---	---	---
Cook Islands					
1950	100.0	---	---	---	---
1960	100.0	---	---	---	---
1970	100.0	---	---	---	---
Fiji					
1950	82.8	17.2	---	---	---
1960	81.6	18.4	---	---	---
1970	80.4	19.6	---	---	---
French Polynesia					
1950	76.9	23.1	---	---	---
1960	76.2	23.7	---	---	---
1970	75.5	24.5	---	---	---
Gilbert and Ellice Is.					
1950	100.0	---	---	---	---
1960	84.3	15.7	---	---	---
1970	79.0	21.0	---	---	---

TABLE C (continued)

REGION AND COUNTRY	RURAL	URBAN CLASS			
		I	II	III	IV
Guam					
1950	97.8	2.2	---	---	---
1960	92.1	7.9	---	---	---
1970	80.0	20.0	---	---	---
Johnston Island					
1950	100.0	---	---	---	---
1960	100.0	---	---	---	---
1970	100.0	---	---	---	---
Midway Island					
1950	100.0	---	---	---	---
1960	100.0	---	---	---	---
1970	100.0	---	---	---	---
Nauru					
1950	100.0	---	---	---	---
1960	100.0	---	---	---	---
1970	100.0	---	---	---	---
New Caledonia					
1950	76.0	24.0	---	---	---
1960	60.9	39.1	---	---	---
1970	45.0	55.0	---	---	---
New Guinea					
1950	100.0	---	---	---	---
1960	100.0	---	---	---	---
1970	100.0	---	---	---	---
New Hebrides					
1950	100.0	---	---	---	---
1960	100.0	---	---	---	---
1970	100.0	---	---	---	---
Niue Island					
1950	100.0	---	---	---	---
1960	100.0	---	---	---	---
1970	100.0	---	---	---	---
Norfolk Island					
1950	100.0	---	---	---	---
1960	100.0	---	---	---	---
1970	100.0	---	---	---	---

TABLE C (continued)

REGION AND COUNTRY	RURAL	URBAN CLASS			
		I	II	III	IV
Pacific Islands					
1950	100.0	---	---	---	---
1960	100.0	---	---	---	---
1970	100.0	---	---	---	---
Papua					
1950	96.8	3.2	---	---	---
1960	97.2	2.8	---	---	---
1970	95.8	4.2	---	---	---
Solomon Is. (U.K.)					
1950	97.8	2.2	---	---	---
1960	96.9	3.1	---	---	---
1970	96.1	3.9	---	---	---
Tokelau Islands					
1950	100.0	---	---	---	---
1960	100.0	---	---	---	---
1970	100.0	---	---	---	---
Tonga					
1950	84.0	16.0	---	---	---
1960	83.8	16.2	---	---	---
1970	84.1	15.9	---	---	---
Wake Island					
1950	100.0	---	---	---	---
1960	100.0	---	---	---	---
1970	100.0	---	---	---	---
Western Samoa					
1950	85.1	14.9	---	---	---
1960	81.2	18.8	---	---	---
1970	77.0	23.0	---	---	---
U.S.S.R.					
U.S.S.R.					
1950	57.5	21.6	11.1	5.1	4.7
1960	49.9	25.2	12.4	7.0	5.4
1970	37.7	31.5	14.7	7.6	8.4

EXPLANATION

Table D presents the average annual change, over each of
two decades, in the total population and in the population classed
as living in places of various sizes. It gives this information
not only for each country but also for each region. The absolute
figures on which the rates are based appear in Tables A and B.

As in previous tables, "town" means an urban place of fewer
than 100,000 inhabitants, and "city" means a place (if possible,
an urbanized area) with that many people or more. These two categories together constitute the urban population, and the rural
population is composed of the total population minus the urban
population.

Except with respect to the total population, the rates
shown here are not strictly growth rates. They are rates of
change in the combined population living in places of a given
size at each date. As noted in the explanation to Table B, the
particular places making up a given size-class at the starting
date may not be identically the same as those making up the class
at the ending date. For instance, the rate of change shown here
for the rural population between 1950 and 1960 is not the combined growth of all places that were rural in 1950, because some
of those places grew so much that they were classified as towns
by 1960. Instead, the rural column gives simply the proportional
change per year in the number of persons classified as rural,
comparing 1960 with 1950 and comparing 1970 with 1960. Similarly,
the "town" rate is not the population increase of the same places
throughout the decade. Some places classed as rural villages in
1950 subsequently entered the town class, and some places defined as towns subsequently became cities.

Above all, the rates shown in Table D are not to be con-
strued as rates of natural increase—that is, as the remainder
when the death rate is subtracted from the birth rate. Not only
does the same class at successive dates not usually include the
same places, but, even when it does do so, it does not include
the same people and their offspring. Thus the change in the size
of the population classed as rural in 1960 and 1970 is not the
natural increase of the people who were rural in 1960. Many of
them, and their offspring, went to towns and cities during the
decade and hence, by 1970, were classified as urban.

Since our files contain data on individual cities of 100,000
or more inhabitants, they make possible the computation of growth

rates for cities classified by their size at the starting date. The results are not shown here but are given in the analytical volume. If the reader wishes, he can utilize the figures for individual cities in Table E to compute such rates for any particular country, region, or class of countries. In the meantime, the change in the size of the various classes is itself an important facet of the process of urbanization.

The average annual rates in the present table are computed in either of two ways that give identical results. One is by use of the compound interest formula,

$$P_2 = P_1(1 + r)^t$$

where P_1 is the starting population, P_2 is the ending population, and t is the time in years. The other method is by use of the exponential formula,

$$P_2 = P_1(e^{"r"t})$$

The "r" in this case is continuously compounding. To convert it to an annually compounding rate, we take advantage of the fact that $_e"r" - 1 = r$.

TABLE D

ANNUAL GROWTH RATE OF POPULATION,
1950 TO 1960 AND 1960 TO 1970
(PER CENT)

REGION AND COUNTRY	TOTAL	RURAL	URBAN	TOWN	CITY
NORTHERN AFRICA					
1950-60	2.4	1.7	4.3	3.9	4.6
1960-70	2.6	1.8	4.2	4.4	4.0
Algeria					
1950-60	1.9	1.0	4.4	3.6	5.2
1960-70	2.4	1.3	4.5	7.7	.5
Ifni					
1950-60	2.7	2.0	4.8	4.8	---
1960-70	.8	---	2.9	2.9	---
Libya					
1950-60	3.0	2.6	4.6	-7.7	9.7
1960-70	3.2	2.7	4.6	-1.4	5.3
Morocco					
1950-60	2.7	1.8	5.0	6.1	4.5
1960-70	2.9	2.0	4.9	4.1	5.4
Sp. North Africa					
1950-60	.7	---	.7	.7	---
1960-70	.8	---	.8	.8	---
Spanish Sahara					
1950-60	1.8	-1.6	10.2	10.2	---
1960-70	7.3	1.5	12.3	12.3	---
Sudan					
1950-60	2.8	2.7	4.2	4.8	3.4
1960-70	2.9	2.8	4.3	4.7	3.5
Tunisia					
1950-60	1.6	.6	3.5	6.5	.5
1960-70	1.6	.5	3.2	1.5	5.3
U.A.R.					
1950-60	2.5	1.5	4.2	3.0	4.9
1960-70	2.5	1.5	4.0	3.3	4.2

TABLE D (cont'd) Rates in Per Cent

REGION AND COUNTRY	TOTAL	RURAL	URBAN	TOWN	CITY
WESTERN AFRICA					
1950-60	3.4	2.9	6.9	5.8	9.4
1960-70	3.1	2.5	6.2	5.6	7.3
Cape Verde Islands					
1950-60	3.1	3.1	2.7	2.7	---
1960-70	2.1	1.7	5.8	5.8	---
Dahomey					
1950-60	2.7	2.3	6.1	6.1	---
1960-70	2.9	2.4	6.0	.8	---
Gambia					
1950-60	1.3	1.1	3.1	3.1	---
1960-70	2.0	1.8	3.8	3.8	---
Ghana					
1950-60	3.3	2.2	8.5	4.8	15.5
1960-70	2.7	1.2	6.8	5.6	8.0
Guinea					
1950-60	3.2	2.9	7.3	.7	---
1960-70	2.7	2.3	6.5	6.1	7.0
Ivory Coast					
1950-60	2.2	1.3	10.0	5.3	---
1960-70	2.9	1.1	9.3	10.6	8.5
Liberia					
1950-60	1.4	.5	11.7	11.7	---
1960-70	1.7	-.4	10.4	10.4	---
Mali					
1950-60	1.9	1.7	5.8	-1.8	---
1960-70	1.9	1.6	5.7	5.7	5.6
Mauritania					
1950-60	3.1	3.1	3.9	3.9	---
1960-70	1.8	1.8	2.4	2.4	---
Niger					
1950-60	3.2	3.1	4.7	4.7	---
1960-70	2.9	2.9	4.5	4.5	---
Nigeria					
1950-60	4.2	3.7	6.8	6.9	6.6
1960-70	3.7	3.2	6.0	5.8	6.5

TABLE D (cont'd) Rates in Per Cent

REGION AND COUNTRY	TOTAL	RURAL	URBAN	TOWN	CITY
Portuguese Guinea					
1950-60	.2	-.2	3.4	3.4	---
1960-70	.2	-.3	3.0	3.0	---
Saint Helena					
1950-60	---	---	---	---	---
1960-70	---	---	---	---	---
Senegal					
1950-60	4.0	3.6	5.8	5.0	6.8
1960-70	2.4	1.9	4.0	2.6	5.3
Sierra Leone					
1950-60	1.1	.8	3.6	-1.9	---
1960-70	1.4	1.0	3.8	2.6	5.1
Togo					
1950-60	2.7	2.3	9.0	9.0	---
1960-70	2.5	1.7	8.2	-1.1	---
Upper Volta					
1950-60	1.7	1.6	4.6	4.6	---
1960-70	2.2	2.1	5.1	5.1	---
EASTERN AFRICA					
1950-60	2.5	2.2	5.5	3.6	10.0
1960-70	2.5	2.2	5.3	3.1	8.3
Burundi					
1950-60	4.6	4.5	10.0	10.0	---
1960-70	2.0	1.9	7.2	7.2	---
Comoro Islands					
1950-60	1.5	1.4	4.9	4.9	---
1960-70	4.1	3.9	7.7	7.7	---
Ethiopia					
1950-60	2.6	2.6	3.2	3.0	3.5
1960-70	1.8	1.8	2.4	1.4	3.6
French Somaliland					
1950-60	3.6	1.6	6.8	6.8	---
1960-70	3.6	1.2	6.0	6.0	---
Kenya					
1950-60	3.0	2.8	6.9	-.3	12.4
1960-70	3.0	2.8	5.1	2.5	6.0

REGION AND COUNTRY	TOTAL	RURAL	URBAN	TOWN	CITY
Madagascar					
1950-60	2.4	2.2	4.4	5.1	3.5
1960-70	2.4	2.2	4.3	3.3	5.6
Malawi					
1950-60	2.4	2.3	10.4	10.4	---
1960-70	2.4	2.1	10.1	-3.2	---
Mauritius					
1950-60	3.3	1.2	7.1	7.1	---
1960-70	2.6	.2	5.3	1.4	---
Mozambique					
1950-60	1.4	1.2	6.7	-6.8	---
1960-70	1.1	.9	6.2	6.3	6.2
Reunion					
1950-60	3.3	2.2	6.2	6.2	---
1960-70	3.1	1.8	5.4	5.4	---
Rwanda					
1950-60	2.7	2.7	7.4	7.4	---
1960-70	3.1	3.1	8.3	8.3	---
Seychelles					
1950-60	1.6	1.8	.8	.8	---
1960-70	1.8	.8	4.3	4.3	---
Somalia					
1950-60	.6	.2	2.9	2.9	---
1960-70	3.9	3.3	6.0	2.5	---
Southern Rhodesia					
1950-60	3.2	2.4	8.7	1.6	14.5
1960-70	3.2	2.7	5.4	5.7	5.2
Tanganyika					
1950-60	1.8	1.6	6.3	2.0	---
1960-70	3.4	3.1	7.8	7.1	9.0
Uganda					
1950-60	2.5	2.3	9.6	1.6	---
1960-70	2.5	2.1	9.2	9.2	9.2
Zambia					
1950-60	2.8	2.0	6.8	6.8	---
1960-70	3.0	2.1	6.4	.5	---

TABLE D (cont'd) Rates in Per Cent

REGION AND COUNTRY	TOTAL	RURAL	URBAN	TOWN	CITY
Zanzibar					
1950-60	1.3	.4	4.0	4.0	---
1960-70	1.9	.9	4.2	4.2	---
MIDDLE AND SOUTHERN AFRICA					
1950-60	1.8	1.3	7.7	5.7	12.0
1960-70	2.0	1.5	4.9	4.8	5.0
Angola					
1950-60	1.5	1.3	4.7	4.7	4.7
1960-70	1.3	1.0	4.3	4.6	4.1
Basutoland (Lesotho)					
1950-60	2.1	2.1	7.0	7.0	---
1960-70	2.9	2.8	7.9	7.9	---
Bachuanaland (Botswana)					
1950-60	2.7	2.6	3.0	3.0	---
1960-70	3.0	2.9	3.3	3.3	---
Cameroon					
1950-60	1.1	.8	6.0	.8	---
1960-70	2.2	1.7	6.8	5.6	8.4
Central African Rep.					
1950-60	1.4	.7	8.2	8.2	---
1960-70	2.6	1.3	8.4	1.7	---
Chad					
1950-60	1.8	1.5	8.5	8.5	---
1960-70	1.5	1.1	7.9	7.9	---
Congo, Brazzaville					
1950-60	1.4	.1	6.5	-3.4	---
1960-70	1.5	-.3	5.4	7.2	4.1
Congo, Dem. Rep.					
1950-60	2.2	1.4	9.2	7.9	11.2
1960-70	2.1	1.8	3.9	4.4	3.3
Gabon					
1950-60	.5	-.1	6.8	6.8	---
1960-70	1.0	-.1	6.5	6.5	---
Sao Tome					
1950-60	.7	.4	2.2	2.2	---
1960-70	-.4	-.8	1.3	1.3	---

TABLE D (cont'd) Rates in Per Cent

REGION AND COUNTRY	TOTAL	RURAL	URBAN	TOWN	CITY
South West Africa					
1950-60	2.3	1.2	7.0	7.0	---
1960-70	1.7	.3	5.5	5.5	---
Sp. Eq. Guinea					
1950-60	2.1	1.7	7.7	7.7	---
1960-70	1.7	1.0	6.8	6.8	---
Swaziland					
1950-60	2.4	2.2	---	---	---
1960-70	4.8	4.7	9.4	9.4	---
SOUTH AFRICA					
South Africa					
1950-60	2.5	1.5	3.9	4.3	3.7
1960-70	2.3	1.2	3.5	2.5	4.1
NORTHERN AMERICA					
1950-60	1.8	.0	2.7	1.5	3.3
1960-70	1.4	-.6	2.2	.2	2.9
Bermuda					
1950-60	1.3	---	1.3	1.3	---
1960-70	2.4	---	2.4	2.4	---
Canada					
1950-60	2.7	.7	3.8	2.9	4.3
1960-70	1.9	-.3	2.8	1.9	3.3
Greenland					
1950-60	3.7	3.5	5.4	5.4	---
1960-70	4.0	4.7	6.5	6.5	---
St. Pierre and Miq.					
1950-60	---	---	---	---	---
1960-70	---	---	---	---	---
U.S.A.					
1950-60	1.8	-.0	2.7	1.4	3.2
1960-70	1.4	-.6	2.1	-.0	2.8
MIDDLE AMERICA					
1950-60	3.1	1.8	4.8	4.4	5.5
1960-70	3.7	2.3	5.1	5.0	5.2

TABLE D (cont'd) Rates in Per Cent

REGION AND COUNTRY	TOTAL	RURAL	URBAN	TOWN	CITY
British Honduras					
1950-60	3.0	3.0	3.0	3.0	---
1960-70	3.2	3.2	3.3	3.3	---
Canal Zone					
1950-60	-2.2	-2.1	-2.5	-2.5	---
1960-70	3.8	2.8	5.6	5.6	---
Costa Rica					
1950-60	3.8	3.6	4.3	1.6	6.3
1960-70	4.2	4.0	4.6	3.2	5.4
El Salvador					
1950-60	2.8	2.6	3.3	3.1	4.0
1960-70	3.6	3.3	4.0	2.8	7.1
Guatemala					
1950-60	3.2	2.3	5.3	5.6	4.9
1960-70	3.1	2.2	4.9	4.9	5.0
Honduras					
1950-60	3.0	2.5	5.1	.2	---
1960-70	3.4	2.8	5.2	4.8	5.9
Mexico					
1950-60	3.1	1.5	4.9	4.7	5.3
1960-70	3.8	2.1	5.2	5.3	5.2
Nicaragua					
1950-60	2.9	2.2	4.2	3.3	6.1
1960-70	3.5	2.7	4.6	3.8	5.9
Panama					
1950-60	2.9	2.0	4.4	.7	7.9
1960-70	3.1	2.2	4.4	3.5	4.9
CARIBBEAN					
1950-60	2.2	1.7	3.1	2.3	4.2
1960-70	2.4	1.7	3.5	2.8	4.2
Bahama Islands					
1950-60	4.1	2.7	6.0	6.0	---
1960-70	2.8	1.3	4.4	4.4	---
Barbados Islands					
1950-60	1.0	.2	2.2	2.2	---
1960-70	.9	.1	2.0	2.0	---

REGION AND COUNTRY	TOTAL	RURAL	URBAN	TOWN	CITY
Cayman Islands					
1950–60	.8	.8	---	---	---
1960–70	1.7	1.7	---	---	---
Cuba					
1950–60	2.2	1.9	2.3	1.4	3.5
1960–70	2.4	2.2	2.6	1.6	3.5
Dominican Republic					
1950–60	3.6	2.7	6.1	5.4	7.3
1960–70	3.6	2.6	5.7	4.3	7.6
Guadeloupe					
1950–60	2.9	2.3	5.4	5.4	---
1960–70	2.2	1.6	4.5	4.5	---
Haiti					
1950–60	2.6	2.3	4.6	3.7	6.0
1960–70	2.0	1.6	3.8	2.7	5.2
Jamaica					
1950–60	1.8	.9	4.3	6.9	3.8
1960–70	2.2	1.2	4.3	5.4	4.0
Leeward Islands					
1950–60	1.2	.5	3.4	3.4	---
1960–70	.5	-.3	2.2	2.2	---
Martinique					
1950–60	2.5	1.0	5.6	5.6	---
1960–70	2.1	.3	4.4	4.4	---
Neth. Antilles					
1950–60	1.6	-.1	3.6	3.6	---
1960–70	1.5	-.3	3.1	3.1	---
Puerto Rico					
1950–60	.6	-.0	1.5	-2.0	4.3
1960–70	2.0	1.3	2.8	.8	3.8
Trinidad and Tobago					
1950–60	2.7	.7	7.2	7.2	---
1960–70	2.9	.3	6.0	6.0	---
Turks and Caicos Is.					
1950–60	-.5	-.5	---	---	---
1960–70	.5	.5	---	---	---

REGION AND COUNTRY	TOTAL	RURAL	URBAN	TOWN	CITY
Virgin Islands (U.S.A.)					
1950-60	1.9	2.4	1.4	1.4	---
1960-70	8.3	6.7	9.3	9.3	---
Windward Islands					
1950-60	1.8	1.7	2.7	2.7	---
1960-70	1.8	1.6	2.6	2.6	---
TROPICAL SOUTH AMERICA					
1950-60	3.1	1.6	5.4	3.9	6.9
1960-70	2.8	1.1	4.6	2.8	6.0
Bolivia					
1950-60	1.4	1.0	2.5	2.1	2.9
1960-70	1.4	1.0	2.4	.4	4.1
Brazil					
1950-60	3.2	1.6	5.5	3.6	7.2
1960-70	2.8	1.1	4.6	2.9	5.7
British Guiana					
1950-60	2.8	2.7	3.2	-19.2	---
1960-70	2.8	2.6	3.2	4.1	3.1
Colombia					
1950-60	3.1	1.5	5.5	4.4	6.6
1960-70	3.2	1.4	5.0	2.1	7.2
Ecuador					
1950-60	3.1	2.5	4.6	4.2	5.0
1960-70	3.4	2.7	4.7	3.9	5.5
French Guiana					
1950-60	2.8	1.7	4.1	4.1	---
1960-70	2.2	1.0	3.3	3.3	---
Peru					
1950-60	2.9	2.0	4.3	3.6	5.7
1960-70	2.1	1.2	3.3	1.4	6.1
Surinam					
1950-60	2.7	2.4	3.2	3.2	---
1960-70	4.0	3.7	4.5	-15.6	---
Venezuela					
1950-60	3.7	-.1	7.1	6.7	7.6
1960-70	3.5	-1.2	5.6	5.4	5.9

REGION AND COUNTRY	TOTAL	RURAL	URBAN	TOWN	CITY
TEMPERATE SOUTH AMERICA					
1950-60	1.9	.3	2.8	1.2	3.6
1960-70	1.9	.3	2.7	1.1	3.3
Argentina					
1950-60	1.6	.5	2.2	-1.7	3.4
1960-70	1.9	.7	2.4	-1.3	3.1
Chile					
1950-60	2.5	-.1	4.3	4.3	4.3
1960-70	2.0	-.9	3.4	3.1	3.7
Falkland Islands					
1950-60	---	---	---	---	---
1960-70	---	---	---	---	---
Paraguay					
1950-60	2.7	2.4	3.1	2.7	3.6
1960-70	3.1	2.9	3.5	3.4	3.6
Uruguay					
1950-60	1.5	-2.9	3.9	3.2	4.7
1960-70	1.3	-4.3	2.9	.4	4.7
EAST ASIA					
1950-60	1.8	1.1	6.0	6.1	5.9
1960-70	1.3	.3	4.8	5.5	4.4
China (Taiwan)					
1950-60	3.4	1.9	4.6	3.5	5.7
1960-70	3.1	1.5	4.1	2.4	5.5
China					
1950-60	1.8	1.2	6.0	6.5	5.8
1960-70	1.1	.3	4.8	5.7	4.3
Hong Kong					
1950-60	4.7	---	7.0	---	7.0
1960-70	2.9	---	2.9	---	2.9
Korea, North					
1950-60	.9	.2	4.7	3.0	5.1
1960-70	2.6	2.2	4.1	7.2	3.5
Korea, South					
1950-60	2.0	.7	6.4	7.5	6.2
1960-70	2.6	.9	6.0	5.0	6.2

TABLE D (cont'd) Rates in Per Cent

REGION AND COUNTRY	TOTAL	RURAL	URBAN	TOWN	CITY
Macau					
1950-60	-1.1	---	-1.1	---	-1.1
1960-70	5.2	---	5.2	---	5.2
Mongolia					
1950-60	2.7	.5	8.7	1.5	---
1960-70	3.0	.0	7.1	6.4	7.9
Ryukyu Islands					
1950-60	2.5	1.6	4.4	-9.0	---
1960-70	1.1	.2	2.7	2.7	2.7
JAPAN					
Japan					
1950-60	1.1	-4.2	6.6	8.4	5.8
1960-70	1.0	-6.6	3.7	3.7	3.7
SOUTHEAST ASIA					
1950-60	2.5	2.1	4.6	3.2	5.7
1960-70	2.7	2.3	4.7	4.1	5.0
Brunei					
1950-60	6.2	6.1	6.3	6.3	---
1960-70	3.5	3.4	3.6	3.6	---
Burma					
1950-60	1.8	1.6	2.8	3.3	2.0
1960-70	2.1	1.9	3.1	2.0	4.6
Cambodia					
1950-60	2.9	2.7	5.6	2.4	8.3
1960-70	2.3	2.0	4.8	-1.8	7.6
Indonesia					
1950-60	2.1	1.8	4.1	.4	7.0
1960-70	2.4	2.0	4.2	3.4	4.7
Laos					
1950-60	5.8	5.6	8.8	.0	---
1960-70	2.5	2.0	7.2	8.2	6.3
West Malaysia					
1950-60	2.9	1.4	6.7	6.7	6.6
1960-70	3.1	1.2	5.9	5.1	7.5

TABLE D (cont'd) Rates in Per Cent

REGION AND COUNTRY	TOTAL	RURAL	URBAN	TOWN	CITY
Maldive Islands					
1950-60	1.2	1.1	1.5	1.5	---
1960-70	1.7	1.6	2.3	2.3	---
Philippines					
1950-60	2.9	2.7	3.7	2.7	4.3
1960-70	3.5	3.3	4.3	3.4	4.7
Portuguese Timor					
1950-60	1.6	1.6	1.8	1.8	---
1960-70	1.4	1.4	1.7	1.7	---
Sabah					
1950-60	3.2	3.0	4.5	4.5	---
1960-70	3.8	3.6	5.0	5.0	---
Sarawak					
1950-60	2.5	2.1	5.2	5.2	---
1960-70	2.8	2.3	5.3	5.3	---
Singapore					
1950-60	4.8	---	4.8	---	4.8
1960-70	2.6	---	2.6	---	2.6
Thailand					
1950-60	2.9	2.8	4.3	4.9	3.9
1960-70	3.2	3.0	4.5	3.5	5.2
Viet-Nam, North					
1950-60	3.0	2.2	9.4	10.2	8.5
1960-70	3.2	2.0	8.7	8.7	8.7
Viet-Nam, South					
1950-60	3.0	2.4	5.6	5.6	5.7
1960-70	2.7	2.0	5.0	5.1	4.9
West Irian					
1950-60	---	-.0	.7	.7	---
1960-70	2.3	2.3	3.0	3.0	---
SOUTHWEST ASIA					
1950-60	2.7	1.9	4.7	3.2	6.5
1960-70	2.5	1.6	4.4	2.1	6.3
Bahrain					
1950-60	3.2	2.4	3.4	3.4	---
1960-70	3.7	3.0	4.0	4.0	---

152

REGION AND COUNTRY	TOTAL	RURAL	URBAN	TOWN	CITY
Cyprus					
1950-60	1.5	-.2	5.6	5.6	---
1960-70	1.0	-1.1	3.9	-.8	---
Fed. of South Arabia (Southern Yemen)					
1950-60	1.0	-.2	5.1	3.8	5.4
1960-70	2.6	2.0	4.2	3.6	4.3
Gaza Strip					
1950-60	3.0	3.0	---	---	---
1960-70	3.1	3.1	---	---	---
Iran					
1950-60	2.8	1.9	5.0	5.0	5.0
1960-70	3.0	2.0	4.8	3.4	5.9
Iraq					
1950-60	2.8	2.1	4.0	1.7	6.5
1960-70	2.9	2.2	4.0	-.6	6.8
Israel					
1950-60	5.3	6.5	5.0	2.5	8.2
1960-70	3.2	1.3	3.7	-.6	6.8
Jordan					
1950-60	2.8	2.0	4.1	-.1	---
1960-70	3.6	2.8	4.8	2.9	7.8
Kuwait					
1950-60	5.0	1.4	7.1	-6.7	---
1960-70	7.1	2.7	8.5	9.1	8.3
Lebanon					
1950-60	1.8	.8	4.0	-1.1	5.8
1960-70	2.1	1.0	4.0	3.3	4.2
Muscat and Oman					
1950-60	.3	.1	4.4	4.4	---
1960-70	---	-.2	4.1	4.1	---
Qatar					
1950-60	8.4	6.1	10.4	10.4	---
1960-70	7.8	5.2	9.2	9.2	---
Saudi Arabia					
1950-60	1.7	.9	7.2	2.7	16.9
1960-70	1.7	.6	6.4	5.1	7.7

153

REGION AND COUNTRY	TOTAL	RURAL	URBAN	TOWN	CITY
Syria					
1950-60	2.9	2.6	3.3	.9	4.5
1960-70	3.0	2.7	3.4	-.2	4.6
Trucial Oman					
1950-60	2.3	---	7.2	7.2	---
1960-70	4.7	1.7	8.1	8.1	---
Turkey					
1950-60	2.8	2.2	4.8	3.2	6.9
1960-70	2.5	1.8	4.2	1.4	6.8
Yemen					
1950-60	2.3	2.1	8.5	8.5	---
1960-70	---	-.3	5.9	5.9	---
SOUTH CENTRAL ASIA					
1950-60	1.9	1.8	2.7	1.8	3.5
1960-70	2.3	2.2	3.1	2.4	3.9
Afghanistan					
1950-60	1.8	1.7	2.6	.6	6.1
1960-70	1.5	1.5	2.3	-2.4	6.5
Bhutan					
1950-60	2.4	2.4	---	---	---
1960-70	2.0	2.0	---	---	---
Ceylon					
1950-60	2.6	2.6	2.5	2.1	2.8
1960-70	2.5	2.3	3.6	3.7	3.6
India					
1950-60	1.9	1.8	2.4	1.7	3.1
1960-70	2.4	2.3	2.9	2.2	3.5
Kashmir-Jammu					
1950-60	.9	.7	2.6	.0	5.0
1960-70	1.4	1.1	3.0	3.7	2.4
Nepal					
1950-60	1.4	1.3	2.9	-3.3	5.4
1960-70	2.0	1.7	8.0	8.2	7.9
Pakistan					
1950-60	2.1	1.8	4.5	2.8	6.1
1960-70	2.1	1.7	4.3	2.0	5.9

REGION AND COUNTRY	TOTAL	RURAL	URBAN	TOWN	CITY
Sikkim					
1950-60	1.6	1.4	9.7	9.7	---
1960-70	1.9	1.5	9.6	9.6	---
NORTHERN EUROPE					
1950-60	.4	-.5	.8	1.6	.6
1960-70	.7	-.3	1.0	1.8	.8
Channel Islands					
1950-60	.6	1.1	-.2	-.2	---
1960-70	.8	-.3	2.5	2.5	---
Denmark					
1950-60	.7	-1.6	1.7	2.4	.9
1960-70	.8	-1.8	1.6	1.3	1.9
Faeroe Islands					
1950-60	.9	.4	2.8	2.8	---
1960-70	1.3	.8	3.1	3.1	---
Finland					
1950-60	1.0	-1.8	4.0	4.6	3.1
1960-70	.7	-2.6	2.7	2.8	2.6
Iceland					
1950-60	2.1	.6	3.0	3.0	---
1960-70	1.9	.2	2.7	2.7	---
Ireland					
1950-60	-.5	-1.4	.7	1.2	.4
1960-70	.4	-.6	1.4	1.2	1.5
Isle of Man					
1950-60	-1.4	-1.7	-1.0	-1.0	---
1960-70	.8	.5	1.1	1.1	---
Norway					
1950-60	.9	-.3	2.4	3.3	1.2
1960-70	.8	-.5	2.0	1.1	3.1
Sweden					
1950-60	.6	-.7	1.6	1.1	2.3
1960-70	.8	-.6	1.6	---	3.5
United Kingdom					
1950-60	.4	---	.5	.2	.5
1960-70	.6	.3	.7	2.9	.5

TABLE D (cont'd) Rates in Per Cent

REGION AND COUNTRY	TOTAL	RURAL	URBAN	TOWN	CITY
WESTERN EUROPE					
1950-60	.9	-.5	1.6	1.1	2.0
1960-70	1.1	-.6	1.8	1.5	2.1
Austria					
1950-60	.2	---	.4	1.1	.2
1960-70	.6	.3	.8	2.3	.2
Belgium					
1950-60	.6	-.2	1.0	1.4	.5
1960-70	.7	-.1	1.1	1.4	.6
France					
1950-60	.9	-.8	2.2	.7	3.5
1960-70	1.2	-.7	2.2	1.2	3.0
Germany, Fed. Rep.					
1950-60	.9	-1.2	1.6	1.7	1.5
1960-70	1.1	-1.2	1.7	1.8	1.6
Liechtenstein					
1950-60	2.0	1.8	2.6	2.6	---
1960-70	2.6	2.3	3.6	3.6	---
Luxembourg					
1950-60	.6	-.2	1.2	1.2	---
1960-70	.9	-.1	1.4	1.4	---
Monaco					
1950-60	.4	---	.4	.4	---
1960-70	1.2	---	1.2	1.2	---
The Netherlands					
1950-60	1.3	2.2	.8	-.2	1.7
1960-70	1.4	-.2	2.0	.4	3.1
Switzerland					
1950-60	1.4	.2	2.6	2.0	3.1
1960-70	1.5	.1	2.5	1.9	2.9
EASTERN EUROPE					
1950-60	.9	-.2	2.2	2.0	2.6
1960-70	.7	-.6	1.9	1.5	2.4
Bulgaria					
1950-60	.8	-.6	3.9	3.2	5.3
1960-70	.7	-1.0	3.1	1.9	4.9

REGION AND COUNTRY	TOTAL	RURAL	URBAN	TOWN	CITY
Czechoslovakia					
1950-60	1.0	.1	2.2	2.6	1.4
1960-70	.7	-.3	1.7	1.8	1.4
Germany, East					
1950-60	-.6	-3.4	.3	.5	-.1
1960-70	-.1	-3.4	.6	.7	.4
Hungary					
1950-60	.6	.2	1.4	1.0	1.8
1960-70	1.1	.6	1.8	1.4	2.1
Poland					
1950-60	1.8	.2	3.8	4.7	3.2
1960-70	1.0	-.7	2.6	2.7	2.5
Romania					
1950-60	1.2	.3	3.5	1.5	6.2
1960-70	.7	-.4	2.6	1.0	4.0
SOUTHERN EUROPE					
1950-60	.8	-.1	2.0	1.2	2.8
1960-70	.9	-.1	2.0	.7	3.0
Albania					
1950-60	2.9	1.5	7.2	3.9	---
1960-70	2.8	2.1	4.1	3.8	4.9
Andorra					
1950-60	3.6	3.6	---	---	---
1960-70	7.2	7.2	---	---	---
Gibraltar					
1950-60	.4	---	.4	.4	---
1960-70	.8	---	.8	.8	---
Greece					
1950-60	1.0	-.3	2.1	1.0	3.4
1960-70	.6	-.7	1.6	.3	2.8
Holy See					
1950-60	---	---	---	---	---
1960-70	---	---	---	---	---
Italy					
1950-60	.6	-.1	1.4	.5	2.4
1960-70	.8	.0	1.5	.1	2.8

REGION AND COUNTRY	TOTAL	RURAL	URBAN	TOWN	CITY
Malta and Gozo Is.					
1950-60	.5	-.6	1.2	1.2	---
1960-70	-.5	-1.6	.0	.0	---
Portugal					
1950-60	.5	.1	1.3	1.3	1.4
1960-70	.9	.5	1.7	2.6	1.2
San Marino					
1950-60	1.4	2.0	---	---	---
1960-70	2.4	3.0	.5	.5	---
Spain					
1950-60	.8	-.2	1.9	1.4	2.3
1960-70	.8	-.3	1.7	.7	2.5
Yugoslavia					
1950-60	1.2	-.1	5.9	6.4	5.7
1960-70	1.2	-.6	4.8	3.0	5.6
AUSTRALIA-NEW ZEALAND					
1950-60	2.3	-.7	3.4	4.0	3.1
1960-70	1.8	-1.7	2.6	1.3	3.2
Australia					
1950-60	2.3	-1.5	3.5	4.4	3.2
1960-70	1.8	-3.2	2.7	2.1	2.9
New Zealand					
1950-60	2.2	1.5	2.6	2.8	2.5
1960-70	1.9	1.2	2.3	-2.0	5.1
OCEANIA					
1950-60	2.7	2.6	4.8	4.8	---
1960-70	2.5	2.3	5.1	5.1	---
American Samoa					
1950-60	.6	.8	-2.1	-2.1	---
1960-70	6.0	6.1	4.4	4.4	---
Christmas Island					
1950-60	11.6	11.6	---	---	---
1960-70	---	---	---	---	---
Cocos Islands					
1950-60	---	---	---	---	---
1960-70	1.6	1.6	---	---	---

REGION AND COUNTRY	TOTAL	RURAL	URBAN	TOWN	CITY
Cook Islands					
1950-60	2.1	2.1	---	---	---
1960-70	1.3	1.3	---	---	---
Fiji					
1950-60	3.1	3.0	3.8	3.8	---
1960-70	3.2	3.0	3.9	3.9	---
French Polynesia					
1950-60	2.7	2.7	3.0	3.0	---
1960-70	2.9	2.7	3.2	3.2	---
Gilbert and Ellice Is.					
1950-60	1.9	.2	---	---	---
1960-70	3.0	2.4	6.1	6.1	---
Guam					
1950-60	1.2	.6	15.1	15.1	---
1960-70	4.1	2.6	14.2	14.2	---
Johnston Island					
1950-60	---	---	---	---	---
1960-70	---	---	---	---	---
Midway Island					
1950-60	---	---	---	---	---
1960-70	---	---	---	---	---
Nauru					
1950-60	2.9	2.9	---	---	---
1960-70	5.8	5.8	---	---	---
New Caledonia					
1950-60	2.2	-.1	7.3	7.3	---
1960-70	2.5	-.5	6.1	6.1	---
New Guinea					
1950-60	2.6	2.6	---	---	---
1960-70	1.7	1.7	---	---	---
New Hebrides					
1950-60	2.0	2.0	---	---	---
1960-70	4.1	4.1	---	---	---
Niue Island					
1950-60	.9	.9	---	---	---
1960-70	.2	.2	---	---	---

159

TABLE D (cont'd) Rates in Per Cent

REGION AND COUNTRY	TOTAL	RURAL	URBAN	TOWN	CITY
Norfolk Island					
1950-60	---	---	---	---	---
1960-70	5.0	5.0	---	---	---
Pacific Islands					
1950-60	3.1	3.1	---	---	---
1960-70	2.5	2.5	---	---	---
Papua					
1950-60	3.0	3.1	1.9	1.9	---
1960-70	3.1	3.0	7.3	7.3	---
Solomon Is. (U.K.)					
1950-60	2.2	2.1	5.6	5.6	---
1960-70	2.1	2.0	4.7	4.7	---
Tokelau Islands					
1950-60	2.9	2.9	---	---	---
1960-70	---	---	---	---	---
Tonga					
1950-60	2.8	2.7	2.9	2.9	---
1960-70	3.4	3.4	3.2	3.2	---
Wake Island					
1950-60	---	---	---	---	---
1960-70	---	---	---	---	---
Western Samoa					
1950-60	3.5	3.0	5.9	5.9	---
1960-70	2.9	2.4	5.0	5.0	---
U.S.S.R.					
U.S.S.R.					
1950-60	1.8	.3	3.5	3.3	3.6
1960-70	1.3	-1.5	3.5	3.6	3.5

TABLE E

EXPLANATION

Table E lists the names of all cities of the world with a population of 100,000 or more in 1950, 1960, or 1970. It gives the population of the city for any or all of the three dates when it reached or exceeded the 100,000 level, but puts a dash (---) in the cell when the population was below that level.

The cities are listed by country, under each region. A list of the regions used, in the order in which they appear, is to be found on page 56, before Table A. Each country's cities are arranged in order of population size in 1960. This is usually also the order of size in 1950 and 1970, but occasionally cities shift in rank.

If a country had no city population at any of the dates in question, it is omitted from the table. Such countries can be readily identified in the previous table--Table D--because they are the countries in that table with a dash (for zero) in the last column (the column showing the percentage in cities).

When the necessary data are available, the "city" is defined as the entire urbanized area, or urban agglomeration; otherwise, it is defined as the political city. The cities delimited in the first sense, as UA's, are marked with an asterisk; those that are delimited as CP's are not so marked. In order to be able to compute growth rates, we have endeavored always to use the same definition of a city for both the beginning and the end of a decade--that is, to have the same definition for both 1950 and 1960 and the same definition for both 1960 and 1970. To attain this consistency over each decade and at the same time to utilize UA data whenever possible, we frequently had to estimate the UA population. Such estimation was necessary when we had only CP information at one date (usually the earlier one) but not at the other date in the decade. In only four cases--three cities of Israel and one (Teheran) in Iran--did we end up with a UA for 1960 but none for 1950 to compare it with. In these cases the table shows both the CP and the UA population for 1960, the first to go with the 1950 data and the second to go with the 1970 data.

The populations of the cities in 1970 were projected on the basis of the latest available censuses and estimates. If, for example, there was a census in 1961 and an estimate in 1967, we obtained the city's 1970 population by assuming a continuance of the 1961-67 growth rate. When we had no recent estimate, either official or unofficial, we fell back upon our 1950 and 1960

161

estimates for the projection. We also frequently used earlier data as a check on possibly inaccurate or unreasonable recent estimates.

An inherent difficulty in our procedure was that new cities just prior to 1970 tended to be overlooked. Since we are dealing with individual cities only when their population equals or exceeds 100,000, and since our chief source (the Demographic Yearbook) lists only cities of that size except when they are capitals, the task of determining whether additional cities would cross the 100,000 mark between the date of the last estimates and the date of the projections (1970) was a difficult one. Although we did include many of these new cities, we undoubtedly missed some as well (see Chapter IV).

As a check on our projections for individual cities, we utilized another kind of projection to 1970. Having for each country the entire city population in 1950 and 1960, we could extrapolate the growth of that population to 1970. This alone would not be accurate, however, because the rate of growth of the city population varies systematically with the proportion of city inhabitants in the national population. Accordingly, we modified our projections of the total city growth for each country on the basis of a specific correction factor for its level, a factor derived from the regression curve for the entire world during 1950-60 (a regression between proportion in cities and the subsequent decade gain in that proportion).

The procedures for the 1970 projections are more fully described in Chapter IV of the present volume. Our first source in assembling the data pertinent to all three dates was the Demographic Yearbook of the United Nations. Other sources, including statistical publications of individual countries, were consulted as needed. Many of the 1950 and 1960 figures are of course estimates, either official estimates or our own. The sources, definitions, and procedures for the data on the urban population as a whole are coded in Table A, and any special features or problems, including those for cities, are referred to, country by country, in the section entitled "Notes on Special Sources, Definitions, and Procedures for Particular Countries," which follows Table H at the end of the present volume.

The growth rates shown in the last two columns are geometric rates, computed in the manner described in the explanation of the previous table (Table D).

TABLE E

POPULATION OF CITIES OF 100,000 OR MORE IN 1950, 1960,
AND (ESTIMATED) 1970, WITH GROWTH RATES

| REGION, COUNTRY AND CITY | POPULATION (Thousands) | | | ANNUAL PER CENT GROWTH | |
	1950	1960	1970	1950-60	1960-70
NORTHERN AFRICA					
Algeria					
Alger*	531	884	988	5.2	1.1
Oran*	289	393	323	3.1	-1.9
Constantine*	131	223	278	5.5	2.2
Bone*	111	165	172	4.0	.4
Sidi-Bel-Abbes*	---	105	100	---	-.5
Libya					
Tripoli	114	183	281	4.8	4.4
Benghasi	---	105	202	---	6.8
Morocco					
Casablanca*	647	965	1,462	4.1	4.2
Marrakech	211	243	334	1.4	3.2
Rabat*	147	228	550	4.5	9.2
Fes	174	216	317	2.2	3.9
Meknes	136	176	265	2.6	4.2
Tanger	100	142	200	3.6	3.5
Oujda	---	129	191	---	4.0
Tetouan	---	101	149	---	4.0
Kenitra	---	---	132	---	---
Safi	---	---	118	---	---
Sudan					
Khartoum*	230	320	450	3.4	3.5
Tunisia					
Tunis	615	648	700	.5	.8

REGION, COUNTRY AND CITY	POPULATION (Thousands)			ANNUAL PER CENT GROWTH	
	1950	1960	1970	1950-60	1960-70
Sfax	---	---	160	---	---
Bizerta	---	---	125	---	---
Sousse	---	---	100	---	---
U.A.R.					
Cairo*	2,502	3,747	5,600	4.1	4.1
Alexandria	1,037	1,516	2,061	3.9	3.1
Port Said	192	245	315	2.5	2.5
Suez	125	204	322	5.0	4.7
Tanta	150	184	254	2.1	3.3
El Mahalla el Kubra	129	178	257	3.3	3.7
Mansura	112	151	214	3.0	3.5
Asyut	---	128	179	---	3.4
Damanhur	---	127	161	---	2.4
Zagazig	---	125	176	---	3.5
Ismailia	---	116	132	---	1.3
Faiyum	---	102	153	---	4.1
Subra-El Khema	---	---	200	---	---
Asswan	---	---	175	---	---
Minya	---	---	122	---	---
WESTERN AFRICA					
Dahomey					
Cotonou	---	---	175	---	---
Ghana					
Accara*	173	389	750	8.4	6.8
Kumasi*	---	218	382	---	5.8

REGION, COUNTRY AND CITY	POPULATION (Thousands)			ANNUAL PER CENT GROWTH	
	1950	1960	1970	1950-60	1960-70
Sekondi-Takoradi*	---	123	241	---	7.0
Tamale*	---	---	100	---	---
Oda-Swedru*	---	---	100	---	---
Guinea					
Conakry*	---	112	220	---	7.0
Ivory Coast					
Abidjan*	---	180	375	---	7.6
Bouake	---	---	120	---	---
Mali					
Bamako*	---	130	225	---	5.6
Nigeria					
Ibadon	459	568	760	2.2	3.0
Lagos	267	420	800	4.6	6.7
Ogbomosho	127	206	336	5.0	5.0
Kano	118	192	313	5.0	5.0
Oshogbo	123	179	287	3.8	4.8
Abeokuta	---	150	287	---	6.7
Iwo	100	137	210	3.2	4.4
Port Harcourt	---	133	130	---	-.2
Onitsha	---	132	120	---	-.9
Ilesha	---	125	286	---	8.6
Ife	111	123	145	1.0	1.7
Enugu	---	106	110	---	.4
Oyo	---	---	145	---	---
Maiduguri	---	---	132	---	---
Benin	---	---	130	---	---
Zaria	---	---	130	---	---

REGION, COUNTRY AND CITY	POPULATION (Thousands) 1950	1960	1970	ANNUAL PER CENT GROWTH 1950-60	1960-70
Kaduna	---	---	100	---	---
Ede	---	---	100	---	---
Llorin	---	---	100	---	---
Senegal					
Dakar*	186	358	600	6.8	5.3
Sierra Leone					
Freetown	---	106	175	---	5.1
Togo					
Lome*	---	---	180	---	---
EASTERN AFRICA					
Ethiopia					
Addis Ababa	392	432	631	1.0	3.9
Asmara	---	119	155	---	2.7
Kenya					
Nairobi*	135	275	500	7.4	6.2
Mombasa*	---	159	279	---	5.8
Madagascar					
Tananarive	177	250	432	3.5	5.6
Malawi					
Blantyre-Limbe	---	---	174	---	---
Mauritius					
Port-Louis*	---	---	146	---	---
Mozambique					
Lourenco Marques*	---	178	325	---	6.2

REGION, COUNTRY AND CITY	POPULATION (Thousands)			ANNUAL PER CENT GROWTH	
	1950	1960	1970	1950-60	1960-70
Somalia					
Mogadiscio	---	---	200	---	---
Southern Rhodesia					
Salisbury*	108	267	400	9.5	4.1
Bulawayo*	---	151	297	---	7.0
Tanganyika					
Dar es Salaam	---	148	350	---	9.0
Uganda					
Kampala*	---	135	325	---	9.2
Zambia					
Lusaka*	---	---	225	---	---
Kitwe*	---	---	150	---	---
Ndola*	---	---	120	---	---
MIDDLE AND SOUTHERN AFRICA					
Angola					
Luanda*	142	225	335	4.7	4.1
Cameroon					
Douala*	---	153	229	---	4.1
Yaounde	---	---	114	---	---
Central African Rep.					
Bangui*	---	---	180	---	---
Congo, Brazzaville					
Brazzaville*	---	127	190	---	4.1

REGION, COUNTRY AND CITY	POPULATION (Thousands) 1950	1960	1970	ANNUAL PER CENT GROWTH 1950-60	1960-70
Congo, Dem. Rep.					
Kinshasa (Leopoldville)	209	417	580	7.2	3.4
Lubumbashi (Elizabethville)	103	190	266	6.3	3.4
Kisangani (Stanleyville)	---	155	147	---	-.5
Luluabourg	---	140	141	---	.1
Jadothville	---	---	111	---	---
SOUTH AFRICA					
South Africa					
Johannesburg*	863	1,153	1,400	2.9	2.0
Cape Town*	560	807	1,100	3.7	3.1
Durban*	477	681	950	3.6	3.4
Pretoria*	278	423	750	4.3	5.9
Port Elizabeth*	182	291	450	4.8	4.5
Germiston*	145	214	235	4.0	.9
Bloemfontein*	105	145	175	3.3	1.9
Springs*	118	142	185	1.9	2.7
Benoni*	105	141	160	3.0	1.3
Pietermaritzburg*	---	129	235	---	6.2
East London*	---	116	155	---	2.9
Vereeniging*	112	---	105	---	---
Welkom*	---	---	130	---	---
Roodepoort-Maraisburg*	---	---	115	---	---
Kimberley*	---	---	105	---	---
Krugersdorp*	---	---	100	---	---

REGION, COUNTRY AND CITY	POPULATION (Thousands) 1950	1960	1970	ANNUAL PER CENT GROWTH 1950-60	1960-70
NORTHERN AMERICA					
Canada					
Montreal*	1,354	2,001	2,437	4.0	2.0
Toronto*	1,075	1,720	2,511	4.8	3.9
Vancouver*	543	763	990	3.5	2.6
Winnipeg*	344	462	543	3.0	1.6
Ottawa*	283	411	559	3.8	3.1
Hamilton*	262	381	501	3.8	2.8
Quebec*	268	348	464	2.6	2.9
Edmonton*	161	318	469	7.0	4.0
Calgary*	131	261	466	7.1	6.0
Windsor*	159	192	226	1.9	1.6
Halifax*	129	180	211	3.4	1.6
London*	124	176	231	3.6	2.8
Victoria*	105	148	193	3.5	2.7
Kitchener*	---	136	242	---	5.9
Regina	---	107	150	---	3.4
Sudbury*	---	106	125	---	1.7
Sydney-Glace Bay*	103	---	---	---	---
Saskatoon	---	---	150	---	---
St. John's*	---	---	110	---	---
Saint John*	---	---	106	---	---
U.S.A.					
New York*	12,331	14,114	16,077	1.4	1.3
Los Angeles-Long Beach*	4,009	6,489	9,473	4.9	3.9
Chicago*	4,935	5,959	6,983	1.9	1.6

REGION, COUNTRY AND CITY	POPULATION (Thousands) 1950	1960	1970	ANNUAL PER CENT GROWTH 1950-60	1960-70
Philadelphia*	2,930	3,635	4,355	2.2	1.8
Detroit*	2,667	3,538	4,447	2.9	2.3
San Francisco-Oakland*	2,028	2,431	4,490	1.8	6.3
Boston*	2,239	2,413	2,600	.8	.7
Washington, D.C.*	1,291	1,808	2,666	3.4	4.0
Pittsburgh*	1,538	1,804	1,958	1.6	.8
Cleveland*	1,388	1,785	2,248	2.5	2.3
St. Louis*	1,404	1,668	1,981	1.7	1.7
Baltimore*	1,165	1,419	1,729	2.0	2.0
Minneapolis-St. Paul*	988	1,377	1,760	3.4	2.5
Milwaukee*	831	1,150	1,496	3.3	2.7
Houston*	703	1,140	1,924	5.0	5.4
Buffalo*	800	1,054	1,244	2.8	1.7
Cincinnati*	815	994	1,331	2.0	3.0
Dallas*	541	932	1,478	5.6	4.7
Kansas City*	700	921	1,206	2.8	2.7
Seattle*	624	864	1,148	3.3	2.9
Miami*	460	853	1,341	6.4	4.6
New Orleans*	662	845	1,064	2.5	2.3
San Diego*	434	836	1,355	6.8	4.9
Denver*	500	804	1,151	4.9	3.7
Atlanta*	510	768	1,116	4.2	3.8
Providence*	585	660	722	1.2	.9
Portland, Ore.*	515	652	813	2.4	2.2
San Antonio*	451	642	892	3.6	3.3
Indianapolis*	503	639	766	2.4	1.8

REGION, COUNTRY AND CITY	POPULATION (Thousands)			ANNUAL PER CENT GROWTH	
	1950	1960	1970	1950-60	1960-70
Columbus, Ohio*	439	617	879	3.5	3.6
San Jose*	176	603	---	13.1	---
Louisville*	474	607	729	2.5	1.8
Phoenix*	217	552	1,102	9.8	7.2
Memphis*	407	545	724	3.0	2.9
Birmingham*	446	521	573	1.6	1.0
Norfolk*	386	508	634	2.8	2.2
Fort Worth*	317	503	699	4.7	3.3
Dayton*	348	502	682	3.7	3.1
Rochester*	410	493	594	1.9	1.9
Akron*	368	458	544	2.2	1.7
Albany-Schenectady-Troy*	416	455	502	.9	1.0
Sacramento*	213	452	781	7.8	5.6
Springfield, Mass.*	358	450	523	2.3	1.5
Toledo*	365	438	501	1.8	1.4
Oklahoma City*	276	429	601	4.5	3.4
Omaha*	311	390	486	2.3	2.2
Hartford*	302	382	475	2.4	2.2
San Bernardino-Riverside*	136	378	813	10.8	8.0
Jacksonville*	244	373	500	4.3	3.0
Youngstown*	299	373	429	2.2	1.4
Bridgeport*	238	367	499	4.4	3.1
Honolulu*	296	351	438	1.7	2.2
Salt Lake City*	228	349	490	4.3	3.5
Nashville*	260	347	442	2.9	2.4
Richmond*	259	333	421	2.5	2.4

REGION, COUNTRY AND CITY	POPULATION (Thousands) 1950	1960	1970	ANNUAL PER CENT GROWTH 1950-60	1960-70
Syracuse*	266	333	400	2.3	1.9
St. Petersburg*	116	325	660	10.9	7.3
Fort Lauderdale-Hollywood*	---	320	643	---	7.2
Tampa*	180	302	435	5.3	3.7
Tulsa*	207	299	382	3.7	2.5
Grand Rapids*	228	294	360	2.6	2.0
Wichita*	194	292	372	4.2	2.5
Wilmington*	187	284	391	4.3	3.2
New Haven*	246	279	317	1.3	1.3
Flint*	199	278	375	3.4	3.0
El Paso*	137	277	446	7.3	4.9
Mobile*	183	268	374	3.9	3.4
Allentown-Bethlehem*	227	256	285	1.2	1.1
Trenton*	190	242	304	2.4	2.3
Albuquerque*	---	241	400	---	5.2
Des Moines*	201	241	269	1.8	1.1
Wilkes-Barre*	273	234	210	-1.5	-1.1
Davenport*	196	227	260	1.5	1.4
Spokane*	176	227	261	2.6	1.4
Tucson*	---	227	682	---	11.6
Worcester*	220	225	235	.2	.4
South Bend*	168	219	251	2.7	1.4
Tacoma*	168	215	271	2.5	2.3
Canton*	175	214	248	2.0	1.5
Fresno*	132	213	309	4.9	3.8
Scranton*	237	211	192	-1.2	-.9

REGION, COUNTRY AND CITY	POPULATION (Thousands) 1950	1960	1970	ANNUAL PER CENT GROWTH 1950-60	1960-70
Harrisburg*	170	210	255	2.1	2.0
Charlotte*	142	210	290	4.0	3.3
Newport News*	---	209	438	---	7.7
Shreveport*	150	209	254	3.4	2.0
Chattanooga*	169	205	235	1.9	1.4
Orlando*	---	201	409	---	7.4
Baton Rouge*	139	193	253	3.3	2.7
Utica-Rome*	117	188	254	4.9	3.1
Pomona-Ontario*	---	187	310	---	5.2
Austin*	136	187	255	3.2	3.2
Little Rock*	154	185	227	1.9	2.1
Peoria*	155	181	200	1.6	1.0
Fort Wayne*	140	180	228	2.5	2.4
Corpus Christi*	123	177	229	3.7	2.6
Erie*	153	177	194	1.5	.9
Knoxville*	149	173	196	1.5	1.3
West Palm Beach*	---	173	244	---	3.5
Rockford*	123	172	219	3.4	2.4
Savannah*	128	170	201	2.9	1.7
Charleston, W. Va.*	131	169	188	2.6	1.1
Lansing*	135	169	213	2.3	2.3
Stamford*	174	167	160	-.4	-.4
Lawrence-Haverhill*	113	166	207	3.9	2.2
Huntington-Ashland*	157	166	174	.6	.5
Columbia*	121	163	210	3.0	2.6
Reading*	155	160	169	.3	.5
Charleston, S.C.*	120	160	214	2.9	3.0

REGION, COUNTRY AND CITY	POPULATION (Thousands)			ANNUAL PER CENT GROWTH	
	1950	1960	1970	1950-60	1960-70
Binghamton*	144	158	173	.9	.9
Columbus, Ga.*	118	158	218	3.0	3.3
Madison*	110	158	222	3.7	3.5
Jackson*	100	147	202	3.9	3.2
Duluth-Superior*	143	145	141	.1	-.3
Evansville*	139	144	147	.4	.2
Lorain-Elyria*	---	143	176	---	2.1
Montgomery*	109	143	170	2.8	1.7
Waterbury*	132	142	151	.7	.6
Stockton*	113	142	174	2.3	2.1
Bakersfield*	---	142	201	---	3.5
Amarillo*	---	138	215	---	4.5
Lincoln*	---	136	166	---	2.0
Lubbock*	---	129	206	---	4.8
Saginaw*	107	129	154	1.9	1.8
Winston-Salem*	---	128	163	---	2.4
Pensacola*	---	128	161	---	2.3
New Bedford*	126	127	128	.1	.1
Greenville*	---	127	141	---	1.1
Atlantic City*	105	125	152	1.8	2.0
Roanoke*	107	125	147	1.6	1.6
Augusta, Ga.*	---	124	162	---	2.7
Fall River*	119	124	127	.4	.2
Greensboro*	---	123	161	---	2.7
Ogden*	---	122	147	---	1.9
Beaumont*	---	119	137	---	1.4
Lowell*	108	119	131	1.0	1.0

REGION, COUNTRY AND CITY	POPULATION (Thousands) 1950	1960	1970	ANNUAL PER CENT GROWTH 1950-60	1960-70
Topeka*	---	119	146	---	2.1
Galveston-Texas City*	---	118	171	---	3.8
Joliet*	---	117	162	---	3.3
Kalamazoo*	---	116	147	---	2.4
Port Arthur*	---	116	143	---	2.1
Waco*	---	116	135	---	1.5
Ann Arbor*	---	115	147	---	2.5
Macon*	---	114	140	---	2.1
Portland, Me.*	113	112	112	-.1	---
Lexington*	---	112	145	---	2.6
Springfield, Ill.*	---	111	124	---	1.1
Brockton*	---	111	134	---	1.9
Cedar Rapids*	---	105	132	---	2.3
Pueblo*	---	103	130	---	2.4
Waterloo*	---	103	116	---	1.2
Wichita Falls*	---	102	127	---	2.2
York*	---	101	121	---	1.8
Colorado Springs*	---	100	152	---	4.3
New Britain*	123	---	---	---	---
Wheeling*	107	---	---	---	---
Las Vegas*	---	---	225	---	---
Odessa*	---	---	170	---	---
Midland*	---	---	160	---	---
Lake Charles*	---	---	140	---	---
Abiline*	---	---	125	---	---
Eugene*	---	---	125	---	---

REGION, COUNTRY AND CITY	POPULATION (Thousands)			ANNUAL PER CENT GROWTH	
	1950	1960	1970	1950-60	1960-70
Hamilton, O.*	---	---	125	---	---
Raleigh, N.C.*	---	---	125	---	---
Santa Barbara*	---	---	125	---	---
Green Bay*	---	---	125	---	---
Huntsville*	---	---	120	---	---
Norwalk*	---	---	120	---	---
Springfield, Mo.*	---	---	120	---	---
Lancaster*	---	---	115	---	---
Racine*	---	---	115	---	---
Reno*	---	---	115	---	---
Decatur*	---	---	105	---	---
High Point*	---	---	105	---	---
Monroe*	---	---	105	---	---
Muskegon*	---	---	105	---	---
Sioux City*	---	---	105	---	---
Albany, Ga.*	---	---	100	---	---
Aurora*	---	---	100	---	---
Harlingen-San Benito*	---	---	100	---	---
Lawton*	---	---	100	---	---
MIDDLE AMERICA					
Costa Rica					
San Jose*	140	257	435	6.3	5.4
El Salvador					
San Salvador*	162	239	375	4.0	4.6
Santa Ana*	---	---	100	---	---

REGION, COUNTRY AND CITY	POPULATION (Thousands) 1950	1960	1970	ANNUAL PER CENT GROWTH 1950-60	1960-70
Guatemala					
Guatemala City*	294	474	770	4.9	5.0
Honduras					
Tegucigalpa*	---	159	281	---	5.9
Mexico					
Mexico City	2,234	2,832	3,541	2.4	2.3
Guadalajara	378	737	1,364	6.9	6.3
Monterrey	332	597	1,009	6.0	5.4
Puebla de Zaragoza	207	289	387	3.4	3.0
Ciudad Juarez	122	262	532	7.9	7.3
Leon	122	210	346	5.6	5.1
Torreon	129	180	245	3.4	3.1
Mexicali	---	174	436	---	9.6
Merida	145	171	202	1.7	1.7
San Luis Potosi	127	160	185	2.3	1.5
Tijuana	---	152	467	---	11.9
Chihuahua	---	150	251	---	5.3
Veracruz Llave	101	145	201	3.7	3.3
Aguascalientes	---	127	168	---	2.8
Tampico	---	122	156	---	2.5
Villa de Guadaloupe Hidalgo	---	103	153	---	4.0
Morelia	---	101	156	---	4.4
Hermosillo	---	---	200	---	---
Matamoros	---	---	178	---	---
Durango	---	---	154	---	---
Culiacan	---	---	148	---	---

REGION, COUNTRY AND CITY	POPULATION (Thousands)			ANNUAL PER CENT GROWTH	
	1950	1960	1970	1950-60	1960-70
Nuevo Laredo	---	---	144	---	---
Saltillo	---	---	137	---	---
Nicaragua					
Managua*	109	197	350	6.1	5.9
Panama					
Panama*	128	273	440	7.9	4.9
CARIBBEAN					
Cuba					
La Habana*	1,081	1,549	1,700	3.7	.9
Santiago de Cuba	150	208	280	3.3	3.0
Camaguey	101	117	225	1.5	6.8
Santa Clara	---	---	180	---	---
Guantanamo	---	---	160	---	---
Cienfuegos	---	---	100	---	---
Dominican Republic					
Santo Domingo	182	367	650	7.3	5.9
Santiago de los Caballeros	---	---	110	---	---
Haiti					
Port-au-Prince	134	240	400	6.0	5.2
Jamaica					
Kingston*	260	377	560	3.8	4.0
Puerto Rico					
San Juan*	429	542	819	2.4	4.2
Ponce*	---	114	131	---	1.4

REGION, COUNTRY AND CITY	POPULATION (Thousands) 1950	1960	1970	ANNUAL PER CENT GROWTH 1950-60	1960-70
TROPICAL SOUTH AMERICA					
Bolivia					
La Paz*	300	400	500	2.9	2.3
Cochabamba	---	---	100	---	---
Brazil					
Rio de Janeiro*	3,052	4,692	7,213	4.4	4.4
Sao Paulo*	2,449	4,537	8,405	6.4	6.4
Recife*	693	1,115	1,794	4.9	4.9
Porto Alegre*	434	894	1,842	7.5	7.5
Belo Horizante*	353	781	1,728	8.3	8.3
Salvador*	417	656	1,032	4.6	4.6
Fortaleza*	270	515	982	6.7	6.7
Santos*	248	409	675	5.1	5.1
Belem*	255	402	634	4.7	4.7
Curitiba*	181	362	724	7.2	7.2
Campos*	---	292	358	---	2.1
Campinas*	153	238	370	4.5	4.5
Campina Grande*	---	207	263	---	2.4
Joao Pessoa*	119	185	288	4.5	4.5
Juiz de Fora*	126	183	266	3.8	3.8
Vitoria*	---	182	345	---	6.6
Pelotas*	---	178	248	---	3.4
Manaus*	---	175	284	---	5.0
Natal*	103	171	284	5.2	5.2
Maceio*	121	170	239	3.5	3.5
Sao Luis*	120	160	213	2.9	2.9

REGION, COUNTRY AND CITY	POPULATION (Thousands) 1950	1960	1970	ANNUAL PER CENT GROWTH 1950-60	1960-70
Goiana*	---	154	456	---	11.5
Volta Redonda*	---	153	330	---	8.0
Teresina*	---	152	248	---	5.0
Petropolis*	---	150	208	---	3.3
Ribeirao Preto*	---	147	235	---	4.8
Brazilia*	---	142	503	---	13.5
Sorocaba*	---	138	214	---	4.5
Florianopolis*	---	130	188	---	3.8
Juazapio do Norte Crato*	---	128	159	---	2.2
Jundai*	---	119	202	---	5.4
Aracaju*	---	116	182	---	4.6
Piracicaba*	---	116	139	---	1.8
Londrina*	---	---	190	---	---
Bauru*	---	---	113	---	---
Santa Maria*	---	---	108	---	---
British Guiana					
Georgetown*	---	148	200	---	3.1
Colombia					
Bogota	607	1,241	2,500	7.4	7.3
Medellin	341	579	1,090	5.4	6.5
Cali	269	486	915	6.1	6.5
Baranquilla	287	414	645	3.7	4.5
Cartagena	124	185	320	4.1	5.6
Bucaramanga	107	177	315	5.2	5.9
Manizales	123	167	285	3.1	5.5
Pereira	113	137	235	1.9	5.5

REGION, COUNTRY AND CITY	POPULATION (Thousands)			ANNUAL PER CENT GROWTH	
	1950	1960	1970	1950-60	1960-70
Cucuta	---	129	235	---	6.2
Ibague	---	116	200	---	5.6
Armenia	---	101	185	---	6.2
Palmira	---	---	150	---	---
Bello	---	---	145	---	---
Santa Marta	---	---	145	---	---
Buenaventura	---	---	100	---	---
Ecuador					
Guayaquil	259	450	800	5.7	5.9
Quito	210	314	500	4.1	4.8
Peru					
Lima-Callao*	947	1,519	2,500	4.8	5.1
Arequipa	---	130	190	---	3.9
Chiclayo	---	---	140	---	---
Trujillo	---	---	140	---	---
Surinam					
Paramaribo	---	---	135	---	---
Venezuela					
Caracas*	694	1,280	2,147	6.3	5.3
Maracaibo	236	405	682	5.5	5.3
Barquisimeto	105	190	281	6.1	4.0
Valencia	---	156	222	---	3.6
Maracay	---	128	191	---	4.1
San Cristobal	---	---	154	---	---
Cabimas	---	---	153	---	---

REGION, COUNTRY AND CITY	POPULATION (Thousands) 1950	1960	1970	ANNUAL PER CENT GROWTH 1950-60	1960-70
TEMPERATE SOUTH AMERICA					
Argentina					
Buenos Aires*	5,213	7,000	9,400	3.0	3.0
Rosario*	560	672	806	1.8	1.8
Cordoba*	426	589	814	3.3	3.3
Mendoza*	256	427	712	5.2	5.2
La Plata*	325	414	527	2.4	2.4
San Miguel de Tucuman*	224	288	370	2.5	2.5
Santa Fe*	217	260	312	1.8	1.8
Mar del Plata*	142	225	357	4.7	4.7
San Juan*	139	212	323	4.3	4.3
Parana*	154	175	199	1.3	1.3
Bahia Blanca*	128	150	176	1.6	1.6
Salta*	---	123	185	---	4.2
San Fernando*	---	120	172	---	3.7
Corrientes*	---	106	161	---	4.3
Santiago del Estero*	---	103	129	---	2.3
Misiones*	---	---	112	---	---
Chile					
Santiago*	1,275	1,907	2,600	4.1	3.1
Valpariso	217	255	300	1.6	1.6
Concepcion	114	166	200	3.8	1.9
Vina del Mar	---	124	155	---	2.3
Antofagasta	---	---	140	---	---
Talcahuano	---	---	125	---	---

TABLE E (continued)

REGION, COUNTRY AND CITY	POPULATION (Thousands) 1950	1960	1970	ANNUAL PER CENT GROWTH 1950-60	1960-70
Paraguay					
Assuncion*	219	311	445	3.6	3.6
Uruguay					
Montevideo	609	962	1,530	4.7	4.7
EAST ASIA					
China (Taiwan)					
Taipei*	750	1,329	2,150	5.9	4.9
Kaohsiung	277	453	735	5.0	5.0
Tainan	226	330	475	3.9	3.7
Taichung	202	292	430	3.8	3.9
Keelung	148	231	330	4.6	3.6
Chiayi	124	175	235	3.5	3.0
Hsinchu	102	147	210	3.7	3.6
Pingtung	---	120	170	---	3.5
Sanchung	---	104	225	---	8.0
Yangmingshan Administration	---	---	190	---	---
Chenghwa	---	---	140	---	---
Chunli	---	---	130	---	---
China					
Shanghai*	5,300	7,200	8,500	3.1	1.7
Peking (Peiping, Pei-ching)*	2,150	5,500	8,000	9.8	3.8
Tientsin (T'ien-ching)*	2,200	3.500	4,500	4.8	2.5
Shenyang (Mukden)*	1,700	2,500	3,750	3.9	4.1

REGION, COUNTRY AND CITY	POPULATION (Thousands) 1950	1960	1970	ANNUAL PER CENT GROWTH 1950-60	1960-70
Wu-han*	1,200	2,500	4,250	7.6	5.4
Chungking* (Ch'ung-ch'ing)	1,400	2,300	3,500	5.1	4.3
Lu-ta (Port Arthur-Dairen)*	700	2,000	4,000	11.1	7.2
Canton (Kuang-chou)*	1,500	1,900	2,300	2.4	1.9
Harbin (Ha-erh-pin)*	1,000	1,800	2,750	6.1	4.3
Nanking (Nan-ching)*	950	1,500	2,000	4.7	2.9
Sian (Hsi-an)*	600	1,500	1,900	9.6	2.4
T'ai-yuan and Yu-tz'u*	600	1,400	2,725	8.8	6.9
Ch'eng-tu*	750	1,200	2,000	4.8	5.2
Tsingtao (Ch'ing-tao)*	850	1,200	1,900	3.5	4.7
Tzepo (Tzu-po)*	250	1,100	1,750	16.0	4.8
Ch'ang-ch'un*	750	1,050	1,500	3.4	3.6
Fu-shun*	650	1,000	1,700	4.4	5.4
K'un-ming*	625	1,000	1,700	4.8	5.4
Lanchow (Lan-chou)*	300	950	1,500	12.2	4.7
Tsitsihan (Ch'i-ch'i-ha-erh)*	300	950	1,500	12.2	4.7
Tsinan (chi-nan)*	650	920	1,500	3.5	5.0
An-shan*	475	900	1,500	6.6	5.2
Suchow (Hsu-chou)*	375	900	1,500	9.1	5.2
Chengchow (Cheng-chou)*	500	850	1,500	5.4	5.8
T'ang-shan*	500	850	1,200	5.4	3.5

REGION, COUNTRY AND CITY	POPULATION (Thousands) 1950	1960	1970	ANNUAL PER CENT GROWTH 1950-60	1960-70
Hangchow (Hang-chou)*	640	837	1,100	2.7	2.8
Shihkiachwang (Shih-chia-chuang)*	275	750	1,500	10.6	7.2
Soochow (Su-chou)*	400	740	1,300	6.3	5.8
Ch'ang-sha*	600	730	850	2.0	1.5
Kweiyang (Kuei-yang)*	260	700	1,500	10.4	7.9
Foochow (Fu-chou)*	475	668	900	3.5	3.0
Kirin (Chi-lin)*	350	650	1,200	6.4	6.3
Wusih (Wu-hsi)*	550	631	900	1.4	3.6
Nan-ch'ang*	340	575	900	5.4	4.6
Ch'ang-chia-k'ou (Kalgan)*	250	500	1,000	7.2	7.2
Pen-ch'i (Penki)*	350	500	750	3.6	4.1
Lo-yang*	150	500	750	12.8	4.1
Chinchow (Chin-chou)*	275	420	750	4.3	6.0
Pa-t'ou (Paotow)*	130	400	800	11.9	7.2
Han-tan*	200	380	500	6.6	2.8
An-tung*	250	370	450	4.0	2.0
Ho-fei*	150	320	400	7.9	2.3
Huhehot (Hu-ho-hao-t'e, Kwe'isui)*	150	320	700	7.9	8.1
K'ai-feng*	300	320	330	.6	.3
Chang-chou (Changchow)*	250	300	400	1.8	2.9
Swatow (Shan-t'ou)*	250	300	400	1.8	2.9

REGION, COUNTRY AND CITY	POPULATION (Thousands) 1950	1960	1970	ANNUAL PER CENT GROWTH 1950-60	1960-70
Urumchi (Wu-lu-mu-ch'i, Tihua)*	100	300	500	11.6	5.2
Pang-fou*	150	300	400	7.2	2.9
Amoy (Hsia-men)*	200	300	400	4.1	2.9
Huai-nan (Hwainan)*	250	290	350	1.5	1.9
Ning-po*	200	280	350	3.4	2.3
Tzu-kung (Tzekung)*	150	275	350	6.2	2.4
Chihshi (Chi-hsi)*	125	250	350	7.2	3.4
Nan-t'ung*	240	250	300	.4	1.8
Pao-ting*	160	250	350	4.6	3.4
Chiao-tso*	200	250	300	2.3	1.8
Fu-hsin (Fou-hsin)*	160	250	350	4.6	3.4
Mu-tan-chiang*	150	250	400	5.2	4.8
Nan-ning*	175	250	375	3.6	4.1
Ta-t'ung*	150	240	300	4.8	2.3
Heng-yang*	200	240	310	1.8	2.6
Wu-hu*	220	240	300	.9	2.3
Kiamusze (Chia-mu-ssu)*	150	230	275	4.4	1.8
Hsing-tan (Hsiang-t'an)*	160	210	300	2.8	3.6
Wenchow (Wen-chou)*	175	210	250	1.8	1.8
Chinghuang* (Ch'in-huang-tao)	160	210	400	2.8	6.7
Hsin-hai-lien*	155	210	300	3.1	3.6
Ho Kang (Hao-kang)*	---	200	350	---	5.8
Nan-ch'ung*	125	200	275	4.8	3.2
Hsin-hsiang*	150	200	300	2.9	4.1

REGION, COUNTRY AND CITY	POPULATION (Thousands)			ANNUAL PER CENT GROWTH	
	1950	1960	1970	1950-60	1960-70
Yang-ch'uan (Yangchuan)*	100	200	350	7.2	5.8
Ching-te-chen*	---	200	300	---	4.1
Hai-k'ou*	100	200	500	7.2	9.6
T'ai-chou*	140	200	275	3.6	3.2
Yumen (Yu-men)*	---	200	325	---	5.0
Chen-chiang (Ching-kiang)*	180	200	250	1.1	2.3
Tsun-i*	125	200	275	4.8	3.2
Chu-chou (Chuchow)*	110	200	350	6.2	5.8
Wu-t'ung-ch'iao*	175	200	250	1.3	2.3
I-pin*	150	190	275	2.4	3.8
Lu-chou*	150	190	225	2.4	1.7
Liu-chow*	150	190	250	2.4	2.8
Wei Fang*	140	190	260	3.1	3.2
Pao-chi (Paoki)*	110	180	275	5.0	4.3
Ko-chiu*	125	180	250	3.7	3.3
Nei-chiang (Neikiang)*	150	180	240	1.8	2.9
Liaoyuan (Liao-yuan)*	110	180	300	5.0	5.2
Liao-yang*	125	175	250	3.4	3.6
Ch'ang-chih*	---	175	300	---	5.5
T'ung-hua*	110	175	275	4.8	4.6
Shao-yang*	110	170	275	4.4	4.9
Chan-chiang (Fort Bayard, Tsankong)*	150	170	220	1.3	2.6
Kuei-lin (Kweilin)*	140	170	225	2.0	2.8

REGION, COUNTRY AND CITY	POPULATION (Thousands) 1950	1960	1970	ANNUAL PER CENT GROWTH 1950-60	1960-70
Yang Chow (Yang-chou)*	150	160	210	.6	2.8
Shao-hsing*	110	160	225	3.8	3.5
Hsi-ning (Sining)*	---	150	250	---	5.2
Shang-ch'iu (Shangkiu)*	110	150	250	3.2	5.2
An-yang*	120	150	225	2.3	4.1
Ying-k'ou*	130	150	215	1.4	3.7
Ch'ang-te*	---	150	225	---	4.1
Chefoo (Yen-t'ai)*	110	140	180	2.4	2.5
Huang-shih (Hwangshih)*	---	130	200	---	4.4
Ssu-p'ing (Szeping)*	100	130	180	2.7	3.3
An-chiang (An-ch'ing, Anking)*	100	125	160	2.3	2.5
Wan-hsien*	---	125	175	---	3.4
Wu-chou (Wuchow)*	100	120	150	1.8	2.3
Ch'eng-te*	---	120	200	---	5.2
Shuang-ya-shan*	---	110	150	---	3.2
Hu-chou*	---	110	160	---	3.8
I-chang*	---	110	150	---	3.2
Chiang Men (Kongmoon)*	---	110	150	---	3.2
Chuan-chow (Ch'uan-chou)*	100	110	130	1.0	1.7
Shih-ch'i*	---	100	135	---	3.0
Kashgar (K'o-shih)*	---	100	175	---	5.8
Kan-chou*	---	100	135	---	3.0
Ch'ang-shu*	---	100	150	---	4.1

REGION, COUNTRY AND CITY	POPULATION (Thousands) 1950	1960	1970	ANNUAL PER CENT GROWTH 1950-60	1960-70
I-ch'un*	---	100	200	---	7.2
Pei-hai*	---	100	175	---	5.8
Chi-ning*	---	100	160	---	4.8
I-ning (Kuldja)*	---	100	160	---	4.8
Lhasa*	---	100	175	---	5.8
Sha-shih*	---	100	125	---	2.3
Shao-kuan*	---	100	125	---	2.3
Yin-ch'uan*	---	100	175	---	5.8
Hsiang Fan*	---	---	150	---	---
Pei-an*	---	---	130	---	---
Yen-chi*	---	---	130	---	---
Hsin-yang*	---	---	125	---	---
Han-chung*	---	---	120	---	---
Hsien-yang*	---	---	120	---	---
Chiu-chiang*	---	---	120	---	---
Ch'ing-ch'iang*	---	---	110	---	---
Ya-an*	---	---	100	---	---
Ulanhot (Wu-lan-hao-t'e)*	---	---	100	---	---
Tien-shui*	---	---	100	---	---
Shang-jao*	---	---	100	---	---
Chou-k'ou*	---	---	100	---	---
Ching-shih*	---	---	100	---	---
Chi-an*	---	---	100	---	---
Hong Kong					
Hong Kong-Kowloon*	1,561	3,075	4,105	7.0	2.9

189

REGION, COUNTRY AND CITY	POPULATION (Thousands) 1950	1960	1970	ANNUAL PER CENT GROWTH 1950-60	1960-70
Korea, North					
Pyong Yang (Pyeongyang)	516	653	800	2.4	2.1
Sinuiju (Sinuyin)	180	226	300	2.3	2.9
Wonson (Wonsan)	176	221	275	2.3	2.2
Chungjin (Chongjin)	158	200	250	2.4	2.3
Hamhung-Heungnam*	---	150	200	---	1.6
Kaesong	---	140	175	---	2.3
Chenampo (Chinnampo, Nampo)	---	100	140	---	3.4
Haeju	---	---	140	---	---
Kimchaek (Songjin)	---	---	100	---	---
Korea, South					
Seoul (Soul)	1,467	2,445	4,661	5.2	6.7
Pusan (Busan)	542	1,164	1,592	7.9	3.2
Taegu (Daegu)	339	677	989	7.2	3.9
Inchon (Incheon)	274	402	636	3.9	4.7
Kwangchu (Gwangju)	152	314	515	7.5	5.1
Taejon (Daejeon)	134	229	367	5.5	4.8
Chonchu (Jeonju, Chonju)	104	188	249	6.1	2.8
Masan	---	158	157	---	-.1
Mokpo	112	130	184	1.5	3.5
Ulsan	---	---	243	---	---
Suweon (Puwan, Suwon)	---	---	140	---	---

190

REGION, COUNTRY AND CITY	POPULATION (Thousands) 1950	1960	1970	ANNUAL PER CENT GROWTH 1950-60	1960-70
Cheongju (Chungju, Chongju)	---	---	137	---	---
Weonju	---	---	123	---	---
Jinju (Jingu, Chinju)	---	---	118	---	---
Yeosu (Yosu)	---	---	112	---	---
Chuncheon (Chunchon)	---	---	111	---	---
Gunsan (Kunsan)	---	---	105	---	---
Macau					
Macau (Macao)*	188	169	280	-1.1	5.2
Mongolia					
Ulan Bator (Ulaan Baatar)	---	164	350	---	7.9
Ryukyu Islands					
Naha	---	223	391	---	2.7
JAPAN					
Japan					
Tokyo*	6,277	9,684	12,199	4.4	2.3
Osaka*	1,956	3,012	3,307	4.4	.9
Nagoya*	1,031	1,592	2,353	4.4	4.0
Yokohama*	951	1,376	2,326	3.8	5.4
Kyoto*	1,102	1,285	1,450	1.5	1.2
Kobe*	765	1,114	1,329	3.8	1.8
Fukuoka*	393	647	869	5.1	3.0
Kawasaki*	319	633	1,154	7.1	6.2

REGION, COUNTRY AND CITY	POPULATION (Thousands) 1950	1960	1970	ANNUAL PER CENT GROWTH 1950-60	1960-70
Sapporo*	314	524	1,206	5.3	8.7
Hiroshima*	286	431	590	4.2	3.2
Sendai*	342	425	544	2.2	2.5
Amagasaki*	279	406	618	3.8	4.3
Kumamoto*	267	374	443	3.4	1.7
Nagasaki*	242	344	478	3.6	3.3
Sakai*	214	340	640	4.7	6.5
Hamamatsu*	152	333	463	8.2	3.4
Yahata*	210	332	---	4.7	---
Himeji*	212	329	411	4.5	2.3
Shizuoka*	239	329	411	3.2	2.3
Niigata*	221	315	403	3.6	2.5
Gifu*	212	304	422	3.7	3.3
Kanazawa*	252	299	377	1.7	2.3
Kagoshima*	229	296	364	2.6	2.1
Yokosuka*	251	287	351	1.3	2.0
Kokura*	199	286	---	3.7	---
Wakayama*	191	285	379	4.1	2.9
Nishinomiya*	127	263	431	7.6	5.1
Sasebo*	194	262	233	3.1	-1.2
Okayama*	163	261	326	4.8	2.2
Shimonoseki*	194	247	262	2.4	.6
Hakodate*	229	243	244	.6	---
Chiba*	134	242	456	6.1	6.5
Matsuyama*	164	239	334	3.8	3.4
Utsunomiya*	107	239	295	8.4	2.1
Takamatsu*	125	228	260	6.2	1.3

REGION, COUNTRY AND CITY	POPULATION (Thousands)			ANNUAL PER CENT GROWTH	
	1950	1960	1970	1950-60	1960-70
Toyohashi*	146	216	264	4.0	2.0
Fuse*	150	213	347	3.6	5.0
Kure*	188	210	241	1.1	1.4
Toyama*	154	207	278	3.0	3.0
Omuta*	192	206	182	.7	-1.2
Akita*	126	204	230	4.9	1.2
Aomori*	106	202	249	6.7	2.1
Otaru*	178	199	195	1.1	-.2
Toyonaka*	---	199	428	---	8.0
Kochi*	162	196	242	1.9	2.1
Yokkaichi*	124	196	245	4.7	2.3
Yamagata*	105	189	199	6.1	.5
Asahikawa*	123	188	320	4.3	5.5
Ichinomiya*	---	183	227	---	2.2
Tokushima*	121	183	204	4.2	1.1
Maebashi*	---	182	217	---	1.8
Hachinohe*	104	174	206	5.3	1.7
Kawaguchi*	125	170	365	3.1	7.9
Omiya*	100	170	274	5.4	4.9
Urawa*	115	169	290	3.9	5.5
Ube*	129	167	151	2.6	-1.0
Okazaki*	---	166	228	---	3.2
Hitachi*	---	161	201	---	2.2
Kofu*	122	161	185	2.8	1.4
Nagano*	101	161	186	4.8	1.5
Hachioji*	---	158	273	---	5.6
Miyazaki*	103	158	212	4.4	3.0

REGION, COUNTRY AND CITY	POPULATION (THOUSANDS) 1950	1960	1970	ANNUAL PER CENT GROWTH 1950-60	1960-70
Ichikawa*	103	157	276	4.3	5.8
Morioka*	118	157	199	2.9	2.4
Kurume*	101	155	163	4.4	.5
Hirosaki*	---	152	151	---	-.1
Moji*	124	152	---	2.1	---
Kushiro*	---	151	201	---	2.9
Fukui (Hukui)*	101	150	192	4.0	2.5
Nagaoka*	---	148	162	---	.9
Matsumoto*	---	148	161	---	.8
Muroran*	110	146	178	2.9	2.0
Numazu*	102	143	179	3.4	2.3
Shimizu*	---	143	334	---	8.9
Takasaki*	---	142	120	---	-1.7
Fukuyama*	---	141	205	---	3.8
Fukushima*	---	139	217	---	4.6
Mito*	---	139	173	---	2.2
Funabashi*	---	135	372	---	10.7
Nara*	---	135	191	---	3.5
Takaoka*	142	135	144	-.5	.6
Saga*	---	130	139	---	.7
Akashi*	---	130	195	---	4.1
Niihama*	---	126	124	---	-.2
Fujisawa*	---	125	246	---	7.0
Kurashiki*	---	125	167	---	2.9
Odawara*	---	125	164	---	2.8
Oita*	---	125	410	---	12.6
Kiryu*	---	123	133	---	.8

REGION, COUNTRY AND CITY	POPULATION (Thousands)			ANNUAL PER CENT GROWTH	
	1950	1960	1970	1950-60	1960-70
Nobeoka*	---	123	125	---	.2
Yao*	---	123	236	---	6.7
Musashino*	---	120	149	---	2.2
Kishiwada*	---	120	172	---	3.7
Suita*	---	117	331	---	11.0
Otsu*	---	114	129	---	1.2
Ashikaga*	---	111	203	---	6.2
Tsu*	---	111	124	---	1.1
Tobata*	---	109	---	---	---
Beppu*	---	108	131	---	1.9
Hiratsuka*	---	108	169	---	4.6
Kawagoe*	---	108	150	---	3.3
Yubari*	---	108	---	---	---
Wakamatsu*	---	107	---	---	---
Matsue*	---	106	115	---	.8
Tattori*	---	105	113	---	.7
Koriyama*	---	103	484	---	16.7
Moriguchi*	---	102	189	---	6.4
Ogaki*	---	102	127	---	2.2
Sagamihara*	---	102	262	---	9.9
Obihiro*	---	101	136	---	3.0
Yatsushiro*	---	101	104	---	.3
Iwakuni*	---	100	112	---	1.1
Imabari*	---	100	109	---	.9
Aizuwakamatsu*	---	---	105	---	---
Chigasaki*	---	---	140	---	---
Chofu*	---	---	190	---	---

REGION, COUNTRY AND CITY	POPULATION (Thousands) 1950	1960	1970	ANNUAL PER CENT GROWTH 1950-60	1960-70
Fuchu*	---	---	195	---	---
Hirakata*	---	---	202	---	---
Kakogawa*	---	---	114	---	---
Ibaraki*	---	---	174	---	---
Ise*	---	---	106	---	---
Itami*	---	---	170	---	---
Kamakura*	---	---	142	---	---
Kashiwa*	---	---	175	---	---
Kasugai*	---	---	169	---	---
Kodaira*	---	---	192	---	---
Kumagaya*	---	---	122	---	---
Machida*	---	---	177	---	---
Matsudo*	---	---	296	---	---
Matsuzaka*	---	---	101	---	---
Mitaka*	---	---	188	---	---
Miyakonojo*	---	---	124	---	---
Neyagawa*	---	---	252	---	---
Suzuka*	---	---	110	---	---
Tachikawa*	---	---	142	---	---
Toyota*	---	---	222	---	---
Yamaguchi*	---	---	121	---	---
Yonago*	---	---	104	---	---
Kitakyushu*	---	---	1,094	---	---

SOUTHEAST ASIA

Burma

| Rangoon | 696 | 884 | 1,200 | 2.4 | 3.1 |

REGION, COUNTRY AND CITY	POPULATION (Thousands) 1950	1960	1970	ANNUAL PER CENT GROWTH 1950-60	1960-70
Mandalay	181	200	300	1.0	4.1
Moulmein	100	110	175	1.0	4.8
Bassein	---	---	105	---	---
Henzada	---	---	100	---	---
Cambodia					
Phnom Penh*	152	337	700	8.3	7.6
Indonesia					
Djakarta	1,452	2,852	4,500	7.0	4.7
Surabaja	679	1,088	1,400	4.8	2.6
Bandung	511	954	1,500	6.4	4.6
Semarang	371	475	700	2.5	4.0
Medan	284	399	850	3.5	7.9
Surakarta	275	397	450	3.7	1.3
Palembang	277	390	800	3.5	7.4
Makasar	228	374	550	5.1	3.9
Malong	202	333	500	5.1	4.1
Jogjakarta	231	304	400	2.8	2.8
Bandjarmasin	127	192	300	4.2	4.6
Padang	---	154	200	---	2.6
Kediri	---	154	200	---	2.6
Tjirebon	---	151	225	---	4.1
Pontianak	---	139	200	---	3.7
Bogor	---	138	200	---	3.8
Menado	---	126	200	---	4.7
Madiun	---	120	150	---	2.3
Teluk Betung	---	120	250	---	7.6

REGION, COUNTRY AND CITY	POPULATION (Thousands)			ANNUAL PER CENT GROWTH	
	1950	1960	1970	1950-60	1960-70
Pematang Siantar	---	112	150	---	3.0
Djambi	---	110	150	---	3.2
Pakalongan	---	---	100	---	---
Baltkpapan	---	---	125	---	---
Samarenda	---	---	115	---	---
Pare-pare	---	---	125	---	---
Laos					
Vientiane*	---	114	210	---	6.3
West Malaysia					
Kuala Lumpur	208	379	650	6.2	5.5
George Town	201	251	325	2.2	2.6
Ipoh	---	144	225	---	4.6
Klang	---	---	150	---	---
Jahore Bahru	---	---	150	---	---
Malacca	---	---	100	---	---
Philippines					
Manila*	1,781	2,704	4,100	4.3	4.3
Cebu	178	251	355	3.5	3.5
Davao*	124	226	320	6.2	3.5
Basilan*	116	156	225	3.0	3.7
Iloili	116	151	215	2.7	3.6
Zamboanga*	107	131	190	2.0	3.8
San Carlos	---	125	175	---	3.4
Bacolod	104	119	170	1.4	3.6
Tarlac	---	---	139	---	---
Butuan	---	---	118	---	---

REGION, COUNTRY AND CITY	POPULATION (Thousands)			ANNUAL PER CENT GROWTH	
	1950	1960	1970	1950-60	1960-70
Bantangas	---	---	117	---	---
Singapore					
Singapore*	1,022	1,634	2,113	4.8	2.6
Thailand					
Bangkok*	891	1,330	2,100	4.1	4.7
Thonburi*	276	375	625	3.1	5.2
Songkla	---	---	100	---	---
Viet-Nam, North					
Hanoi*	280	644	1,400	8.7	8.1
Haiphong*	168	369	600	8.2	5.0
Nam Dinh	---	---	125	---	---
Thai Nguyen	---	---	110	---	---
Hon Gay	---	---	100	---	---
Viet-Nam, South					
Saigon	850	1,264	1,750	4.0	3.3
Danang	---	105	400	---	14.3
Hue	---	104	130	---	2.3
Cantho	---	---	100	---	---
SOUTHWEST ASIA					
Cyprus					
Nicosia*	---	---	112	---	---
Fed. of South Arabia (Southern Yemen)					
Aden*	107	181	275	5.4	4.3

REGION, COUNTRY AND CITY	POPULATION (Thousands) 1950	1960	1970	ANNUAL PER CENT GROWTH 1950-60	1960-70
Iran					
Teheran	1,073	1,839	---	5.5	---
Ibid.*	---	1,923	3,250	---	5.4
Tabriz	249	316	460	2.4	3.8
Esfahan	219	278	510	2.4	6.3
Mashhad	208	264	500	2.4	6.6
Abadan	194	247	290	2.4	1.6
Shiraz	147	186	320	2.4	5.6
Kermanshah	108	137	210	2.4	4.4
Ahvaz	103	132	225	2.5	5.5
Rasht	---	119	150	---	2.3
Hamedan	---	109	130	---	1.8
Ghom	---	105	150	---	3.6
Rai	---	---	130	---	---
Razaeyeh	---	---	125	---	---
Tajrish	---	---	180	---	---
Iraq					
Baghdad*	540	815	1,250	4.2	4.4
Basra*	100	210	450	7.7	7.9
Mosul*	140	200	300	3.6	4.1
Kirkuk*	---	135	200	---	4.0
Najaf*	---	100	150	---	4.1
Sulaimaniyah	---	---	125	---	---
Arbil	---	---	125	---	---
Hilla*	---	---	110	---	---
Kerbela (Karbela, Karbala)	---	---	100	---	---

REGION, COUNTRY AND CITY	POPULATION (Thousands) 1950	1960	1970	ANNUAL PER CENT GROWTH 1950-60	1960-70
Israel					
Tel-Aviv	270	384	---	3.6	---
Ibid.*	---	699	900	---	2.6
Haifa	108	177	---	5.1	---
Ibid.*	---	276	355	---	2.5
Jerusalem	---	167	---	---	---
Ibid.*	---	192	350	---	6.2
Ramat Gan	---	105	---	---	---
Jordan					
Amman	---	225	350	---	4.5
Zarqa	---	---	125	---	---
Kuwait					
Kuwait City*	---	146	325	---	8.3
Lebanon					
Beirut*	321	450	600	3.4	2.9
Tripoli*	---	115	150	---	2.7
Zahle*	---	---	100	---	---
Saudi Arabia					
Riyadh	---	169	300	---	5.9
Mecca	100	159	215	4.7	3.1
Jeddah	---	148	255	---	5.6
Al Hufuf	---	---	125	---	---
Medina	---	---	100	---	---
Syria					
Damascus	359	530	670	4.0	2.4

REGION, COUNTRY AND CITY	POPULATION (Thousands) 1950	1960	1970	ANNUAL PER CENT GROWTH 1950-60	1960-70
Aleppo	314	425	680	3.1	4.8
Homs	102	137	260	3.0	6.6
Hama	---	111	170	---	4.4
Latakia	---	---	100	---	---
Turkey					
Istanbul*	983	1,467	2,600	4.1	5.9
Ankara*	289	650	1,250	8.4	6.8
Izmir*	228	361	750	4.7	7.6
Adana	118	232	325	7.0	3.4
Bursa	104	154	250	4.0	5.0
Eskisehir	---	150	175	---	1.6
Gaziantep	---	122	175	---	3.7
Konya	---	118	175	---	4.0
Kayseri	---	101	150	---	4.0
Diyarbakir	---	---	125	---	---
Samsun	---	---	125	---	---
Malatya	---	---	125	---	---
Erzurum	---	---	120	---	---
Sivas	---	---	120	---	---
SOUTH CENTRAL ASIA					
Afghanistan					
Kabul	218	290	---	2.9	---
Ibid.*	---	364	500	---	3.2
Kandahar	---	103	135	---	2.7
Herat	---	---	100	---	---

TABLE E (continued)

REGION, COUNTRY AND CITY	POPULATION (Thousands) 1950	1960	1970	ANNUAL PER CENT GROWTH 1950-60	1960-70
Ceylon					
Colombo*	722	950	1,250	2.8	2.8
Jaffna	---	---	100	---	---
India					
Calcutta*	5,153	6,138	7,350	1.8	1.8
Bombay*	3,335	4,089	5,100	2.1	2.2
Delhi*	1,737	2,309	3,100	2.9	3.0
Madras*	1,700	2,090	2,600	2.1	2.2
Hyderabad*	1,074	1,238	1,500	1.4	1.9
Bangalore*	922	1,184	1,550	2.5	2.7
Ahmedabad*	904	1,182	1,550	2.7	2.7
Kanpur*	689	948	1,325	3.2	3.4
Poona*	585	726	925	2.2	2.5
Nagpur*	435	668	1,030	4.4	4.4
Lucknow*	487	642	850	2.8	2.8
Agra*	348	495	710	3.6	3.7
Varanasi* (Banaras)	347	478	660	3.3	3.3
Allahabad*	326	422	550	2.6	2.7
Madurai*	357	420	500	1.6	1.8
Jaipur*	284	394	550	3.3	3.4
Amritsar*	321	392	500	2.0	2.5
Indore*	305	388	500	2.4	2.6
Patna*	278	358	475	2.6	2.9
Jabalpur*	250	357	525	3.6	3.9
Sholapur*	273	333	410	2.0	2.1
Jamshedpur*	212	318	500	4.1	4.6

REGION, COUNTRY AND CITY	POPULATION (Thousands)			ANNUAL PER CENT GROWTH	
	1950	1960	1970	1950-60	1960-70
Ernakulam*	187	302	500	4.9	5.2
Gwalior*	238	296	375	2.2	2.4
Trivandrum*	180	292	475	5.0	5.0
Baroda*	206	291	415	3.5	3.6
Surat*	219	283	375	2.6	2.9
Meerut*	230	280	350	2.0	2.3
Coimbatore*	192	278	405	3.8	3.8
Bareilly*	204	267	355	2.7	2.9
Jullundur* (Jullunder)	163	256	405	4.6	4.7
Mysore*	244	253	265	.4	.5
Trichurapalli* (Tiruchirapalli)	217	247	285	1.3	1.4
Salem*	199	245	305	2.1	2.2
Kozhikode* (Calicut)	153	240	380	4.6	4.7
Hubli*	123	237	450	6.8	6.6
Ludhiana*	149	236	375	4.7	4.7
Ajmer*	194	228	275	1.6	1.9
Vijayawada* (Vijayavada)	157	224	325	3.6	3.8
Jodhpur*	178	221	275	2.2	2.2
Nasik*	153	210	290	3.2	3.3
Bhopal*	---	210	440	---	7.7
Dhanbad*	115	193	325	5.3	5.3
Ulhasnagar* (Kalyan Camp)	109	191	335	5.8	5.8
Rajkot*	128	189	280	4.0	4.0
Kolhapur*	133	188	270	3.5	3.7

REGION, COUNTRY AND CITY	POPULATION (Thousands)			ANNUAL PER CENT GROWTH	
	1950	1960	1970	1950-60	1960-70
Tirunelveli*	109	183	310	5.3	5.4
Saharanpur*	146	182	230	2.2	2.4
Guntur (Guntar)*	122	182	275	4.1	4.2
Aligarh*	139	181	240	2.7	2.9
Ambala*	150	179	215	1.8	1.8
Moradabad*	161	179	200	1.1	1.1
Gorakhpur*	129	176	240	3.2	3.2
Visakhapatnam*	104	175	295	5.3	5.4
Bhaunagar*	135	173	225	2.5	2.7
Jhansi*	125	166	225	2.9	3.1
Mangalore*	114	166	245	3.8	4.0
Asansol*	---	162	285	---	5.8
Dehra Dun*	143	155	175	.8	1.2
Warangal*	132	154	185	1.6	1.9
Gaya*	132	150	170	1.3	1.3
Bikaner*	129	149	175	1.5	1.6
Kolar Gold Fields*	160	148	145	-.8	-.2
Kharagpur*	128	146	170	1.3	1.5
Jamnagar*	102	145	205	3.6	3.5
Monghyr*	117	144	180	2.1	2.3
Belgaum*	116	144	180	2.2	2.3
Ujjain*	129	143	165	1.0	1.4
Cuttack*	100	142	205	3.6	3.7
Bhagalpur*	113	141	180	2.2	2.5
Ranchi*	105	137	185	2.7	3.0
Alleppey*	115	137	165	1.8	1.9

REGION, COUNTRY AND CITY	POPULATION (Thousands)			ANNUAL PER CENT GROWTH	
	1950	1960	1970	1950-60	1960-70
Amravati* (Amraoti, Amaravati)	123	137	155	1.1	1.2
Rampur*	134	135	140	.1	.4
Raipur*	---	135	210	---	4.5
Rajamundry*	104	128	160	2.1	2.3
Durg*	---	125	275	---	8.2
Tuticorin*	---	125	165	---	2.8
Sangli*	---	124	175	---	3.5
Patiala*	---	123	160	---	2.7
Kakinada*	---	121	150	---	2.2
Chandigarh*	113	117	125	.3	.7
Shahjahanpur*	104	117	135	1.2	1.4
Mathura*	105	116	130	1.0	1.1
Ahmednagar*	---	116	170	---	3.9
Kotah*	---	115	210	---	6.2
Malegoon*	---	114	225	---	7.0
Akola*	---	114	150	---	2.8
Vellore*	105	113	125	.7	1.0
Thanjavur* (Tanjore, Tanjavrur)	100	110	125	1.0	1.3
Udaipur*	---	109	140	---	2.5
Eluru (Ellore)*	---	107	135	---	2.4
Thana*	---	106	150	---	3.5
Muzaffarpur*	---	106	155	---	3.9
Burdwan*	---	105	155	---	4.0
Nellore*	---	105	140	---	2.9

REGION, COUNTRY AND CITY	POPULATION (Thousands)			ANNUAL PER CENT GROWTH	
	1950	1960	1970	1950-60	1960-70
Sagar*	---	103	130	---	2.4
Darbhanga*	---	102	125	---	2.1
Gauhati*	---	---	200	---	---
Bilaspur*	---	---	178	---	---
Shillong*	---	---	170	---	---
Panhati*	---	---	167	---	---
Jagadhri*	---	---	166	---	---
Kurnool*	---	---	160	---	---
Barauni-Teghra*	---	---	150	---	---
Firozabad*	---	---	143	---	---
Bandar* (Masulipatnam)	---	---	130	---	---
Aurangabad*	---	---	138	---	---
Dhulia*	---	---	124	---	---
Quilon*	---	---	121	---	---
Gulbarga*	---	---	119	---	---
Hooghly-Chinsura*	---	---	117	---	---
Ratlam*	---	---	117	---	---
Tiruppur*	---	---	116	---	---
Muzaffarnagar*	---	---	116	---	---
Mirzapur-cum-Vindhayachal* (Mirzapur-Vindhyachal)	---	---	115	---	---
Ferozepur*	---	---	113	---	---
Bhusawal*	---	---	111	---	---
Serampore*	---	---	110	---	---
Farrukhabad-cum-Fatehgarh*	---	---	110	---	---

REGION, COUNTRY AND CITY	POPULATION (Thousands)			ANNUAL PER CENT GROWTH	
	1950	1960	1970	1950-60	1960-70
Dindigul*	---	---	108	---	---
Ghaziabad*	---	---	108	---	---
Rhotak*	---	---	106	---	---
Bellary*	---	---	102	---	---
Kumbakonam*	---	---	102	---	---
Kanchipuram*	---	---	100	---	---
Kashmir-Jammu					
Srinagar*	242	292	350	1.9	1.8
Jammu	---	101	150	---	4.0
Nepal					
Katmandu*	121	205	440	5.4	7.9
Pakistan					
Karachi*	1,086	1,884	3,246	5.7	5.6
Lahore*	826	1,262	1,902	4.3	4.2
Dacca*	322	531	854	5.1	4.9
Hyderabad*	232	419	741	6.1	5.9
Lyalpur*	169	402	931	9.1	8.8
Chittagong*	290	361	447	2.2	2.2
Multan*	182	344	636	6.6	6.3
Rawalpindi*	147	277	472	6.5	5.5
Peshawar*	148	214	307	3.8	3.7
Gujranwala*	110	186	304	5.4	5.0
Sialkot*	156	165	176	.6	.6
Narayanganj*	---	148	367	---	9.5
Saragodha*	---	125	207	---	5.2
Khulna*	---	119	350	---	11.4

REGION, COUNTRY AND CITY	POPULATION (Thousands) 1950	1960	1970	ANNUAL PER CENT GROWTH 1950-60	1960-70
Quetta*	---	105	135	---	2.5
Sukkur*	---	101	136	---	3.0
Jhang*	---	---	127	---	---
Bahawalpur*	---	---	161	---	---
Mardan*	---	---	121	---	---
Okara*	---	---	127	---	---
NORTHERN EUROPE					
Denmark					
Kobenhavn* (Copenhagen)	1,168	1,262	1,480	.8	1.6
Arhus*	151	177	190	1.6	.7
Odense*	114	130	133	1.3	.2
Aalborg*	---	---	100	---	---
Finland					
Helsinki*	414	566	757	3.2	3.0
Tampere*	129	166	198	2.6	1.8
Turku*	117	165	205	3.5	2.2
Ireland					
Dublin*	632	661	775	.4	1.6
Cork*	112	115	130	.3	1.2
Norway					
Oslo*	505	580	590	1.4	.2
Bergen*	144	149	152	.3	.2
Trondheim	---	---	127	---	---
Sor-Trondelag	---	---	120	---	---

REGION, COUNTRY AND CITY	POPULATION (Thousands) 1950	1960	1970	ANNUAL PER CENT GROWTH 1950-60	1960-70
Sweden					
Stockholm*	928	1,149	1,350	2.2	1.6
Goteborg*	380	486	650	2.5	3.0
Malmo*	196	246	410	2.3	5.2
Vasteras	---	---	128	---	---
Upsalaas	---	---	106	---	---
United Kingdom					
London*	10,393	10,953	11,544	.5	.5
Birmingham*	2,583	2,775	2,981	.7	.7
Manchester*	2,509	2,525	2,541	.1	.1
Glasgow*	1,911	1,959	2,008	.2	.2
Leeds-Bradford*	1,907	1,926	1,945	.1	.1
Liverpool*	1,665	1,742	1,823	.5	.5
Newcastle upon Tyne*	1,125	1,159	1,193	.3	.3
Sheffield*	756	766	776	.1	.1
Cardiff-Rhondda*	692	705	719	.2	.2
Nottingham*	599	641	686	.7	.7
Bristol*	595	639	687	.7	.7
Edinburgh*	565	600	637	.6	.6
Coventry*	510	591	686	1.5	1.5
Middlesbrough-Stockton-West Hartlepool*	479	533	594	1.1	1.1
Stoke on Trent*	503	520	538	.3	.3
Leicester*	425	463	505	.9	.9
Newport-Pontypool*	414	427	440	.3	.3
Portsmouth*	367	407	452	1.0	1.1

REGION, COUNTRY AND CITY	POPULATION (Thousands)			ANNUAL PER CENT GROWTH	
	1950	1960	1970	1950-60	1960-70
Southampton*	353	398	448	1.2	1.2
Brighton-Worthing*	361	397	436	1.0	.9
Derby*	357	377	399	.5	.6
Kingston upon Hull*	334	345	356	.3	.3
Swansea-Neath*	305	307	310	.1	.1
Bournemouth*	273	303	336	1.0	1.0
Wigan-Leigh*	300	297	295	-.1	-.1
Preston*	272	282	293	.4	.4
Plymouth*	264	256	248	-.3	-.3
Doncaster*	232	253	276	.9	.9
Blackpool*	229	251	275	.9	.9
Sunderland*	232	243	254	.5	.4
Reading*	203	238	280	1.6	1.6
Mansfield-Sutton*	222	236	250	.6	.6
Norwich*	219	232	245	.6	.5
Blackburn*	237	231	224	-.3	-.3
Chesterfield*	199	225	256	1.2	1.3
Aberdeen*	212	215	219	.1	.2
Barnesley*	204	207	210	.1	.1
Dundee*	195	200	206	.3	.3
Chatan-Rochester-Gillingham*	178	199	222	1.1	1.1
Oxford*	169	195	224	1.4	1.4
Luton*	144	189	249	2.8	2.8
Warrington*	182	176	171	-.3	-.3
Burnley-Nelson*	182	173	164	-.5	-.5

REGION, COUNTRY AND CITY	POPULATION (Thousands)			ANNUAL PER CENT GROWTH	
	1950	1960	1970	1950-60	1960-70
Darlington- Auckland*	147	157	167	.7	.6
Aldershot- Farnborough*	139	155	172	1.1	1.0
Northampton*	141	150	160	.6	.6
Port Talbot*	133	149	167	1.1	1.1
Grimsby*	136	146	157	.7	.7
Exeter*	135	146	158	.8	.8
Cambridge*	119	138	161	1.5	1.6
Swindon*	104	134	174	2.6	2.6
York*	125	133	140	.6	.5
Saint Helen's*	129	126	124	-.2	-.2
Ipswich*	107	117	127	.9	.8
Gloucester*	103	115	129	1.1	1.2
Greenock*	108	107	106	-.1	-.1
Lancaster- Morecambe*	104	106	109	.2	.3
WESTERN EUROPE					
Austria					
Wien (Vienna)*	1,861	1,874	1,890	.1	.1
Linz*	251	251	255	---	.2
Graz*	225	236	250	.5	.6
Innsbruck*	172	182	195	.6	.7
Salzburg*	102	108	115	.6	.6
Belgium					
Bruxelles* (Brussel)	967	1,013	1,104	.5	.9

REGION, COUNTRY AND CITY	POPULATION (Thousands)			ANNUAL PER CENT GROWTH	
	1950	1960	1970	1950-60	1960-70
Antwerpen* (Anvers)	595	637	674	.7	.6
Liege (Luik)*	429	446	447	.4	---
Charleroi*	264	276	304	.4	1.0
Gent (Grand)*	228	229	239	---	.4
France					
Paris*	5,998	7,287	8,714	2.0	1.8
Lyon*	583	827	1,226	3.6	4.0
Marseille*	674	762	1,061	1.2	3.4
Bordeaux*	385	451	519	1.6	1.4
Lille*	322	414	522	2.5	2.3
Roubaix*	230	322	438	3.4	3.1
Toulouse*	270	311	429	1.4	3.3
Rouen*	210	306	435	3.8	3.6
Nantes*	212	306	452	3.7	4.0
Nice*	241	293	405	2.0	3.3
Strasbourg*	212	287	386	3.1	3.0
Saint-Etienne*	180	262	468	3.8	6.0
Lens*	---	246	343	---	3.4
Grenoble*	128	210	383	5.1	6.2
Le Havre*	157	210	293	3.0	3.4
Toulon*	183	209	291	1.3	3.4
Nancy*	157	201	249	2.5	2.2
Valenciennes*	---	163	225	---	3.3
Clermont-Ferrand*	133	154	189	1.5	2.1
Mulhouse*	---	151	250	---	5.2
Rennes*	123	148	204	1.9	3.3

REGION, COUNTRY AND CITY	POPULATION (Thousands)			ANNUAL PER CENT GROWTH	
	1950	1960	1970	1950-60	1960-70
Dijon*	107	144	209	3.0	3.8
Tours*	107	143	198	2.9	3.3
Reims*	119	139	168	1.6	1.9
Metz*	---	139	193	---	3.3
Le Mans*	106	135	180	2.4	2.9
Brest	---	130	169	---	2.7
Douai*	---	127	175	---	3.3
Angers*	---	126	176	---	3.4
Orleans*	---	119	165	---	3.3
Thionville*	---	118	166	---	3.5
Montpellier*	---	117	162	---	3.3
Dunkerque*	---	115	159	---	3.3
Limoges*	109	113	159	.4	3.5
Caen*	---	111	153	---	3.3
Amiens*	---	107	149	---	3.4
Bruay-en-Artois*	---	104	141	---	3.1
Troyes*	---	---	112	---	---
Nimes	---	---	112	---	---
Montreuil	---	---	112	---	---
Avignon*	---	---	101	---	---
Besancon*	---	---	100	---	---
Germany, Fed. Rep.					
Essen-Dortmund-Duisberg*	4,597	5,587	6,789	2.0	2.0
West Berlin*	2,147	2,193	2,240	.2	.2
Hamburg*	1,952	2,168	2,407	1.1	1.1
Stuttgart*	1,129	1,478	1,935	2.7	2.7

REGION, COUNTRY AND CITY	POPULATION (Thousands)			ANNUAL PER CENT GROWTH	
	1950	1960	1970	1950-60	1960-70
Frankfurt-am-Main*	1,309	1,378	1,452	.5	.5
Koln (Cologne)*	1,060	1,376	1,788	2.6	2.7
Mannheim-Ludwigshafen-Heidelberg*	1,146	1,345	1,578	1.6	1.6
Munchen* (Munich)	1,110	1,291	1,502	1.5	1.5
Dusseldorf*	708	946	1,264	2.9	2.9
Wuppertal-Solingen-Remsheid*	763	888	1,032	1.5	1.5
Hanover*	787	856	931	.8	.8
Nuremburg*	632	734	852	1.5	1.5
Bremen*	617	709	814	1.4	1.4
Krefeld*	598	697	812	1.5	1.5
Bonn*	460	562	687	2.0	2.0
Karlsruhe*	445	519	606	1.6	1.6
Braunschweig*	445	452	459	.2	.2
Wiesbaden-Mainz*	365	438	525	1.8	1.8
Aachen*	352	421	504	1.8	1.8
Saarbrucken*	356	387	422	.8	.9
Lubeck*	235	334	473	3.6	3.5
Kassel*	333	329	325	-.1	-.1
Darmstadt*	268	325	393	1.9	1.9
Ausburg*	267	308	355	1.4	1.4
Bielefeld*	255	286	322	1.2	1.2
Munster*	210	274	358	2.7	2.7
Kiel*	254	272	290	.7	.6

REGION, COUNTRY AND CITY	POPULATION (Thousands)			ANNUAL PER CENT GROWTH	
	1950	1960	1970	1950-60	1960-70
Osnaburuck*	227	256	290	1.2	1.3
Hildesheim*	199	205	210	.3	.2
Koblenz*	134	171	219	2.5	2.5
Flensburg*	182	163	147	-1.1	-1.0
Hamm*	133	154	179	1.5	1.5
Pforzheim*	110	142	183	2.6	2.6
Freiburg*	110	141	182	2.5	2.6
Bremerhaven*	114	139	170	2.0	2.0
Oldenburg*	123	125	127	.2	.2
Regensburg*	117	124	132	.6	.6
Wurzburg*	102	114	128	1.1	1.2
Salgitter*	101	109	119	.8	.9
Wilhemshaven*	101	100	103	-.1	.3
Leverhusen	---	---	114	---	---
The Netherlands					
Amsterdam*	890	911	1,139	.2	2.3
Rotterdam*	777	827	1,222	.6	4.0
S' Gravenhage* (The Hague)	654	692	778	.6	1.2
Utrecht*	196	252	289	2.5	1.4
Haarlem*	218	224	249	.3	1.1
Enschede-Hengelo*	171	202	239	1.7	1.7
Eindhoven-Tivoli*	142	166	195	1.6	1.6
Arnhem*	129	152	189	1.7	2.2
Groningen*	132	140	243	.6	5.7
Nijmegen*	125	133	243	.6	6.2
Tilburg*	123	131	248	.6	6.6
Leiden*	110	117	185	.6	4.7

REGION, COUNTRY AND CITY	POPULATION (Thousands)			ANNUAL PER CENT GROWTH	
	1950	1960	1970	1950-60	1960-70
Apeldoorn	---	105	125	---	1.8
Breda*	---	102	173	---	5.4
Hilversum	---	102	129	---	2.4
Dordrecht*	---	100	133	---	2.9
Maastrict*	---	---	145	---	---
Switzerland					
Zurich*	447	537	667	1.9	2.2
Basel (Bale)*	234	300	370	2.5	2.1
Geneve*	174	238	307	3.2	2.6
Berne*	183	221	256	1.9	1.5
Lausanne*	---	163	215	---	2.8
Luzeyn (Lucerne)*	121	120	152	-.1	2.4
Winthertur*	---	---	129	---	---
EASTERN EUROPE					
Bulgaria					
Sofia*	520	687	920	2.8	3.0
Plovdiv	138	178	265	2.6	4.1
Varna	---	138	215	---	4.5
Rousse	---	103	150	---	3.8
Bourgas	---	---	120	---	---
Stara Zagora	---	---	115	---	---
Czechoslovakia					
Praha	931	998	1,050	.7	.5
Brno	285	321	345	1.2	.7
Bratislava	193	265	300	3.2	1.2
Ostrava	189	249	300	2.8	1.9
Plzen	124	139	140	1.1	.1

REGION, COUNTRY AND CITY	POPULATION (Thousands) 1950	1960	1970	ANNUAL PER CENT GROWTH 1950-60	1960-70
Kosice	---	---	125	---	---
Germany, East					
East Berlin	1,189	1,077	1,100	-1.0	.2
Leipzig	618	590	605	-.5	.3
Dresden	494	495	522	---	.5
Karl-Marx-Stadt	293	286	303	-.2	.6
Halle	289	278	275	-.4	-.1
Magdeburg	244	261	271	.7	.4
Erfurt	189	186	197	-.2	.6
Rostock	133	159	208	1.8	2.7
Zwickau	135	129	128	-.5	-.1
Potsdam	118	115	110	-.3	-.4
Gera	---	101	115	---	1.3
Hungary					
Budapest	1,600	1,804	2,060	1.2	1.3
Miskolc	108	144	195	2.9	3.1
Debrecen	121	130	165	.7	2.4
Pecs	---	115	150	---	2.7
Szeged	---	---	130	---	---
Poland					
Katowice-Zabreze-Bytom*	1,675	2,006	2,424	1.8	1.9
Warzawa*	1,300	1,845	2,664	3.6	3.7
Lodz*	768	887	1,031	1.5	1.5
Gdansk-Gdynia*	335	479	696	3.6	3.8
Krakow*	344	479	696	3.4	1.6

TABLE E (continued)

REGION, COUNTRY AND CITY	POPULATION (Thousands) 1950	1960	1970	ANNUAL PER CENT GROWTH 1950-60	1960-70
Wroclaw*	309	429	500	3.3	1.5
Poznan*	321	408	460	2.4	1.2
Szczecin*	179	269	350	4.2	2.7
Bydgoszcz*	163	231	280	3.5	1.9
Walbrzych*	148	185	233	2.3	2.3
Lublin*	117	181	225	4.5	2.2
Czestochow*	112	164	190	3.9	1.5
Radom	---	130	155	---	1.8
Bialystok	---	121	160	---	2.8
Torun	---	105	123	---	1.6
Kielce	---	---	120	---	---
Romania					
Bucaresti*	1,111	1,349	1,700	2.0	2.3
Brasov*	---	219	320	---	3.9
Cluj*	158	200	250	2.4	2.3
Ploiesti*	131	163	220	2.2	3.0
Timisoara*	133	163	230	2.1	3.5
Iasi*	---	154	250	---	5.0
Constanta*	107	145	260	3.1	6.0
Craiova*	---	129	230	---	6.0
Arad*	---	122	155	---	2.4
Oradea*	---	118	160	---	3.1
Braila*	---	115	180	---	4.6
Galati*	---	105	225	---	7.9
Sibiu*	---	---	125	---	---
Tirgu Mures	---	---	115	---	---

REGION, COUNTRY AND CITY	POPULATION (Thousands)			ANNUAL PER CENT GROWTH	
	1950	1960	1970	1950-60	1960-70
SOUTHERN EUROPE					
Albania					
Tirane	---	136	220	---	4.9
Greece					
Athinai (Athens)*	1,345	1,812	2,425	3.0	3.0
Salonika*	291	371	470	2.5	2.4
Patrai*	---	102	110	---	.8
Italy					
Roma*	1,605	2,020	2,920	2.3	3.8
Milano*	1,252	1,491	1,750	1.8	1.6
Napoli*	988	1,160	1,300	1.6	1.1
Torino*	686	963	1,175	3.4	2.0
Genova*	678	764	930	1.2	2.0
Palermo*	473	596	688	2.3	1.4
Bologna*	328	434	520	2.8	1.8
Firenze*	367	433	470	1.7	.8
Catania*	290	368	432	2.4	1.6
Venezia*	312	347	383	1.1	1.0
Bari*	260	317	364	2.0	1.4
Trieste*	269	283	292	.5	.3
Messina*	216	251	275	1.5	.9
Verona*	174	213	273	2.0	2.5
Padova*	163	197	234	1.9	1.7
Taranto*	165	194	230	1.6	1.7
Cagliari*	134	175	234	2.7	2.9
Brescia*	140	166	220	1.7	2.9

TABLE E (continued)

REGION, COUNTRY AND CITY	POPULATION (Thousands) 1950	1960	1970	ANNUAL PER CENT GROWTH 1950-60	1960-70
Livorno*	140	160	180	1.3	1.2
Reggio di Calabria*	106	153	165	3.7	.8
Ferrara*	132	150	164	1.3	.9
Parma*	122	136	185	1.1	3.1
Modena*	109	134	175	2.1	2.7
La Spezia*	111	122	137	.9	1.2
Foggia*	---	118	150	---	2.4
Bergamo*	101	114	128	1.2	1.2
Reggio nell'Emilia*	139	114	131	-2.0	1.4
Salerno*	---	113	160	---	3.5
Ravenna*	---	111	137	---	2.1
Perugia*	---	110	130	---	1.7
Prato*	---	104	145	---	3.4
Pescara*	---	---	125	---	---
Rimini*	---	---	117	---	---
Vicenza*	---	---	116	---	---
Ancona*	---	---	113	---	---
Bolzano*	---	---	110	---	---
Terni*	---	---	109	---	---
Pisa*	---	---	109	---	---
Piacenza*	---	---	109	---	---
Sassari*	---	---	108	---	---
Forli*	---	---	108	---	---
Portugal					
Lisboa*	1,161	1,335	1,500	1.4	1.2
Porto*	655	746	850	1.3	1.3

REGION, COUNTRY AND CITY	POPULATION (Thousands) 1950	1960	1970	ANNUAL PER CENT GROWTH 1950-60	1960-70
Spain					
Madrid*	1,618	2,260	2,990	3.4	2.8
Barcelona*	1,281	1,558	1,850	2.0	1.7
Valencia*	509	505	498	-.1	-.1
Sevilla*	377	442	510	1.6	1.4
Zaragoza*	264	326	392	2.1	1.9
Malaga*	276	301	323	.9	.7
Bilbao*	229	298	375	2.7	2.3
Murcia*	218	250	280	1.4	1.1
Cordoba*	166	198	232	1.8	1.6
Las Palmas* (Canarias)	153	194	238	2.4	2.1
La Coruna*	134	177	229	2.8	2.6
Palma de Mallorca* (Baleares)	137	159	180	1.5	1.2
Granada*	154	157	159	.2	.1
Valladolid*	124	152	180	2.1	1.7
Vigo*	138	145	190	.5	2.7
San Sebastian*	114	135	157	1.7	1.5
Santa Cruz de Tenerife*	103	133	167	2.6	2.3
Jerez de la Frontera*	108	131	150	1.9	1.4
Oviedo*	106	127	149	1.8	1.6
Gijon*	111	125	144	1.2	1.4
Cartagena*	113	124	139	.9	1.1
Hospitalet*	---	123	190	---	4.4
Alicante*	104	122	139	1.6	1.3

REGION, COUNTRY AND CITY	POPULATION (Thousands) 1950	1960	1970	ANNUAL PER CENT GROWTH 1950-60	1960-70
Santander*	103	118	134	1.4	1.3
Cadiz*	100	118	135	1.7	1.4
Sabadell*	---	105	158	---	4.2
Badalona*	---	---	135	---	---
Pamplona*	---	---	125	---	---
Tarrasa*	---	---	125	---	---
Salamanca*	---	---	115	---	---
Badajoz*	---	---	112	---	---
Yugoslavia					
Boegrad*	568	813	1,165	3.7	3.7
Zagreb*	529	797	1,178	4.2	4.0
Skopje*	156	260	423	5.2	5.0
Ljubljana*	171	204	241	1.8	1.7
Sarajevo*	138	192	268	3.4	3.4
Novi Sad*	103	157	237	4.3	4.2
Maribor*	130	151	175	1.5	1.5
Nis*	---	139	229	---	5.1
Split*	---	130	175	---	3.0
Banja Luka*	120	127	204	.6	4.9
Rijeka-Susak*	---	123	184	---	4.1
Subotica*	---	119	167	---	3.4
Osijek*	---	115	165	---	3.7
Pancevo*	---	---	175	---	---
Peistina*	---	---	171	---	---
Tuzla*	---	---	166	---	---
Sombor*	---	---	161	---	---

REGION, COUNTRY AND CITY	POPULATION (Thousands) 1950	1960	1970	ANNUAL PER CENT GROWTH 1950-60	1960-70
Kragujevac*	---	---	131	---	---
Zrenjanin*	---	---	127	---	---
AUSTRALIA-NEW ZEALAND					
Australia					
Sydney*	1,702	2,134	2,720	2.3	2.5
Melbourne*	1,338	1,850	2,200	3.3	1.7
Brisbane*	444	603	800	3.1	2.9
Adelaide*	432	571	900	2.8	4.7
Perth*	313	409	580	2.7	3.6
Newcastle*	163	204	260	2.3	2.5
Greater Wollongong*	---	125	190	---	4.3
Hobart*	---	113	122	---	.8
Canberra*	---	---	130	---	---
Geelong*	---	---	121	---	---
New Zealand					
Aukland*	322	437	635	3.1	3.8
Christchurch*	172	216	265	2.3	2.1
Wellington*	133	148	180	1.1	2.0
Hutt*	---	---	130	---	---
Dunedin*	---	---	110	---	---
U.S.S.R.					
U.S.S.R.					
Moscow (Moskva)*	5,522	6,099	6,750	1.0	1.0
Leningrad* (Sankt-Peterburg, Petrograd)	2,956	3,390	3,850	1.4	1.3

TABLE E (continued)

REGION, COUNTRY AND CITY	POPULATION (Thousands) 1950	1960	1970	ANNUAL PER CENT GROWTH 1950-60	1960-70
Kiev (Kiyev)	849	1,156	1,560	3.1	3.0
Baku*	778	1,010	1,300	2.6	2.6
Gorky (Nizhniy Novgorod)	784	973	1,195	2.2	2.1
Kharkov	766	967	1,215	2.4	2.3
Tashkent	659	966	1,450	3.9	4.1
Novosibirsk (Gusevka, Novonikolayevsk)	729	917	1,130	2.3	2.1
Kuybyshev (Samara)	646	838	1,070	2.6	2.5
Sverdlovsk (Yekaterinburg)	623	810	1,040	2.7	2.5
Donetsk (Yuzovka, Stalino)	575	724	900	2.3	2.2
Tbilisi (Tiflis)	567	720	905	2.4	2.3
Chelyabins	561	714	895	2.4	2.3
Dnepropetrovsk (Yekaterinoslav)	527	687	890	2.7	2.6
Odessa	568	686	835	1.9	2.0
Kazan	502	677	915	3.0	3.1
Perm (Molotov)	490	657	865	3.0	2.8
Rostov-na	469	627	825	2.9	2.8
Volgograd (Tsaritsyn, Stalingrad)	465	618	815	2.9	2.8
Omsk	428	613	870	3.7	3.6
Saratov	463	605	785	2.7	2.6
Riga	490	598	722	2.0	1.9
Ufa	418	574	775	3.2	3.0
Minsk	327	550	900	5.3	5.0

REGION, COUNTRY AND CITY	POPULATION (Thousands) 1950	1960	1970	ANNUAL PER CENT GROWTH 1950-60	1960-70
Yeveran	383	535	738	3.4	3.3
Alma-Ata (Vernyy)	312	488	735	4.6	4.2
Voronezh	322	475	680	4.0	3.7
Zaporozhye (Aleksandrovsk)	312	461	675	4.0	3.9
Krasnoyarsk	289	439	650	4.3	4.0
Lvov (Lemberg, Lwow)	325	428	550	2.8	2.5
Yaroslavl	328	423	536	2.6	2.4
Krivoy Rog	290	408	560	3.5	3.2
Karaganda	296	406	540	3.2	2.9
Novokuznetsk	284	396	535	3.4	3.1
Irkutsk	316	376	448	1.8	1.8
Makeyevka (Dmitriyevka)	307	368	438	1.8	1.8
Ivanovo	272	347	439	2.5	2.4
Nizhny Tagil	303	346	391	1.3	1.2
Kharbarous (Kharbarovsk)	235	342	486	3.8	3.6
Krasnodar (Yekaterinodar)	237	329	449	3.3	3.2
Tula	262	327	400	2.2	2.0
Barnaul	224	322	454	3.7	3.5
Magnitogorsk	269	319	375	1.7	1.6
Vladivostok	209	308	550	4.0	6.0
Astrakhan	235	308	410	2.7	2.9
Gorlovka	248	302	360	2.0	1.8
Zhdanov (Mariupol)	206	301	431	3.9	3.7
Izhevsk	212	300	420	3.5	3.4

REGION, COUNTRY AND CITY	POPULATION (Thousands)			ANNUAL PER CENT GROWTH	
	1950	1960	1970	1950-60	1960-70
Kemerovo (Shcheglovsk)	209	292	395	3.4	3.1
Tallin	231	292	363	2.4	2.2
Lugansk (Voroshilovgrad)	212	288	390	3.1	3.1
Prokopyeus (Prokopyevsk)	274	283	291	.3	.3
Orenburg (Chkalov)	216	277	357	2.5	2.6
Kalinin (Tver)	212	271	347	2.5	2.5
Penza	192	268	367	3.4	3.2
Arkhangelsk	209	265	330	2.4	2.2
Tomsk	188	262	361	3.4	3.3
Kirov (Vyatka)	203	262	333	2.6	2.4
Grozny	174	257	368	4.0	3.7
Vilnyus (Vilnius)	173	249	355	3.7	3.6
Frunze	118	246	485	7.6	7.0
Dushanbe	147	241	380	5.1	4.7
Nikolayev (Nikolaevskaya Oblast)	167	238	335	3.6	3.5
Murmansk	169	233	315	3.3	3.1
Ryazan	144	230	357	4.8	4.5
Kishinev	151	230	345	4.3	4.1
Kaunas	158	226	313	3.6	3.3
Ulyanovsk (Simbirsk)	141	220	344	4.5	4.6
Bryansk	146	220	326	4.2	4.0
Kaliningrad (Konigsberg)	151	215	300	3.6	3.4

REGION, COUNTRY AND CITY	POPULATION (Thousands) 1950	1960	1970	ANNUAL PER CENT GROWTH 1950-60	1960-70
Kursk	163	214	275	2.8	2.5
Taganrog	165	209	264	2.4	2.4
Samarkand	153	205	273	3.0	2.9
Dneproderzhinsk (Kamenskoye)	167	199	235	1.8	1.7
Shakhty (Aleksandrovsk-Grushevskiy)	183	198	213	.8	.7
Simferopol	153	192	240	2.3	2.3
Rybinsk	155	187	222	1.9	1.7
Ulan-Ude (Verkhneudinsk)	133	184	252	3.3	3.2
Orsk	142	183	228	2.6	2.2
Komsomolsk-na-Amure	148	183	220	2.1	1.9
Ashkhabad (Poltoratsk)	119	181	268	4.3	4.0
Gomel	117	179	273	4.3	4.3
Tambov	138	179	226	2.6	2.4
Kostroma	140	178	223	2.4	2.3
Chita	144	177	215	2.1	2.0
Ordzhonikidze (Severo-Osetinskaya ASSR)	121	173	242	3.6	3.4
Lipetsk	---	172	304	---	5.9
Kadiyevka	237	171	200	-3.2	1.6
Kherson	104	170	278	5.0	5.0
Dzerzhinsk (Gorkovskaya Oblast)	132	170	216	2.6	2.4

REGION, COUNTRY AND CITY	POPULATION (Thousands)			ANNUAL PER CENT GROWTH	
	1950	1960	1970	1950-60	1960-70
Tyumen	---	164	305	---	6.4
Chimkent	105	164	253	4.6	4.4
Semipalatinsk	117	164	226	3.4	3.3
Zlatoust	145	164	184	1.2	1.2
Vladimir	110	163	238	4.0	3.9
Kopeysk (Goskopi, Kopi)	156	162	165	.4	.2
Ust-Kamenogorsk	104	160	238	4.4	4.1
Orel	105	160	235	4.3	3.9
Sevastopol	103	158	239	4.4	4.2
Kurgan	---	157	248	---	4.7
Vitebsk	106	157	230	4.0	3.9
Smolensk	108	155	212	3.7	3.2
Syzran	130	153	177	1.6	1.5
Biysk	116	152	194	2.7	2.5
Chernovtsy (Chernauti)	118	152	190	2.6	2.3
Poltava	109	150	207	3.2	3.3
Stravropol (Voroshilovsk)	111	147	196	2.8	2.9
Kamensk-Uralsky	122	145	168	1.7	1.5
Volobda	112	144	187	2.5	2.6
Petrozavodsk	107	142	192	2.9	3.1
Angarsk	---	143	200	---	3.4
Kaluga	---	141	198	---	3.5
Sochi	---	137	212	---	4.5
Andizhan	---	137	187	---	3.2

REGION, COUNTRY AND CITY	POPULATION (Thousands)			ANNUAL PER CENT GROWTH	
	1950	1960	1970	1950-60	1960-70
Petropaulovsk (Petropavlovsk)	102	137	181	3.0	2.8
Kirovograd (Zinovyevsk)	---	135	192	---	3.6
Kutaisi (Kutais)	102	133	170	2.7	2.5
Leninsk-Kuznetsky	126	133	138	.5	.4
Mogilev-na-Dnepre	---	131	208	---	4.7
Podolsk	---	131	178	---	3.1
Kiselevsk	122	131	138	.7	.5
Vinnitsa	---	129	187	---	3.8
Namagan	---	129	173	---	3.0
Makhachkala (Petrovsk)	---	127	188	---	4.0
Kirovobad (Yelisavetpol)	---	125	210	---	5.3
Sterlitams (Sterlitamak)	---	120	185	---	4.4
Dzhambul (Auliye-Ata, Mirzoyan)	---	120	178	---	4.0
Cheremkhovo	140	120	104	-1.5	-1.4
Kramatorsk	---	119	152	---	2.5
Rubtsovsk (Rubtsov)	---	116	155	---	2.9
Armavir	---	116	152	---	2.7
Anzhero	116	116	114	---	-.2
Cheboksary	---	115	213	---	6.4
Tselinograd (Akmolinsk)	---	113	213	---	6.5
Zhitomir	---	112	160	---	3.6

REGION, COUNTRY AND CITY	POPULATION (Thousands) 1950	1960	1970	ANNUAL PER CENT GROWTH 1950-60	1960-70
Norilsk	---	112	138	---	2.1
Leninakan (Aleksandropol)	---	112	144	---	2.5
Berezniki	---	111	142	---	2.5
Novomoskovsk (Stalinogorsk)	---	110	133	---	1.9
Orekhovo	---	110	120	---	.9
Kokand	---	109	141	---	2.6
Serpukhov	---	109	125	---	1.4
Belovo	---	109	119	---	.9
Ussuriysk (Ussurusk)	---	107	131	---	2.0
Uralsk	---	107	132	---	2.1
Novocherkassk	---	105	195	---	6.4
Sumy	---	105	160	---	4.3
Koloma	---	105	140	---	2.9
Novoshaktinsk	101	105	106	.4	.1
Cheropovets	---	103	200	---	6.9
Aktyubinsk	---	103	152	---	4.0
Miass (Miyasskoye Selo)	---	103	131	---	2.4
Novorossiysk	---	102	137	---	3.0
Bobruysk	---	102	129	---	2.4
Kovrov	---	102	122	---	1.8
Kerch	---	101	126	---	2.2
Mytishchi	---	101	116	---	1.4
Saransk	---	100	185	---	6.3
Elektrostal (Zatishye)	---	100	125	---	2.3

REGION, COUNTRY AND CITY	POPULATION (Thousands) 1950	1960	1970	ANNUAL PER CENT GROWTH 1950-60	1960-70
Tolyatti	---	---	190	---	---
Pavlodar	---	---	185	---	---
Temir Tau	---	---	173	---	---
Chernihov (Chernigov)	---	---	164	---	---
Belgorod	---	---	160	---	---
Bratsk	---	---	160	---	---
Kremenchug	---	---	155	---	---
Yoshkar-Ola (Ioshkar-Ola)	---	---	155	---	---
Klaipeda	---	---	151	---	---
Cherkassy	---	---	152	---	---
Osh	---	---	152	---	---
Petropavlovsk-Kamchatsky	---	---	140	---	---
Severodvinsk	---	---	140	---	---
Volzhsky	---	---	140	---	---
Kommunarsk	---	---	135	---	---
Lisichansk	---	---	135	---	---
Lyubertsy	---	---	135	---	---
Sumgait	---	---	135	---	---
Blagoveshehensk (Amurskaya Oblast)	---	---	133	---	---
Nalchick	---	---	133	---	---
Kustanai	---	---	132	---	---
Grodno	---	---	133	---	---
Melitopol	---	---	130	---	---

REGION, COUNTRY AND CITY	POPULATION (Thousands)			ANNUAL PER CENT GROWTH	
	1950	1960	1970	1950-60	1960-70
Novgorod	---	---	130	---	---
Novokubyshevsk	---	---	130	---	---
Engels	---	---	130	---	---
Pskov	---	---	124	---	---
Slavyansk	---	---	125	---	---
Nikopol	---	---	122	---	---
Buchaza (Buchara)	---	---	120	---	---
Syktyvkar	---	---	120	---	---
Chirchik (Circik)	---	---	119	---	---
Maikop	---	---	117	---	---
Pervouralsk	---	---	116	---	---
Gruryev (Gurjev)	---	---	113	---	---
Konstantinovka	---	---	110	---	---
Rovno	---	---	110	---	---
Batumi	---	---	109	---	---
Leninabad	---	---	105	---	---
Noginsk	---	---	105	---	---
Serov	---	---	105	---	---
Krasni Luch	---	---	104	---	---

TABLE F

EXPLANATION

Table F gives the population and rank of each of the world's hundred largest cities at each date--1950, 1960, and 1970. For convenience, it lists them in order of their rank at each date. In addition, to enable the reader to pursue the fate of any particular great city, the table provides a supplementary list of cities that made the hundred-largest group at one of the three dates but not at another.

It can be seen that Table F represents a rearrangement of the information contained in Table E. Table E gives the population of all cities of 100,000 or more, not just that of the hundred largest, and it lists them by country and region, not by order of size.

As in Table E, the present table employs an asterisk by the name of the city to designate those cities that are defined as urbanized areas or urban agglomerations, the others being cities proper. Since the biggest cities tend to be the ones whose inhabitants have spilled over the political boundaries to the greatest extent, a majority of the "hundred largest" are UA's. At each of the three dates, 90 of the top hundred cities bear an asterisk.

The hundred cities comprise, of course, only a small fraction of the total number of cities at each date. They made up 10.4 per cent of the total number of cities in 1950, 7.7 per cent in 1960, and 6.3 per cent in 1970. However, since they are the largest places, they embrace a far greater proportion of the total population living in cities than they do of the sheer number of cities. For instance, in 1950 the hundred largest places had 200 million inhabitants, which was 49 per cent of the entire population living in cities of 100,000 or more at that date; in 1970 they had 348 million inhabitants, or 42 per cent of the entire city population. Thus, with continued world urbanization, the hundred largest cities diminish sharply as a proportion of the total number of cities but decline only slowly as a proportion of the total population living in cities. It is their importance as world centers with a disproportionate share of the world's city population that has led us to give them the special listing in Table F.

Our office has a list of all the cities of the world, by population and rank, for each of the three dates. The lists are available upon request.

234

TABLE F, PART 1

POPULATION° AND RANK OF WORLD'S
HUNDRED LARGEST CITIES IN 1950

CITY	POPULATION	RANK	CITY	POPULATION	RANK
New York*	12,331	1	West Berlin*	2,147	25
London*	10,393	2	San Francisco-		
Tokyo*	6,277	3	Oakland*	2,028	26
Paris*	5,998	4	Osaka*	1,956	27
Moscow*	5,522	5	Hamburg*	1,952	28
Shanghai*	5,300	6	Glasgow*	1,911	29
Buenos Aires*	5,213	7	Leeds-Bradford*	1,907	30
Calcutta*	5,153	8	Wien (Vienna)*	1,861	31
Chicago*	4,935	9	Manila*	1,781	32
Essen-Dortmund-			Delhi*	1,737	33
Duisburg*	4,597	10	Sydney*	1,702	34
Los Angeles*	4,009	11	Madras*	1,700	35
Bombay*	3,335	12	Shen-yang (Mukden)*	1,700	36
Rio de Janeiro*	3,052	13	Katowice-Zabreze-		
Leningrad*	2,956	14	Bytom*	1,675	37
Philadelphia*	2,930	15	Liverpool*	1,665	38
Detroit*	2,667	16	Madrid*	1,618	39
Birmingham (U.K.)*	2,583	17	Roma*	1,605	40
Manchester*	2,509	18	Budapest	1,600	41
Cairo*	2,502	19	Hong Kong*	1,561	42
Sao Paulo*	2,449	20	Pittsburgh*	1,538	43
Boston*	2,239	21	Canton		
Mexico City	2,234	22	(Kuang-chou)*	1,500	44
Tientsin			Seoul	1,467	45
(T'ien-ching)*	2,200	23	Djakarta	1,452	46
Peking*	2,150	24	St. Louis*	1,404	47
			Chungking*	1,400	48

° Populations all in thousands
* Urban agglomerations

235

CITY	POPULATION	RANK	CITY	POPULATION	RANK
Cleveland*	1,388	49	Koln (Cologne)*	1,060	75
Montreal*	1,354	50	Alexandria	1,037	76
Athens*	1,345	51	Nagoya*	1,031	77
Melbourne*	1,338	52	Singapore*	1,022	78
Frankfurt-am-Main*	1,309	53	Harbin		
Warszawa*	1,300	54	(Ha-erh-pin)*	1,000	79
Washington, D.C.*	1,291	55	Napoli*	988	80
Barcelona*	1,281	56	Minneapolis-St. Paul*	988	81
Santiago*	1,275	57	Istanbul*	983	82
Milano*	1,252	58	Bruxelles*	967	83
Wu-han*	1,200	59	Yokohama*	951	84
East Berlin	1,189	60	Nanking*	950	85
Copenhagen*	1,168	61	Lima-Callao*	947	86
Baltimore*	1,165	62	Praha	931	87
Lisboa*	1,161	63	Stockholm*	928	88
Mannheim-Ludwigshafen-Heidelberg*	1,146	64	Bangalore*	922	89
			Ahmedabad*	904	90
Stuttgart*	1,129	65	Bangkok*	891	91
Newcastle Upon Tyne*	1,125	66	Amsterdam*	890	92
Bucaresti*	1,111	67	Johannesburg*	863	93
Munchen (Munich)*	1,110	68	Saigon	850	94
Kyoto*	1,102	69	Tsingtao*	850	95
Karachi*	1,086	70	Kiev	849	96
Habana*	1,081	71	Milwaukee*	831	97
Toronto*	1,075	72	Lahore*	826	98
Hyderabad*	1,074	73	Cincinnati*	815	99
Teheran	1,073	74	Buffalo*	800	100

POPULATION° AND RANK OF WORLD'S
HUNDRED LARGEST CITIES IN 1960

CITY	POPULATION IN 1960	RANK	CITY	POPULATION IN 1960	RANK
New York*	14,114	1	Birmingham (U.K.)*	2,775	25
London*	10,953	2	Manila*	2,704	26
Tokyo*	9,684	3	Manchester*	2,525	27
Paris*	7,287	4	Shen-yang (Mukden)*	2,500	28
Shanghai*	7,200	5	Wu-han*	2,500	29
Buenos Aires*	7,000	6	Seoul	2,445	30
Los Angeles*	6,489	7	San Francisco-Oakland*	2,431	31
Calcutta*	6,138	8	Boston*	2,413	32
Moscow*	6,099	9	Delhi*	2,309	33
Chicago*	5,959	10	Chungking*	2,300	34
Essen-Dortmund-Duisburg*	5,587	11	Madrid*	2,260	35
Peking*	5,500	12	West Berlin*	2,193	36
Rio de Janeiro*	4,692	13	Hamburg*	2,168	37
Sao Paulo*	4,537	14	Sydney*	2,134	38
Bombay*	4,089	15	Madras*	2,090	39
Cairo*	3,747	16	Roma*	2,020	40
Philadelphia*	3,635	17	Katowice-Zabreze-Bytom*	2,006	41
Detroit*	3,538	18	Montreal*	2,001	42
Tientsin (T'ien-ching)*	3,500	19	Lu-ta (Port Arthur-Dairen)*	2,000	43
Leningrad*	3,390	20	Glasgow*	1,959	44
Hong Kong*	3,075	21	Leeds-Bradford*	1,926	45
Osaka*	3,012	22	Santiago*	1,907	46
Djakarta	2,852	23	Canton (Kuang-chou)*	1,900	47
Mexico City	2,832	24			

° Populations all in thousands
* Urban agglomerations

CITY	POPULATION IN 1960	RANK	CITY	POPULATION IN 1960	RANK
Karachi*	1,884	48	Minneapolis-St. Paul*	1,377	76
Wien (Vienna)*	1,874	49	Koln (Cologne)*	1,376	77
Melbourne*	1,850	50	Yokohama*	1,376	78
Warszawa*	1,845	51	Bucaresti*	1,349	79
Teheran	1,839	52	Mannheim-Ludwigshafen-Heidelberg*	1,345	80
Athens*	1,812	53			
Washington, D.C.*	1,808	54	Lisboa*	1,335	81
Pittsburgh*	1,804	55	Bangkok*	1,330	82
Budapest	1,804	56	Taipei*	1,329	83
Harbin (Ha-erh-pin)*	1,800	57	Munchen (Munich)*	1,291	84
Cleveland*	1,785	58	Kyoto*	1,285	85
Liverpool*	1,742	59	Caracas*	1,280	86
Toronto*	1,720	60	Saigon	1,264	87
St. Louis*	1,668	61	Lahore*	1,262	88
Singapore*	1,634	62	Copenhagen*	1,262	89
Nagoya*	1,592	63	Bogota	1,241	90
Barcelona*	1,558	64	Hyderabad*	1,238	91
Habana*	1,549	65	Ch'eng-Tu*	1,200	92
Lima-Callao*	1,519	66	Tsingtao*	1,200	93
Alexandria	1,516	67	Bangalore*	1,184	94
Nanking*	1,500	68	Ahmedabad*	1,182	95
Sian (Hsi-an)*	1,500	69	Pusan	1,164	96
Milano*	1,491	70	Napoli*	1,160	97
Stuttgart*	1,478	71	Newcastle Upon Tyne*	1,159	98
Istanbul*	1,467	72	Kiev	1,156	99
Baltimore*	1,419	73	Johannesburg*	1,153	100
T'ai-yuan,Yu-tz'u*	1,400	74			
Frankfurt-am-Main*	1,378	75			

TABLE F, PART 3

PROJECTED POPULATION° AND RANK OF WORLD'S HUNDRED LARGEST CITIES IN 1970

CITY	POPULATION IN 1970	RANK	CITY	POPULATION IN 1970	RANK
New York*	16,077	1	Hong Kong*	4,105	24
Tokyo*	12,199	2	Manila*	4,100	25
London*	11,544	3	Lu-ta (Port		
Los Angeles*	9,473	4	Arthur-Dairen)*	4,000	26
Buenos Aires*	9,400	5	Leningrad*	3,850	27
Paris*	8,714	6	Shen-yang (Mukden)*	3,750	28
Shanghai*	8,500	7	Mexico City	3,541	21
Sao Paulo*	8,405	8	Chungking*	3,500	30
Peking*	8,000	9	Osaka*	3,307	31
Calcutta*	7,350	10	Teheran*	3,250	32
Rio de Janeiro*	7,213	11	Karachi*	3,246	33
Chicago*	6,983	12	Delhi*	3,100	34
Essen-Dortmund-			Madrid*	2,990	35
Duisburg*	6,789	13	Birmingham (U.K.)*	2,981	36
Moscow*	6,750	14	Roma*	2,920	37
Cairo*	5,600	15	Harbin		
Bombay*	5,100	16	(Ha-erh-pin)*	2,750	38
Seoul	4,661	17	T'ai-yuan,Yu-tz'u*	2,725	39
Tientsin			Sydney*	2,720	40
(T'ien-ching)*	4,500	18	Washington, D.C.*	2,666	41
Djakarta	4,500	19	Warszawa*	2,664	42
San Francisco-			Istanbul*	2,600	43
Oakland*	4,490	20	Madras*	2,600	44
Detroit*	4,447	21	Boston*	2,600	45
Philadelphia*	4,355	22	Santiago*	2,600	46
Wu-han*	4,250	23	Manchester*	2,541	47

° Populations all in thousands
* Urban agglomerations

CITY	POPULATION IN 1970	RANK	CITY	POPULATION IN 1970	RANK
Toronto*	2,511	48	Lahore*	1,902	75
Bogota	2,500	49	Tsingtao*	1,900	76
Lima-Callao*	2,500	50	Sian (Hsi-an)*	1,900	77
Montreal*	2,437	51	Wien (Vienna)*	1,890	78
Athens*	2,425	52	Barcelona*	1,850	79
Katowice-Zabreze-Bytom*	2,424	53	Porto Alegre*	1,842	80
			Liverpool*	1,823	81
Hamburg*	2,407	54	Recife*	1,794	82
Nagoya*	2,353	55	Koln (Cologne)*	1,788	83
Yokohama*	2,326	56	Minneapolis-St. Paul*	1,760	84
Canton (Kuang-chou)*	2,300	57	Tzepo (Tzu-po)*	1,750	85
Cleveland*	2,248	58	Milano*	1,750	86
West Berlin*	2,240	59	Saigon	1,750	87
Melbourne*	2,200	60	Baltimore*	1,729	88
Taipei*	2,150	61	Belo Horizonte*	1,728	89
Caracas	2,147	62	Bucaresti*	1,700	90
Singapore*	2,113	63	Habana*	1,700	91
Bangkok*	2,100	64	K'un-ming*	1,700	92
Alexandria	2,061	65	Fu-shun*	1,700	93
Budapest	2,060	66	Pusan	1,592	94
Glasgow*	2,008	67	Mannheim-Ludwigshafen-Heidelberg*	1,578	95
Nanking*	2,000	68			
Ch'eng-tu*	2,000	69	Kiev	1,560	96
St. Louis*	1,981	70	Ahmedabad*	1,550	97
Pittsburgh*	1,958	71	Bangalore*	1,550	98
Leeds-Bradford*	1,945	72	Montevideo	1,530	99
Stuttgart*	1,935	73	Munich*	1,502	100
Houston*	1,924	74			

TABLE F, SUPPLEMENT

POPULATION° AND RANK OF CITIES THAT FELL
BELOW THE TOP HUNDRED LIST ON ONE OR TWO
OF THE THREE DATES

CITY	POPULATION	RANK	CITY	POPULATION	RANK
1950			Bruxelles*	1,013	111
Taipei*	760	110	Fu-shun*	1,000	113
Ch'eng Tu*	750	111	K'un-ming*	1,000	114
Houston*	703	116	Praha	998	115
Lu-ta (Port			Cincinnati*	994	116
Arthur-Dairen)*	700	117	Montevideo	962	122
Caracas*	694	120	Amsterdam*	911	133
Recife*	693	121	Porto Alegre	894	136
Fu-shun*	650	133	Belo Horizante*	781	158
K'un-ming*	625	139			
Montevideo	609	145	**1970**		
Bogota	607	146	Lisboa*	1,500	101
Sian (Hsi-an)*	600	147	Hyderabad*	1,500	102
T'ai-yuan, Yu-tz'u*	600	148	Milwaukee*	1,496	113
Pusan	542	167	Copenhagen*	1,480	114
Porto Alegre	434	212	Frankfurt-Main*	1,452	117
Belo Horizante*	353	248	Kyoto*	1,450	119
Tzepo (Tzu-po)*	250	339	Johannesburg	1,400	122
			Stockholm*	1,350	125
1960			Cincinnati*	1,331	127
Milwaukee*	1,150	101	Napoli*	1,300	131
Stockholm*	1,149	102	Buffalo*	1,244	137
Houston*	1,140	103	Newcastle-Tyne*	1,193	147
Recife*	1,115	104	Amsterdam*	1,139	154
Tzepo (Tzu-po)*	1,100	106	Bruxelles*	1,104	157
East Berlin	1,077	108	East Berlin	1,100	159
Buffalo	1,054	109	Praha	1,050	167

° Populations all in thousands
* Urban agglomerations

241

TABLE G

EXPLANATION

By definition, the largest city in a country contains a greater share of the total urban population, or total city population, than any other place. Its share is in fact nearly always impressive. For this reason, concern over urban problems or the growth of cities is often phrased in terms of the "dominance" of the principal city. To help provide facts bearing on this concern, Table G presents one index of first-city primacy.

The index used is simply the population of the first city divided by the combined population of the next three. Since only four cities are utilized in its construction, it is called the Four-City Index.

The basic rationale for this type of index lies in the fact that, from one country to another, it is composed of the _same_ number of cities. In each nation the principal city's share of the total population living in cities depends on the sheer number of cities as well as upon the peculiarities of the nation's city hierarchy. In the Soviet Union, for example, our projections turned up 201 cities with 100,000 or more inhabitants in 1970. Every city is thus less than half of 1 per cent of the total number of cities, yet one, Moscow, has 9 per cent of the total city population. Moscow has more than 18 times its pro rata share of city inhabitants. This is impressive enough, but when we turn to Switzerland in 1970, we find that Zurich has 32 per cent of the total city population of that country. At first glance, the Swiss thus seem to have a greater concentration in the first city than does the Soviet Union, but the truth is that Switzerland has only seven cities, not 201. Taking this fact into account, we find that Zurich has only a little more than two times its pro rata share of the city population, in contrast to Moscow's eighteen times.

Obviously needed is an index of first-city primacy that is independent of the total number of cities. The four-city index meets this need. Furthermore, it includes enough cities to give a good idea of the main city's position, but not so many as to make the necessary data for computing the index hard to find. An index placing the first city in relation to the next nine--a ten-city index--is of course feasible, but it would be impractical to try to compute it for a large number of countries whose settlements are mostly obscure towns. The four-city index provides enough of the top portion of the rank-size distribution to give an idea of the main city's prominence, without causing difficulties of application. In any case, as we have found, it is highly correlated with the ten-city and even with the two-city index.

Our index can be applied to any country in which we know the population of the four largest places, regardless of how small those places may be. In Table G, however, we have provided index values only for those countries that have at least four cities with 100,000 or more inhabitants. It turns out that there are only 38 such countries in 1950, 46 in 1960, and 58 in 1970.

In strict terms, the index should be computed only for countries in which the "cities" are delimited by similar criteria. That is, the cities should be either all urbanized areas or all cities proper. Our data as they stand allow us to adhere to this rule in most cases, but for the rest of the countries we have not made an effort to adjust the figures especially for the primacy scoring. There are 6 countries in 1950, 8 in 1960, and 16 in 1970 for which the strict requirement of comparability in delimitation was not met. One should recall that in some cases it is hard to tell whether one is dealing with a UA or a CP; a few of the "mixed" countries fall in that category.

Mathematically, the minimum value of the four-city index must exceed .33, but there is no necessary maximum value. In practice, the index seldom falls below .50 and seldom rises above 8.00. The methodological aspects of primacy indices, together with comparative international data and a theory of the causes of international variations, are presented in a forthcoming monograph dealing specifically with first-city primacy.*

---

* Kingsley Davis and Gerald L. Fox, <u>Primary Cities: An International Analysis of First-City Primacy.</u>

TABLE G

THE FOUR-CITY INDEX OF FIRST-CITY PRIMACY

REGION AND COUNTRY	1950	1960	1970
Northern Africa			
Algeria	1.00	1.13	1.28
Morocco	1.22	1.40	1.22
Tunisia	----	----	1.82
U.A.R.	1.81	1.91	2.08
Western Africa			
Ghana	----	----	1.04
Nigeria	.89	.69	.57
Middle and Southern Africa			
Congo, Dem. Rep.	----	.86	1.05
South Africa			
South Africa	.66	.60	.50
Northern America			
Canada	.69	.68	.63
U.S.A.	1.04	.88	.77
Middle America			
Mexico	2.44	1.74	1.22
Caribbean			
Cuba	----	----	2.48
Tropical South America			
Brazil	.85	.72	.77
Colombia	.68	.84	.94
Peru	----	----	5.32
Venezuela	----	1.70	1.81

REGION AND COUNTRY	1950	1960	1970
Temperate South America			
Argentina	3.98	4.15	4.03
Chile	----	3.50	3.97
East Asia			
Taiwan	1.06	1.24	1.31
China	.88	.63	.51
Korea, North	1.00	1.01	.97
Korea, South	1.27	1.09	1.45
Japan			
Japan	1.54	1.62	1.53
Southeast Asia			
Burma	----	----	2.07
Indonesia	.93	1.13	1.20
West Malaysia	----	----	.93
Philippines	4.26	4.27	4.56
Viet-Nam, North	----	----	1.68
Viet-Nam, South	----	----	2.78
Southwest Asia			
Iran	1.59	2.14	2.21
Iraq	----	1.50	1.32
Israel	----	.86	----
Saudi Arabia	----	----	.50
Syria	----	.79	.62
Turkey	1.55	1.18	1.12
South Central Asia			
India	.76	.72	.68
Pakistan	.76	.85	.88
Northern Europe			
Denmark	----	----	3.50
Norway	----	----	1.48

REGION AND COUNTRY	1950	1960	1970
Sweden	----	----	1.14
United Kingdom	1.48	1.51	1.53
Western Europe			
Austria	2.87	2.80	2.70
Belgium	.75	.75	.77
France	3.65	3.57	3.10
Germany, Fed. Rep.	.85	.96	1.03
The Netherlands	.54	.51	.50
Switzerland	.76	.71	.71
Eastern Europe			
Bulgaria	----	1.64	1.46
Czechoslovakia	1.40	1.20	1.11
Germany, East	.85	.79	.77
Hungary	----	4.64	4.04
Poland	.69	.62	.55
Romania	2.63	2.32	2.05
Southern Europe			
Italy	.55	.56	.69
Spain	.75	.90	1.05
Yugoslavia	.66	.64	.63
Australia-New Zealand			
Australia	.77	.71	.70
New Zealand	----	----	1.10
U.S.S.R.			
U.S.S.R.	1.20	1.10	.98

TABLE H

EXPLANATION

The first table in the series, Table A, gave the total population and the rural population of each region and country. The present table, the last in the book, gives the total territory-- in thousands of square kilometers under the name of each country; and on the basis of the land and population figures, it gives two indices of density for the dates in question.

One density index, which we call "Overall Density," is the familiar division of the total population by the total territory. The second index is less conventional. It is the rural population divided by the total national territory. The rationale for this index arises from the fact that urban settlements, by definition, represent dense aggregates. As such, they occupy little territory, whereas rural inhabitants tend to be spread out over the land, either in small villages or in isolated homesteads. Furthermore, a high proportion of rural inhabitants are dependent on agriculture or extractive industry for their living--activities that utilize land as a factor in production. The rural population thus "uses" the national physical territory more than the urban population does.

The concentration of urban inhabitants in a small area can be illustrated with respect to the United States in 1960. Although the Urbanized Areas of America are unusually spread out in territory compared to those of most other countries, the 213 UA's of 1960 occupied less than 1 per cent of the nation's total land area, despite the fact that they contained 53 per cent of the nation's total population.

The density of persons living in UA's was 1,449 per square kilometer, whereas that of people living outside UA's was only 9 per square kilometer. The non-UA population had almost the same density regardless of whether the denominator included or excluded the land on which the UA's stood. The density ratio was 9.08 per square kilometer with the UA land included as against 9.15 with it excluded. There is accordingly little distortion in taking the entire national territory as the denominator in computing rural density. Yet to make the procedure clear, we call this density figure the "Approximate Rural Density."

Since the total area of each nation does not change in our table (the boundaries being taken as those of 1960), the growth of the two density indices is purely a function of the growth of the total and the rural populations. These rates are given in Table D.

247

Neither of the density indices tells much about resources in relation to population. Of the two, the rural index probably tells more than the overall index, but it too is greatly affected by adventitious factors governing the proportion of the national territory that is usable for agricultural and other productive purposes. The fact that Egypt has an approximate rural density less than one-seventh that of Taiwan does not mean that her farmers have a tremendous advantage over the Taiwanese peasants. It means, rather, that Egypt is composed mostly of desert, whereas Formosa is composed mostly of green hills. The density indices must therefore be used with care, especially since they are averages around which there is great dispersion. Yet they constitute a part of the basic demographic picture in each country; even the deserts of Egypt have significance for that country. The rise of the density indices from 1950 to 1970 gives evidence of the increasingly "containerized" character of the earth's human population.

AREA, AVERAGE DENSITY, AND "APPROXIMATE RURAL DENSITY" OF REGIONS AND COUNTRIES (in Square Kilometers)

REGION, COUNTRY, AND AREA (in thousands)	OVERALL DENSITY			"RURAL DENSITY"		
	1950	1960	1970	1950	1960	1970
<u>NORTHERN AFRICA</u> 8,524	6	8	10	5	5	7
Algeria 2,382	4	5	6	3	3	4
Ifni 1.5	26	33	36	20	25	25
Libya 1,760	1	1	1	---	1	1
Morocco 445	20	26	35	15	19	23
Sp. North Africa 0.0*	4,437	4,781	5,156	---	---	---
Spanish Sahara 266	---	---	---	---	---	---
Sudan 2,506	4	5	6	3	4	6
Tunisia 164	22	25	30	15	16	17
U.A.R. 1,000	20	26	33	14	16	19
<u>WESTERN AFRICA</u> 6,104	10	13	18	9	11	15
Cape Verde Islands 4.0	37	50	61	34	46	55
Dahomey 113	14	18	24	13	16	20
Gambia 11	23	26	32	22	24	29

* See end of table for areas of countries with fewer than 500 km^2.

REGION, COUNTRY, AND AREA (in thousands)	OVERALL DENSITY			"RURAL DENSITY"		
	1950	1960	1970	1950	1960	1970
Ghana 239	20	28	37	17	22	24
Guinea 246	9	12	16	9	12	14
Ivory Coast 322	8	10	13	7	8	9
Liberia 111	8	9	10	7	8	7
Mali 1,202	3	3	4	3	3	4
Mauritania 1,031	1	1	1	1	1	1
Niger 1,267	2	2	3	2	2	3
Nigeria 924	33	50	71	29	41	56
Portuguese Guinea 36	14	14	15	13	12	12
Saint Helena 0.1	43	43	43	43	43	43
Senegal 196	11	16	20	9	12	15
Sierra Leone 72	28	31	36	25	28	30
Togo 57	19	25	33	18	23	27
Upper Volta 274	13	16	20	13	15	19
EASTERN AFRICA 6,326	9	12	15	9	11	14
Burundi 28	67	104	127	66	103	124

REGION, COUNTRY, AND AREA (in thousands)	OVERALL DENSITY			"RURAL DENSITY"		
	1950	1960	1970	1950	1960	1970
Comoro Islands 2.1	76	88	133	73	84	123
Ethiopia 1,222	13	17	20	12	16	19
French Somaliland 22	3	4	5	2	2	2
Kenya 583	10	14	19	10	13	17
Madagascar 587	7	9	12	7	8	10
Malawi 119	23	29	37	23	28	35
Mauritius 2.0	243	335	434	171	193	197
Mozambique 783	7	8	9	7	8	9
Reunion 2.5	97	134	182	74	92	110
Rwanda 26	78	101	138	78	101	137
Seychelles 0.4	89	104	124	65	78	84
Somalia 638	3	3	5	2	3	3
Southern Rhodesia 389	7	9	13	6	8	10
Tanganyika 937	8	10	14	8	9	13
Uganda 236	22	28	36	22	27	34
Zambia 746	3	4	6	3	3	4
Zanzibar 2.6	103	117	142	81	84	92

REGION, COUNTRY, AND AREA (in thousands)	OVERALL DENSITY			"RURAL DENSITY"		
	1950	1960	1970	1950	1960	1970
MIDDLE AND SOUTHERN AFRICA 8,055	3	4	5	3	3	4
Angola 1,247	3	4	4	3	4	4
Basutoland (Lesotho) 30	19	24	32	19	24	31
Bechuanaland (Botswana) 570	1	1	1	1	1	1
Cameroon 475	9	10	12	8	9	11
Central African Rep. 623	2	2	3	2	2	2
Chad 1,284	2	2	3	2	2	3
Congo, Brazzaville 342	2	2	3	2	2	2
Congo, Dem. Rep. 2,345	5	6	7	4	5	6
Gabon 268	2	2	2	1	1	1
Sao Tome 1.0	62	67	64	54	57	52
SOUTH WEST AFRICA 824	1	1	1	---	---	1
Sp. Eq. Guinea 28	7	9	10	7	8	9
Swaziland 17	12	15	24	12	15	23
SOUTH AFRICA 1,221	10	13	16	6	7	8
NORTHERN AMERICA 21,515	8	9	11	3	3	3

REGION, COUNTRY, AND AREA (in thousands)	OVERALL DENSITY			"RURAL DENSITY"		
	1950	1960	1970	1950	1960	1970
Bermuda 0.5	706	804	1,019	---	---	---
Canada 9,976	1	2	2	1	1	1
Greenland 2,176	---	---	---	---	---	---
St. Pierre and Miq. 0.2	21	21	21	21	21	21
U.S.A. 9,363	16	19	22	6	6	5
MIDDLE AMERICA 2,505	14	19	27	8	10	13
British Honduras 23	3	4	5	2	2	3
Canal Zone 1.4	37	29	43	25	20	27
Costa Rica 51	16	23	35	11	15	22
El Salvador 21	87	115	164	55	71	98
Guatemala 109	26	35	47	19	24	30
Honduras 112	13	17	24	11	14	18
Mexico 1,973	13	18	26	8	9	11
Nicaragua 140	8	10	14	5	6	8
Panama 76	11	14	19	7	8	10
CARIBBEAN 236	69	86	109	45	53	63

REGION, COUNTRY, AND AREA (in thousands)	OVERALL DENSITY			"RURAL DENSITY"		
	1950	1960	1970	1950	1960	1970
Bahama Islands 11	7	10	14	4	6	6
Barbados Islands 0.4	491	540	588	316	322	323
Cayman Islands 0.3	27	29	35	27	29	35
Cuba 115	48	60	76	21	25	31
Dominican Republic 49	44	62	89	33	43	56
Guadeloupe 1.8	116	153	191	99	125	146
Haiti 28	112	144	175	98	123	144
Jamaica 11	125	149	184	96	105	118
Leeward Islands 1.1	110	124	130	84	89	86
Martinique 1.1	201	259	319	143	157	162
Neth. Antilles 1.0	169	197	229	100	99	96
Puerto Rico 8.9	249	264	321	148	148	168
Trinidad + Tobago 5.1	123	161	216	91	98	101
Turks + Caicos Is. 0.4	14	13	14	14	13	14
Virgin Islands (U.S.) 0.3	78	93	206	32	41	78
Windward Islands 2.1	128	154	184	108	127	149

REGION, COUNTRY, AND AREA (in thousands)	OVERALL DENSITY			"RURAL DENSITY"		
	1950	1960	1970	1950	1960	1970
TROPICAL SOUTH AMERICA 13,679	6	8	11	4	5	5
Bolivia 1,099	3	3	4	2	2	3
Brazil 8,512	6	8	11	4	5	5
British Guiana 215	2	3	3	1	2	2
Colombia 1,138	10	14	19	6	7	8
Ecuador 284	11	15	21	8	10	13
French Guiana 91	---	---	---	---	---	---
Peru 1,285	6	9	11	4	5	6
Surinam 143	1	2	3	1	1	2
Venezuela 912	6	8	11	3	3	3
TEMPERATE SOUTH AMERICA 4,139	6	8	9	3	3	3
Argentina 2,777	6	7	9	2	2	3
Chile 757	8	10	13	4	4	3
Falkland Islands 12	---	---	---	---	---	---
Paraguay 407	3	4	6	2	3	4
Uruguay 187	12	14	15	5	4	2

REGION, COUNTRY, AND AREA (in thousands)	OVERALL DENSITY			"RURAL DENSITY"		
	1950	1960	1970	1950	1960	1970
EAST ASIA 11,354	53	64	72	47	52	54
China (Taiwan) 36	212	295	400	101	122	143
China 9,561	59	70	79	52	58	60
Hong Kong 1.0	1,890	2,980	3,978	377	---	---
Korea, North 121	80	88	114	70	71	89
Korea, South 98	208	254	327	170	183	199
Macau 0.0*	11,750	10,562	17,500	---	---	---
Mongolia 1,535	---	1	1	---	---	---
Ryukyu Islands 2.2	314	402	448	226	266	271
JAPAN 370	226	253	278	141	92	47
SOUTHEAST ASIA 4,498	38	49	63	33	40	51
Brunei 5.8	8	15	20	5	8	11
Burma 678	28	33	40	24	28	34
Cambodia 181	23	30	38	21	27	38
Indonesia 1,492	51	63	79	45	53	65

* See end of table for areas of countries with fewer than 500 km^2.

REGION, COUNTRY, AND AREA	OVERALL DENSITY			"RURAL DENSITY"		
(in thousands)	1950	1960	1970	1950	1960	1970
Laos 237	6	10	13	5	9	11
West Malaysia 131	40	53	71	30	34	39
Maldive Islands 0.3	275	309	366	245	274	322
Philippines 300	68	98	128	54	71	98
Portuguese Timor 15	30	35	40	27	31	36
Sabah 76	4	6	9	4	5	7
Sarawak 125	5	6	8	4	5	6
Singapore 0.6	1,759	2,812	3,637	---	---	---
Thailand 514	38	51	70	34	45	61
Viet-Nam, North 159	76	101	139	70	87	106
Viet-Nam, South 171	61	83	108	52	65	80
West Irian 413	2	2	2	2	2	2
SOUTHWEST ASIA 5,976	10	13	17	8	9	11
Bahrain 0.6	184	251	361	54	69	92
Cyprus 9.2	53	62	68	40	40	36
Fed. of South Arabia (Southern Yemen) 0.2	3,588	3,974	5,155	2,912	2,861	3,479

REGION, COUNTRY, AND AREA (in thousands)	OVERALL DENSITY			"RURAL DENSITY"		
	1950	1960	1970	1950	1960	1970
Gaza Strip 0.4	741	997	1,360	741	997	1,360
Iran 1,648	10	13	17	7	9	11
Iraq 449	12	15	20	8	9	11
Israel 21	61	102	140	12	23	26
Jordan 90	14	19	27	9	11	15
Kuwait 16	11	17	34	5	5	7
Lebanon 10	170	203	250	125	136	151
Muscat and Oman 212	3	3	3	3	3	3
Qatar 22	1	2	4	---	1	1
Saudi Arabia 2,253	2	3	3	2	2	2
Syria 185	19	25	33	12	16	20
Trucial Oman 84	1	1	2	1	1	1
Turkey 781	27	35	45	21	26	31
Yemen 195	21	26	26	20	25	24
SOUTH CENTRAL ASIA 5,124	90	109	138	76	91	113
Afghanistan 647	19	22	26	17	21	24

REGION, COUNTRY, AND AREA (in thousands)	OVERALL DENSITY			"RURAL DENSITY"		
	1950	1960	1970	1950	1960	1970
Bhutan 47	11	14	18	11	14	18
Ceylon 66	117	151	193	100	128	161
India 3,046	117	141	179	97	116	145
Kashmir-Jammu 223	20	22	25	17	19	21
Nepal 141	57	65	79	55	63	75
Pakistan 947	79	98	121	71	85	101
Sikkim 7.1	19	23	27	19	22	25
NORTHERN EUROPE 1,574	46	48	52	14	13	13
Channel Islands 0.2	533	564	610	319	355	344
Denmark 43	99	107	115	33	28	23
Faeroe Islands 1.4	23	25	29	19	20	21
Finland 337	12	13	14	7	6	4
Iceland 103	1	2	2	1	1	1
Ireland 70	42	40	42	25	22	21
Isle of Man 0.6	94	82	88	43	36	37
Norway 324	10	11	12	6	6	5

REGION, COUNTRY, AND AREA (in thousands)	OVERALL DENSITY			"RURAL DENSITY"		
	1950	1960	1970	1950	1960	1970
Sweden 450	16	17	18	7	7	6
United Kingdom 244	207	215	230	47	47	48
WESTERN EUROPE 987	125	136	152	46	44	41
Austria 84	83	84	89	42	42	43
Belgium 31	283	300	321	104	101	100
France 547	76	84	94	35	32	30
Germany, Fed. Rep. 248	204	223	249	56	50	44
Liechtenstein 0.2	89	108	140	72	86	108
Luxembourg 2.6	114	122	133	47	46	46
Monaco 0.0*	22,000	23,000	26,000	---	---	---
The Netherlands 34	301	341	390	89	111	109
Switzerland 41	114	131	152	59	60	61
EASTERN EUROPE 990	90	98	105	52	51	48
Bulgaria 111	66	71	77	48	45	41
Czechoslovakia 128	96	107	114	56	56	55

* See end of table for areas of countries with fewer than 500 km^2.

REGION, COUNTRY, AND AREA (in thousands)	OVERALL DENSITY			"RURAL DENSITY"		
	1950	1960	1970	1950	1960	1970
Germany, East 108	170	159	157	50	35	25
Hungary 93	100	107	119	63	65	68
Poland 313	80	95	106	49	50	47
Romania 237	69	77	83	51	53	51
SOUTHERN EUROPE 1,315	83	89	98	49	49	48
Albania 29	42	57	74	34	39	48
Andorra 0.5	12	18	35	12	18	35
Gibraltar 0.0*	3,833	4,000	4,333	---	---	---
Greece 132	57	63	67	28	27	25
Holy See 0.0*	1,000	1,000	1,000	---	---	---
Italy 301	155	165	178	87	86	86
Malta + Gozo Is. 0.3	987	1,041	987	399	377	320
Portugal 92	92	97	106	63	64	67
San Marino 0.0*	213	246	311	151	184	246
Spain 505	55	60	65	28	28	27
Yugoslavia 256	64	72	81	53	52	50

* See end of table for areas of countries with fewer than 500 km^2.

REGION, COUNTRY, AND AREA (in thousands)	OVERALL DENSITY			"RURAL DENSITY"		
	1950	1960	1970	1950	1960	1970
AUSTRALIA-NEW ZEALAND 7,955	1	2	2	---	---	---
Australia 7,687	1	1	2	---	---	---
New Zealand 269	7	9	11	3	3	4
OCEANIA 555	4	6	7	4	5	7
American Samoa 0.2	96	102	183	88	95	173
Christmas Island 0.1	7	22	22	7	22	22
Cocos Islands 0.0*	43	43	50	43	43	50
Cook Islands 0.2	64	79	90	64	79	90
Fiji 18	16	22	30	13	18	24
French Polynesia 4.0	15	20	26	12	15	20
Gilbert + Ellice Is. 0.9	43	52	70	43	44	55
Guam 0.5	108	122	182	106	112	146
Johnston Island 0.0*	200	200	200	200	200	200
Midway Island 0.0*	80	480	480	80	480	480
Nauru 0.0*	143	190	333	143	190	333
New Caledonia 19	3	4	5	3	3	2

* See end of table for areas of countries with fewer than 500 km^2.

REGION, COUNTRY, AND AREA (in thousands)	OVERALL DENSITY			"RURAL DENSITY"		
	1950	1960	1970	1950	1960	1970
New Guinea 239	5	6	7	5	6	7
New Hebrides 15	3	4	6	3	4	6
Niue Island 0.3	17	19	19	17	19	19
Norfolk Island 0.0*	22	22	36	22	22	36
Pacific Islands 1.8	32	43	56	32	43	56
Papua 223	2	2	3	2	2	3
Solomon Is. (U.K.) 30	3	4	5	3	4	5
Tokelau Islands 0.0*	150	200	200	150	200	200
Tonga 0.7	69	90	126	58	76	106
Wake Island 0.0*	37	137	137	37	137	137
Western Samoa 2.8	28	39	52	24	32	40
U.S.S.R. 22,402	8	10	11	5	5	4

* Areas of Countries with Fewer than 500 Km^2:

Sp. North Africa	32	Johnston Island	1
Macau	16	Midway Island	5
Monaco	1	Nauru	21
Gibraltar	6	Norfolk Island	36
Holy See	1	Tokelau Islands	10
San Marino	61	Wake Island	8
Cocos Islands	14		

NOTES ON SPECIAL SOURCES, DEFINITIONS, AND PROCEDURES
FOR PARTICULAR COUNTRIES

EXPLANATION

The reader will recall that in Table A a three-digit code
appears in parentheses under the name of each country. The
nature of this code is described in the "Explanation" of Table A.
In general, the code characterizes the information for each
country in 1950 and 1960 in sufficient detail to enable one to
evaluate the data satisfactorily, and therefore, for many
countries, nothing more need to be said. However, there are
many countries whose data cannot be characterized adequately by
our code. They are countries with unusual definitions of
"urban," with changing boundaries, with conflicting estimates of
their total population, with partial or grossly inadequate censuses, or with some other peculiarity requiring special attention
with respect either to sources or to procedures. The present
section gives for these countries the special information required. It can be viewed as a set of footnotes to all the tables
in the present volume.

The notes are given under the name of the country concerned,
and the countries are listed alphabetically by region in the same
order that they appear in the tables. For convenience, the notes
for each country are introduced with standard headings, showing
at a glance what the notes are about. Since these headings are
repeated, they have been abbreviated in order to conserve space
and to facilitate quick reference. The abbreviations are as
follows:

"Tot. Pop."   for Total Population
"Urb. Pop."   for Urban Population
"City Pop."   for City Population
"Urb. Def."   for Urban Definition
"'50"   for 1950
"'60"   for 1960
"'70"   for 1970

In addition to these abbreviations in headings, we have
abbreviated the names of the three serial publications most frequently used as sources. UNDY stands for the United Nations
Demographic Yearbook, StY for Statesman's Yearbook, and OM for
Outre Mer. The digits following the abbreviations designate the
year of issue. Other sources were of course used but they are
referred to so infrequently as not to require abbreviation.

264

In general, the most frequent reason for a country's being
dealt with in these footnotes is an absence of census data, and
this is more serious for us with respect to the urban or city
population than with respect to the total population. Admittedly,
even the total population of a country may well be in doubt, but
we have usually solved that problem by accepting the midyear population estimate given in the United Nations Demographic Yearbook;
in some instances, however, when the Yearbook was silent on the
subject, disagreed with itself, or seemed to us to be in error,
we made our own estimate of the total population and thus were
under the necessity of stating in the present set of notes how
we made it.

The absence of census data is more serious for us in the
case of the urban population than in the case of the total population, because the Demographic Yearbook does not normally provide annual estimates of the urban population as it does for the
entire population. Instead, it simply gives, as a rule, only the
figures from censuses. If, for a particular country, there was
no census available for 1950 and 1960, but other censuses for
other years were available, we made estimates ourselves of the
urban population at the two dates in question by interpolation
and extrapolation, and the second and third digits of our data
code adequately describes the situation. But if only one census
was available, or if there was none at all, we relied on special
procedures and sources for making our 1950 and 1960 estimates--
and these are described below on a case-by-case basis.

In regard to the projections to 1970, Chapter IV describes our regular procedures and checks. Only when there were
peculiar difficulties in the projections are they discussed in
the present notes.

Regardless of the source and quality of the urban data, the
question remains as to how "urban" is defined. In most instances,
it is defined in terms of the lower limit in the size of place
that will be called urban. In this case our data code adequately
describes the definition, although the notes below refer to cases
that do not fit the size-category as coded. However, many countries qualify the size-limit definition by adding a political or
economic criterion. For instance, all places of 3,000 and over
may be regarded as urban, except that places of less than that
size may also be included if they are administrative centers of
provinces or districts. Our special notes are designed to acquaint the reader with these additional criteria as well as with
any other peculiarities or ambiguities of definition that may
characterize a particular country.

Our effort to include in our tables all the countries of
the world has forced us to adopt some unusual procedures. We
have tried in all cases to state briefly the logic of the method,
given the situation with which we were faced. Undoubtedly we
have not always succeeded in finding the best sources or in using
the best means of estimation, but we have tried conscientiously
to reveal our methods so as to facilitate checking by other social
scientists and to promote progress toward improvement of the data.

NOTES ON SPECIAL SOURCES, DEFINITIONS, AND PROCEDURES
FOR PARTICULAR COUNTRIES

NORTHERN AFRICA

Algeria

URB. DEF.: 55 most important communes. Approximately 660 communes in whole country. Smallest was estimated at 8,100 in
1950 and 1,300 in 1960.

Ifni

URB. DEF.: Capital city, Sidi Ifni. Population 8,000 in 1950
and 12,800 in 1960.

Libya

TOT. POP. '50: The growth rate of the North Africa region, 1950-
58, was applied to the 1954 census figure for Libya to estimate the 1950 total population.

URB. POP. '50: Since most of the urban growth probably occurred
after 1954, the growth rate 1954-64, was thought to be too
fast to be used in extrapolation back to 1950. Therefore,
the average between the growth rate of the urban population,
1954-64, and the growth rate of Tripoli, 1936-54, was applied
to the 1954 census figure to find the 1950 urban estimate.

URB. DEF.: Towns 8,000+.

CITY POP. '50: The average of Tripoli's growth rate, 1936-54,
and 1954-60, was applied to the 1954 figure to estimate the
1950 population.

Morocco

URB. POP. '50: The country was split into three parts in 1950:
the Southern Zone (French), the Northern Zone (Spanish), and
the Tangier Zone.

For the Southern Zone, an urban population was given for IV:1952 (UNDY:60), but it excluded the Jewish and foreign populations. An estimate was made for these populations by assuming that they were the same percentage of the IV:1952 urban population as of the cities 100,000+ for that year. This was then added to the Muslim IV:1952 urban population to form an estimate for the whole zone, which was then interpolated with the 1936 estimate (UNDY:52), to find the 1950 urban population.

The Northern Zone, in the absence of data, was assumed to be the same percentage urban as the Southern Zone.

The Tangier CP population was used as the urban and was extrapolated for 1950 by using the growth rate of the five other cities 100,000+, 1951-60, as a basis for extrapolation back from the 1960 figure for Tangier (UNDY:65).

CITY POP.: We considered Casablanca and Rabat as UA's because they were given as prefectures in the censuses.

Spanish Sahara

TOT. POP. '50: Estimated at 20,000 due to the variable estimates for the nomad population.

Sudan

TOT. POP. '50: The 1950 estimate is the average of 1953-60 and 1953-55 extrapolations (UNDY:65).

URB. POP. '50: Extrapolated from the 1956 census and the 1960 estimate (see below).

URB. POP. '60: The growth rate of the total population, 1956-60, was applied to the 1956 census figure for urban-minus-Port Sudan and Khartoum, to find the 1960 estimate for urban-minus-cities. Port Sudan was interpolated from the 1956 census figure and the 1964 estimate (UNDY:64). Khartoum was estimated for 1960 by applying the growth rate of Khartoum and Omdurman CP's, 1956-63, to the 1956 UA figure for Khartoum. The cities were then added to the urban-minus-cities estimate for 1960 to find the 1960 urban.

CITY POP. '60: See urban 1960 above.

Tunisia

CITY POP. '60: Interpolated from 1946 census and the 1964 estimate (UNDY:65).

U.A.R.

URB. DEF.: Cities, including the five largest cities which are also governates, and the capitals of provinces and districts.

WESTERN AFRICA

Cape Verde Islands

URB. DEF.: Capital city, Praia. Population 10,000 in 1950 and 13,100 in 1960.

Dahomey

URB. POP. '50: The growth rate of the four main centers, 1948-57 (OM:1939-49, p. 79 and OM:1958, p. 747) was applied to the total for the nine main urban centers, 1957 (indigenous population, OM:1958, p. 747, and non-indigenous population, UNDY:63), to find the estimated urban population for 1950.

URB. POP. '60: The growth rate of Canton and Porto Novo, 1957-64 (1957 estimates from OM:1958 and 1964 estimates from UNDY:64) was used with the 1957 population of the nine urban centers combined (see above) to reach the 1960 urban estimate.

URB. DEF.: Nine urban centers. Smallest was 4,100 in 1957. It was approximately 3,100 in 1950 and 5,600 in 1960.

Gambia

URB. DEF.: Capital city, Bathurst. Population 18,800 in 1950 and 25,500 in 1960.

Guinea

URB. POP.: For 1951, StY:60-61 gives the populations of nine

towns 5,000+. For 1948, OM:1939-49, p. 79, gives populations
for five of these towns; the remaining four are estimated by
taking the average differences between the five at both dates
and applying it to the 1951 populations of the four not given
for 1948. Thus, the urban population for 1948 is the population of the nine towns. Six of these towns are given for
1960 in StY:63-64. The growth rate of these six towns, 1948-
60, is applied to the 1948 estimate for the remaining three
to find the 1960 urban population. The 1950 population is
then interpolated from the 1948 and the 1960 estimates.

Ivory Coast

TOT. POP. '50: Since UNDY's midyear estimates go back only to
1951, the 1950 total population was calculated on the basis
of the 1951-52 increase, from UNDY:65.

URB. POP. '50: It was assumed that the populations of the two
main cities, Abidjan and Bouake, were the same percentage of
the urban population in 1948 as in 1955 (UNDY:60) to find the
1948 urban population. The percentages urban, 1948 and 1955,
were then interpolated to find the 1950 percent urban.

Liberia

URB. POP.: The capital, Monrovia, was extrapolated to 1950 and
1960 from the 1956 and 1962 censuses. The Central African
Republic ratio of capital city to urban population in 1958
was then applied to the 1950 and 1960 estimates of Monrovia
to find the 1950 and 1960 urban populations.

Mali

URB. POP.: We had the 1955 urban population (places 3,000+) from
OM:1958, p. 734; and we also had 1963 estimates for the eight
main towns from StY:66-67. The ratio of the eight main towns
to the total urban population as of 1955 was applied to the
1963 estimates to find the 1963 urban estimate. The 1950
and 1960 populations were then calculated on the basis of the
1955-63 annual rate of growth.

Mauritania

TOT. POP. '50: The growth rate of Angola's total population,

1950-60, was applied to the 1958 estimate of Mauritania's population (UNDY:65) to find the 1950 estimate.

URB. POP.: Interpolated from the 1948 estimate of places 3,000+ (OM:1939-49, p. 170) and a 1963 estimate for 3,000+ (StY: 66-67 and UNDY:64).

Niger

TOT. POP. '50: Estimated on the basis of the growth rate calculated from the 1951 estimate (UNDY:65) and the 1960 estimate (UNDY:66).

URB. POP.: The urban population was the five main cities, 4,000+. For 1950 and 1960, Niamey was extrapolated from its 1959 census and the 1955 estimate (UNDY:62). Zinder, the Tahoma, and Maradi were estimated for 1950 and 1960 from the 1948 estimates (OM:1939-49, p. 79) and the 1956 estimates (OM: 1958, p. 760). The last city, Agades, was estimated by applying the growth rate of Zinder, Tahoma and Maradi, 1948-56, to the 1956 estimate for Agades (OM:1958, p. 760).

URB. DEF.: Five main cities, 4,000+. The smallest was Agades with estimated population of 4,489 in 1950 and 4,965 in 1960.

Nigeria

URB. POP. '50: Mexico's ratio of 20,000+ to total urban population was applied to the 20,000+ population in the 1952-53 census of Nigeria (Nigerian Federal Office of Statistics, Nigeria Annual Abstract of Statistics, 1961; Lagos, 1963; p. 20) to find the 1952 urban estimate. This estimate was then interpolated with the 1931 urban population to find the 1950 urban population figure.

URB. POP. '60: The 23 CPs combined were interpolated for 1960 from the 1952-53 census and the 1963 census figures. The city population was assumed to be in the same ratio to the 20,000+ in 1960 as it was in 1952. The 20,000+ estimate was then used in the Mexican ratio of 20,000+ to total urban population to find the 1960 estimate for urban.

CITY POP.: The 1963 census figures (UNDY:64) for several cities were judged to be inflated. The population of Lagos in 1963 was therefore scaled down to 500,000, and the 1950 and 1960 estimates made by interpolation and extrapolation, using the lowered 1963 estimate and the 1952 census. The other cities were given a growth rate of 5%, somewhat lower than the 1963 census data would indicate, and their 1950 and 1960 populations were calculated from the 1952 census. In projecting city populations to 1970, we modified the 1963 census figures as above, but gave the projected population for Lagos 50,000 more on account of the civil war.

URB. DEF.: Approximately 2,500+.

Portuguese Guinea

URB. POP. '60: The average of the growth rates of the proportion urban during 1950-60 in five neighboring countries (Gambia, Guinea, Liberia, Senegal, and Sierra Leone) was applied to the percentage urban in the 1950 census of Portuguese Guinea to find the 1960 percentage urban.

URB. DEF.: Two main ports, Brissau and Cacheu. Smaller was 14,321 in 1950 and approximately 20,000 in 1960.

Saint Helena

TOT. POP.: The 1956 census was accepted for both dates since the
UNDY:65 midyear estimates gave it 5,000 for each year, 1946-51.

Senegal

URB. POP.: We began with the size-class 10,000+, but since the 10,000+ seemed to be too high a cut-off point for the urban, an estimate was made for towns 5,000+ for 1950 and 1960. The 10,000+ figure for 1960 was estimated by interpolation of the eight cities 10,000+ in 1956 (OM:1958, p. 727) and the XII: 1960 figures for the same cities. The 1950 figure for 10,000+ was calculated by interpolating the 1948 estimate for the eight cities (OM:1939-49, p. 79, together with an estimate for Saint Louis extrapolated from 1951-56 data in OM:1958 and OM:1955). To find the 5,000+ figure, the ratio of 5,000-10,000 / 10,000+ in 1956 was applied to the 1960 estimate for 10,000+ calculated above.

To find the 1950 estimate for urban, the same ratio of 5,000-10,000 / 10,000+ in 1956 was applied to the 10,000+

figure in 1948 to find the urban estimate for 1948. The 1950 figure was then interpolated from the 1948 and 1960 estimates.

CITY POP. '50: Interpolation from a 1948 estimate (OM:1939-49, p. 79) and the 1955 census.

Sierra Leone

URB. POP. '50: The growth rate of the capital city, 1950-60, was used with the 1960 estimate for urban (see below) to find the 1950 urban population.

URB. POP. '60: The 1960 ratio of Angola's capital city to the total urban population of Angola was applied to the 1960 estimate for Sierra Leone's capital city to find the estimated 5,000+ population in Sierra Leone.

Togo

TOT. POP. '50: Extrapolated from the 1956 and 1965 estimates in UNDY:65.

URB. POP. '50: The capital city was interpolated for 1950 from the 1949 estimate (UNDY:52) and the 1958 census. The ratio of the capital city to urban in 1960 was applied to the 1950 estimate for the capital city to calculate the 1950 urban population.

URB. DEF.: Seven urban communes. Smallest was approximately 3,800 in 1950 and 9,166 in 1960.

Upper Volta

TOT. POP. '50: The UNDY:65 midyear estimates, which are the latest for Upper Volta and which we wished to use, go back only to 1957. The old estimates (UNDY:63), however, go back to 1947 and end in 1956. We decided, first, to get an estimate for 1956 based on the rate of change shown in the UNDY: 65 estimates. Having this, we subtracted the population difference between the old 1950-56 estimates, and subtracted it from the new 1956 estimate to find the 1950 total population estimate.

URB. POP.: The five main cities were estimated for 1950 and 1960 in various ways. Bobo-Dioulasso was interpolated for 1950 and

1960 from 1946 and 1956 estimates (OM:1950-55, p. 80).
Ouagodougou was interpolated for 1950 from 1946 (Ibid.) and
1957 (StY:59) estimates; and the 1960 estimate was from UNDY:
62. Koudougou was interpolated for 1950 from a 1948 estimate
(OM:1939-49, p. 79) and a 1958 estimate (OM:1958, p. 740); its
population came out as 9,000 for 1960 on the basis of the 1958
figure above. Ouahigouya was calculated from the 1948 and
1955 figures (same sources as for Koudougou) for both dates.
The population of Banfora was estimated for both dates by
applying the growth rate of the preceding four cities during
the decade 1950-60 to the 1958 estimate (OM:1958, p. 740) for
Banfora.

EASTERN AFRICA

Burundi

TOT. POP. '50: The 1950 estimated population is given for Rwanda
and Burundi combined. For Burundi, the African population is
estimated at 1,902,000 for VII:1952 (UNDY:64). The non-
African population, estimated at 6,000 in 1958, is assumed to
be approximately 4,000 in 1952, giving 1,906,000 as the entire
population of Burundi in 1952. For Rwanda, the population is
given as 2,128,000 in 1953 (UNDY:65); so we assume it is
2,100,000 in 1952. We take the ratio of Rwanda to Rwanda-
plus-Burundi for 1952 and apply it to the 1950 combined population of 3,193,000 (UNDY:51) to find Rwanda's population;
the remainder is the 1950 estimate of Burundi.

URB. POP. '50: The 1949 estimate for the capital city, Usumbura,
was rounded up and accepted as the 1950 population.

URB. POP. '60: The 1960 estimate for Usumbura from UNDY:63 was
accepted as urban.

URB. DEF.: Capital city, Usumbura. Population 18,000 in 1950
and 46,600 in 1960.

Comoro Islands

URB. POP: The two main cities, Dzoudzi and Moroni. Dzoudzi is
estimated for 1950 and 1960 by applying the growth rate of
the total population, 1950-60, to the 1958 census figure.
Moroni is calculated for both dates by using the average

growth rate of the five city populations in neighboring countries (Basutoland; Congo, Brazzaville; Guinea; Kenya; and
Mali) with the 1962 estimate (UNDY:63).

URB. DEF.: Two cities, Dzoudzi and Moroni. The smaller one had
a population of 2,470 in 1950 and 2,998 in 1960, according
to our estimates.

Ethiopia and Eritrea

TOT. POP. '50: Estimates vary widely. We made a round guess of
16 million which includes the dependency of Eritrea. The
resulting growth rate for the total population is 2.61% per
year for the decade.

URB. POP. '50: The ratios of 100,000+ to the total urban population for Kenya, Uganda, Sudan, and Tanganyika are averaged
and applied to the 1950 estimate for cities 100,000+ to calculate the urban population.

URB. POP. '60: The same ratio as in the 1950 calculation is used,
substituting the 1960 estimate for cities 100,000+.

URB. DEF.: Places 4,000+ by derivation from neighboring countries.

CITY POP. '60: Asmara is extrapolated from the 1963 estimate
(UNDY:63) and the 1964 estimate (UNDY:64); and Addis Ababa is
calculated from the 1961 census and the 1964 estimate (UNDY:
64).

French Somaliland

URB. POP. '50: Extrapolation from a 1944 estimate (StY:48) and
a 1948 estimate (StY:55).

URB. POP. '60: Interpolation from a 1957 estimate (UNDY:60) and
a 1963 estimate (UNDY:64).

URB. DEF.: Capital city, Kjibouti. Population 19,000 in 1950
and 36,800 in 1960.

Kenya

URB. POP. '70: The projection from 1950 to 1960 gave a figure for the urban population that was judged to be too high, in view of the city/urban ratio. For this reason, the 1970 urban population was scaled down by 12.7 per cent.

CITY POP. '60: Nairobi was interpolated from a 1960 estimate (UNDY:62) and the 1962 census figure; Mombasa was extrapolated from the 1958 and 1959 estimates (UNDY:60).

Madagascar

URB. POP.: Interpolated and extrapolated from the 1949 estimate (OM:1939-49, p. 83) and a 1958 estimate (OM:1958, p. 805).

URB. DEF.: Cities, 6,000+

CITY POP. '50: Interpolated from 1949 estimate (UNDY:52) and 1955 estimate (UNDY:55).

CITY POP. '60: Interpolated from 1959 estimate (UNDY:62) and 1962 estimate (UNDY:63).

Malawi

TOT. POP. '50: The upgrading of the midyear estimates by UNDY: 65 was used as a basis for raising the UNDY:63 estimate for 1950.

URB. POP. '50: Zomba is interpolated from the 1956 and 1948 estimates (UNDY:52). Blantyre-Limbe's population is estimated by averaging the result of a 1956-60 interpolation (African Handbook, 1960, p. 282) and the result of assuming the same ratio of Blantyre-Limbe to Zomba in 1950 as in 1956. Luluankwe is estimated on the basis of the same percentage increase as Blantyre-Limbe from 1950-60, using the 1960 estimate (see below).

URB. POP. '60: Zomba is interpolated from the 1956 estimate (UNDY:62) and a 1962 estimate (UNDY:65). Blantyre-Limbe is approximated from figures in StY:63-64 and the Encyclopedia Britannica Atlas, 1962. Lulankwe is estimated on the basis of the same percentage increase as Blantyre-Limbe from 1956-60, using the 1956 estimate (African Handbook, 1960).

URB. DEF.: Three largest towns. The smallest in 1950 had a population of 3,600 and in 1960, a population of 9,600.

Mozambique

URB. POP. '50: The ratio of the capital city to the total urban population in 1960 (see below) was applied to the 1950 census population of the capital city to find the 1950 urban population.

URB. POP. '60: The ratio of 20,000+ / total urban population in 1961 in India, was applied to the 20,000+ census population of Mozambique (one place) to calculate the 1960 urban estimate.

CITY POP. '70: The projection of the city population was 473,000. Since Laurenço Marques is the only city exceeding 100,000 inhabitants, this represented a dubiously high figure. Also, the urban projection showed only 439,000 urban population by 1970. Accordingly, we did not accept the projected figure for the city, but lowered it to 325,000.

Reunion

URB. POP. '50: Extrapolated from the 1954 census figure and the 1960 estimate (see below).

URB. POP. '60: The growth rate of the CP of St. Denis was applied to the 1954 UA figure to find the UA in 1960. Then the ratio of the capital city to urban in 1954 was applied to the 1960 estimate for the capital UA to find the 1960 urban.

URB. DEF.: Administrative centres of communes 2,000+.

Rwanda

URB. POP.: Estimates are extrapolated from 1955 and 1959 estimates (UNDY:62) for the capital city, Kigali.

URB. DEF.: Capital city, Kigali. Population 2,200 in 1950 and 4,500 in 1960.

Seychelles

URB. DEF.: Port Victoria. Population 9,700 in 1950 and 10,500 in 1960.

Somalia

URB. POP. '50:   The growth rate of the two main cities, Mogadiscio and Hargeisa, 1950-60, and the growth rate of the total population, 1950-60, are averaged and applied to the 1960 estimate for urban (see below) to find the 1950 urban estimate.

URBAN POP. '60:   Estimate for places 5,000+ are taken from StY: 66-67 and S. Touval's Somali Nationalism (Cambridge: Harvard University Press, 1963), p. 12.

Southern Rhodesia

TOT. POP. '50:   The estimate for 1954 in UNDY:65 was reduced by 3% per year to find the 1950 estimate for total population.

URB. POP. '60, '70:   The non-African population in the nine main towns 3,000+ was extrapolated to 1962 from the 1956 and 1961 censuses.   This was added to the 1962 population of Africans in the same nine towns to get a 1962 figure for urban which was then interpolated with the 1951 urban population for the 1960 urban estimate.

  For 1970, the urban projection was judged to be too high in view of the city/urban ratio to which it gave rise. Accordingly, the urban projection was scaled down by 20.4 per cent.

CITY POP. '60:   Basically, the same method as for urban was followed.   The non-African population was calculated, added to the 1962 census figure, and then interpolated with the 1951 census data for 1960 estimates.

Tanganyika

URB. POP. '50:   Interpolated from 1948 and 1952 estimates (K.M. Barbour and R.M. Prothro, eds., Essays on African Population; New York: Praeger, 1962; p. 56).

URB. POP. '60:   Extrapolated from the 1952 estimate (see above) and the 1957 census.

URB. DEF.:   Approximately 33 declared townships.   Smallest in 1957 was 512.   Approximately 330 in 1950 and 610 in 1960.

CITY POP. '60:   Interpolated from 1957 census and 1965 estimate (UNDY:65).

Uganda

URB. POP.: We had 1959 populations for places 4,000+ from 1962 Atlas of Uganda, but no comparable data for the 1948 census. There were data for three of the main cities at both dates; the 1948 populations of Entebbe and Jinja from the East African Statistical Department's Quarterly Economic and Statistical Bulletin, 1948, p. 4; and the population of Kampala UA which came from UNDY:65 for 1959 and for 1948 was assumed to be twice the CP population. As for the other cities, Kabale was estimated for 1948 by applying the growth rate of Entebbe, 1948-59, to the 1950 population; Mbale was estimated for 1948 by applying the average of the growth rates of Jinja and Entebbe to the 1959 population. Thus, for 1948, we had a figure for places of 7,000+. To find the 4,000-7,000 size-class for 1948, it was assumed that the ratio of 4,000-7,000 / 7,000+ in 1959 was the same in 1948.

The urban-minus-Kampala figure for 1950 and 1960 was then obtained by extrapolation and interpolation from the 1948 and 1959 populations. Kampala UA was estimated for the two dates by applying the growth rate of the three main cities, Kampala, Jinja, and Entebbe, to the 1948 estimate and 1959 population as given in the census. These estimates for Kampala UA were then added to the urban-minus-Kampala populations at each date, and the 1950 and 1960 populations for urban were obtained.

URB. DEF.: 4,000+.

Zambia

URB. POP.: Since data for the African and the non-African populations were given separately, the urban population had to be estimated in two steps. First, the African urban population and the total population were interpolated from the 1950 estimate (UNDY:60) and the 1963 census. The 1960 non-African urban population was estimated by assuming the non-African population was as urban in 1960 as in 1961. The 1960 and 1950 total non-African population was interpolated from the 1951 and 1961 censuses.

The non-African and the African estimates for 1950 and 1960 were added, both for the urban and the total populations, and the percentage urban was calculated. The percentage urban was also computed by using the total population estimates from the UNDY:65 and UNDY:66 in place of the interpolated figures. The two percentages for each date were then averaged and applied to the UNDY:65 and UNDY:66 midyear estimates to find the final urban figures for 1950 and 1960.

URB. DEF.: Main towns including the suburbs and adjoining nine townships. Population of the smallest in 1950 was 4,400; in 1960, approximately 8,500.

Zanzibar

URB. DEF.: Town of Zanzibar; townships of Wete, Chake, Mkoani; township-planning areas of Bububu, Kemara, Mkweni and Mombasa.

MIDDLE AND SOUTHERN AFRICA

Angola

URB. POP. '60: The ratio of Luanda to all "cidades" 5,000+ in 1950 was applied to the 1960 census figure of Luanda.

URB. DEF.: Cidades 5,000+.

Basutoland

URB. DEF.: Capital city, Maseru. Population 3,800 in 1950 and 7,500 in 1960.

Bechuanaland

URB. POP.: The 1946 census gave urban size-class data only for the indigenous population. We assumed that the European population, given in toto, in the same census, was 3/4 urban, and added it to the indigenous urban population. This was then interpolated with the 1964 census figure to get the 1950 and 1960 estimates for urban.

URB. DEF.: Four largest villages, all over 10,000 in 1946.

Cameroons

URB. POP. '50: We had estimates of two main towns, Younde and Douala, for 1950 (OM:1939-49, p. 26). The ratio of these two towns to the total urban in 1960 (see below) was applied to the 1950 estimates to find the 1950 estimate for urban.

URB. POP. '60: We had 1957 estimates of all 14 towns, 3,000+ from StY:63-64. In addition, we had for Younde, 1956 (UNDY:62) and 1962 (UNDY:64) estimates, and for Douala, a 1956 census and a 1964 estimate (UNDY:64). We assumed that the 12 towns other than Younde and Douala, grew at a rate that was an average of the rate of the total population (1957-60) and the rate of Douala (1956-64), to find their population in 1960. Younde and Douala, interpolated for 1960 from the above data, were then added to form the 1960 urban estimate.

Central African Republic

URB. POP.: Bangui was interpolated and extrapolated for 1950 and 1960 from the 1958 estimate (UNDY:60) and the 1964 census figure. Then the 1958 ratio of Bangui to places 5,000+ was applied to the 1950 and 1960 estimates to find the 1950 and 1960 urban populations.

Chad

URB. POP.: The 1950 population of Fort Laramie was derived by extrapolation and the 1960 population by interpolation, from the 1958 estimate (UNDY:60) and the 1962 census. The 1957 population of Fort Laramie was subtracted from the "urbain centres" total in OM:1958, p. 799, to find the "rest of urban" at that date. The growth rate halfway between that for the total population, 1950-60, and that for Fort Laramie (computed by taking the average of the rates between 1950-57 and 1958-62) was applied to the "rest of the urban" to find its population in 1950 and 1960. These were added to the Fort Laramie estimates to find the total urban population at both dates.

TOT. POP. '50: The percent change between the 1950 estimate in the StY:52 and the 1957 estimate in StY:63-64 was calculated and applied to the midyear estimate for 1957 in UNDY:65 to find the 1950 total population estimate.

URB. DEF.: Urban centers. Smallest in 1957 was 7,800; in 1950, approximately 4,500; and in 1960 approximately 10,200.

Congo, Brazzaville

TOT. POP. '50: The estimate from StY:52 was accepted for the 1950 total population estimate.

URB. POP. '50: Defined as the three cities--Brazzaville, Pointe Noire, and Dolisie. The 1950 estimate for Brazzaville from UNDY:52 was used. Pointe Noire's 1950 population was extrapolated on the basis of the 1956 estimate (OM:1958, p. 785) and the 1962 estimate (UNDY:63). Dolisie was estimated by holding the ratio of its population to the total urban in 1956 (OM:1958, p. 785) constant to 1950.

URB. POP. '60: Brazzaville was estimated for 1960 by assuming a 7% growth per year and applying this to the 1961 municipal census. Pointe Noire was interpolated between the 1959 estimate (StY:60-61) and the 1962 estimate. Dolisie was estimated as in urban 1950 by holding the ratio of its population to the total urban population constant, 1956-60.

URB. DEF.: Three main cities: Brazzaville, Pointe Noire, and Dolisie. Smallest in 1950 was 7,005; in 1960, 13,150.

Congo, Dem. Rep.

URB. POP. '50: The ratio of the 20,000+ to total urban population in 1956 (UNDY:60) was assumed to be the same in 1950, and was applied to the 20,000+ figure for that date (UNDY:60) to estimate the 1950 urban.

URB. POP. '60: The same ratio was applied to the 1959 figure for 20,000+ to find a 1959 urban estimate. This was then extrapolated with the 1950 estimate to find the 1960 urban population.

URB. POP. '70: The curve-projection yielded an incredibly high estimate. It was incompatible with the city estimates, no matter how derived. Accordingly, the projected urban population for 1970 was scaled down to 3,000,000. This is still high in relation to the official 1966 estimates for cities; but, of course, the latter may prove to have been too low.

URB. DEF.: Agglomerations of 2,000+ where predominant economic activity is non-agricultural.

CITY POP. '60: The four cities were extrapolated from the 1959 estimates (for all four from UNDY:60) and the 1950 estimates (Leopoldville and Elizabethville from StY:52 and IPUR estimates for Stanleyville and Luluabourg. These two cities were calculated for 1950 by subtracting Leopoldville and Elizabethville from the 20,000+ figure for five cities in UNDY:60 to find the population of the remaining three cities. By assuming that the smallest had just 20,000, and subtracting that from the sum for the three cities, the population remaining can be assumed to be the 1950 population for Stanleyville and Luluabourg.)

Gabon

URB. POP.: Three main cities, Libreville, Port Gentil, and Moanda-Mouana. There is a 1960 census, but it is not for the midyear, so it had to be adjusted. Libreville was interpolated for 1950 and 1960 from the 1957-61 estimates (UNDY: 62). Port Gentil was extrapolated from the 1950 estimate (Haut Comissariat de l'Afrique Equatorial Francaise, Annuaire Statistique de l'Afrique Equatorial Francaise, 1950; Vol. 1, p. 34) and the 1958 estimate (OM:1958, p. 793). The third city was found by subtracting the two other cities from the urban population figure given in the census. It was estimated for 1950 by assuming that it was in the same ratio to Port Gentil and Libreville in 1950 as it was in 1960.

The three 1950 estimates were added to find the urban population for 1950. The 1960 midyear percentage urban was found by interpolating the 1960 census percent and the 1950 estimate percent and applying it to the 1960 midyear estimate for total population.

URB. DEF.: Three main cities. Smallest in 1950 was Moanda-Mouana with 2,712 in 1950 and 5,459 in 1960.

Sao Tome

URB. DEF.: Capital city, Sao Tome. Population 7,800 in 1950 and 9,700 in 1960.

South West Africa

URB. DEF.: Localities large enough to be treated as separate units, whether having local government or not.

Swaziland

URB. DEF.: Capital city, Mbane. Population 7,300 in 1960.

NORTHERN AMERICA

Canada

URB. DEF.: Cities, towns, and villages 1,000+, incorporated and
    unincorporated, including urbanized fringes of cities classed
    as MA's and other major urban areas. For the census, 1961,
    urbanized fringes of certain smaller cities if the population
    of the city and its fringes was 10,000+ were included.

Greenland

URB. POP. '50: Extrapolated from the 1956 estimate (Denmark
    Statistical Department, Danmark Statistic Arbog, 1958;
    Copenhagen, 1959; p. 363) and the 1960 census figure.

URB. DEF.: Capital city, Godthab. Population 1,900 in 1950 and
    3,200 in 1960.

U.S.A.

URB. DEF.: Incorporated and unincorporated places of 2,500+
    including the urbanized zones around central cities of
    50,000+.

CITY POP. '70: No post-1960 figures were available for UA's.
    However, estimates were variously available for metropolitan
    areas, or SMSA's, for 1965, 1966, and 1967 from the Current
    Population Reports of the Census Bureau. They did not in-
    clude all the places that would have reached 100,000 by 1970,
    but did include most of them. For each city for which an
    SMSA estimate was available, the growth rate of the SMSA from
    1960 to the latest available estimate was calculated and
    applied to the 1960 UA to find an estimate for the UA in 1970.
    An alternate estimate for the UA in 1970 was calculated on
    the basis of the UA growth rate between 1950 and 1960. The
    two estimates were averaged and rounded to get final figures
    for 1970.

For places for which we had a UA population from the
1960 census but no subsequent SMSA official estimate, we took
the 1950-60 growth rate, as modified by the 1960-70/1950-60
ratio for the rest of the UA's for the country as a whole
(as estimated according to procedures just described), to get
1970 estimates. In some cases, however, we had no UA population in 1950 and so could not calculate a 1950-60 growth
rate for the UA. In these instances we took the growth of
the central city, and expanded it according to the CP/UA
ratio of the country at large, to get a rate applicable to
the 1960 UA in order to reach 1970.

MIDDLE AMERICA

British Honduras

URB. DEF.: Principal city, Belize. Population 24,600 in 1950
and 33,100 in 1960.

Costa Rica

URB. DEF.: "Metropolitan area" of San Jose City (excluding rural
sector of district of Las Pavas), Cartago City, and administrative centres of all cantons except San Pablo (province of
Heredia), Nadayure (province of Guanacaste), and Buenos
Aires (province of Puntarenas).

CITY POP. '60: Interpolated from 1958 estimate (UNDY:60) and
1963 census.

El Salvador

URB. DEF.: Administrative centres of departments, districts, and
municipios. Smallest in 1950 was 83 inhabitants.

CITY POP. '50, '60: San Salvador was considered a UA, because
the figures given in the 1950 and 1960 censuses are for the
departamento.

Guatemala

URB. DEF.: Localities of 2,000+ and those of 1,500-2,000 if running water is supplied to houses.

Honduras

URB. POP.: The growth rate of seven cities, 10,000+, 1950-61 (IPUR estimate) is applied to the 1961 census urban population, to find the 1950 and 1960 urban estimates.

URB. DEF.: 1,000+ with urban characteristics.

Mexico

URB. DEF.: Agglomerations 2,500+.

Nicaragua

URB. DEF.: Administrative centres of departments and municipalities. Smallest was 118 in 1950 (places less than 2,000 were 19.8% of the total urban population) and estimated as 119 in 1960.

Panama

URB. DEF.: Localities 1,500+ with urban characteristics.

CITY POP.: Although UNDY lists Panama City as a CP, we define it as a UA, because, as given in the 1960 census, it includes an area of 60 square miles, embracing suburbs as rural territories.

CARIBBEAN

Bahama Islands

URB. POP.: The growth rate of New Providence, 1953-63 (StY:62-63 and StY:66-67), was applied to the 1953 census population of Nassau to find the 1950 and 1960 urban populations.

286

NOTES: CARIBBEAN (continued)

URB. DEF.:   Nassau CP.   Population 30,400 in 1950 and 54,600 in 1960.

Barbados Islands

URB. DEF.:   Bridgetown-St. Michael Parish.   Population 75,300 in 1950 and 93,700 in 1960.

Cuba

URB. POP. '60:   The growth rate of Havana, Camaguey, and Santiago, 1953-1962 censuses, was applied to the 1953 census figure for urban to interpolate the 1960 urban estimate.

URB. DEF.:   Localities 150+ having urban characteristics, such as electricity and legal and medical services.

CITY POP. '60:   Extrapolated from 1962 census and 1964 estimate (UNDY:65).

Dominican Republic

URB. DEF.:   Administrative centres of municipios and municipal districts, some of which include suburban zones of rural character.   Smallest was approximately 240 in 1950 and approximately 430 in 1960.

Guadeloupe

URB. POP.:   We had a CP population for Point-a-Pitre from VII: 1954 census.   The Basse-Terre commune (StY:62-63) was added to form an urban estimate for 1954.   For 1961, the average percent between the 20,000+ percent (Population, Vol. 18, April-June, 1963, p. 367) and the "two principal centers" percent (Population, Vol. 21, January-February, 1966, p. 122) was applied to the 1961 total population to find an urban population estimate.   The 1950 and 1960 populations were then interpolated from the 1954-61 data.

URB. DEF.:   Basse-Terre-St. Claude and Point-a-Pitre-Les Abymes.

Haiti

URB. POP. '60: The growth rate of major towns, 1950 census to 1961 estimates (StY:63-64) was applied to the 1950 census figure for urban to interpolate the 1960 urban population.

URB. DEF.: Administrative centers of communes. Smallest was 72 in 1950, and approximately 112 in 1960.

Jamaica

TOT. POP. '50: No census between 1943 and 1960. To estimate the 1950 total population we applied a growth rate of 1.8% per year 1958-64 (UNDY:65) to the 1960 census figure.

URB. DEF.: Kingston MA and 22 commercial or administrative centers with 2,000+.

Martinique

URB. POP.: Estimate for the 1954 census and the 1961 census. The 1961 census figure for the urban population was adjusted by assuming that the difference between the total population figure given in the urban table and the one given in Table 2 of UNDY:66 represented double-counting in the urban sector.

URB. DEF.: Commune of Fort de France and agglomerations of communes 2,000+.

Netherland Antilles

URB. DEF.: Willemstad agglomeration. Population 66,000 in 1950 and 94,100 in 1960.

Puerto Rico

URB. DEF.: Places 2,500+ and dense urban fringes.

CITY POP. '50: The San Juan UA for 1950 was calculated by applying the growth rate of the SMSA during 1950-60 to the 1960 UA census figure.

Trinidad and Tobago

URB. DEF.: Main cities and their suburbs. Smallest was 28,842 in 1948 and approximately 36,400 in 1950; 39,830 in 1960.

Virgin Islands

URB. DEF.: Places 2,500+.

Windward Islands

URB. POP. '50: The 1946 census figure for the urban population was accepted as the 1950 figure as there was little growth assumed in the islands' urban population.

URB. POP. '60: The ratio of the major city to the total population of each island in 1946 was applied to the 1960 census total population to find the 1960 urban estimate.

TROPICAL SOUTH AMERICA

Bolivia

URB. POP. '50: The ratio of the six largest cities to the nine cities 2,000+ in 1960 (see below) was applied to the 1950 census figures for the six largest cities (America en Cifras: 1960; No.1, "Estadisticas Demograficas," p. 8) to find the population of the nine cities over 2,000 in 1950.

URB. POP. '60: Estimates for the nine cities 2,000+ were taken from the StY:62-63 with an adjustment of the La Paz population. Its population was the average of the UNDY:62 estimate and the StY:62-63 estimate for 1960.

URB. DEF.: Nine cities, 2,000+.

CITY POP. '50: La Paz CP had 321,073 inhabitants according to the 1950 census, but this included a 20.4 per cent adjustment for underenumeration (UNDY:60). The CP population was scaled down to the population actually counted, then rounded up slightly to 275,000. The UA was formed by adding the suburbs for 1950 as given in The World's Metropolitan Areas.

Brazil

URB. DEF.: Urban and suburban zones of administrative centers of municipios.

British Guiana

URB. DEF.: City of Georgetown and New Amsterdam. Smaller was 9,567 in 1946; approximately 10,900 in 1950; and 14,070 in 1960.

Colombia

URB. DEF.: Administrative centers of districts and municipios having 1,500+.

Ecuador

URB. DEF.: Cities, capitals of provinces and cantons. Smallest was approximately 250 in 1950, and approximately 390 in 1960.

French Guiana

TOT. POP. '50: The 1952 midyear estimate from UNDY:62 is accepted as the 1950 population.

URB. DEF.: Capital, Cayenne. Population 11,200 in 1950 and 16,700 in 1960.

Peru

URB. POP.: The growth rate of Colombia's urban population, 1938-51, was applied to the 1961 census urban population of Peru to estimate the 1950 and 1960 populations.

URB. DEF.: Capitals of districts and those populated centers with such urban characteristics as streets, plazas, water and sewer systems, electric lights, et cetera.

Surinam

URB. DEF.: Paramaibo. Population 71,500 in 1950 and 98,400 in 1960.

Venezuela

URB. POP. '50: To find an estimated 1950 population in places of 2,500+, we adjusted the 1950 census figure by assuming that 1/6 of those living in places 2,000-5,000 were in places under 2,500.

URB. DEF.: Places 2,500+.

TEMPERATE SOUTH AMERICA

Argentina

CITY POP.: Using the censuses of 1947 and 1960, Valerie Herr, while at IPUR, delimited metropolitan areas for Argentina. We have used these MA's as UA's in the present study, interpolating between 1947 and 1960 to get the 1950 populations. In the case of Tucuman, however, only CP data were available for 1947. We estimated an MA for that city by assuming that the CP/MA ratio was the same in 1950 as it was later in 1960.

Chile

URB. DEF.: Populated centers which have definite urban characteristics contributed by certain public and municipal services. The smallest urban area was 54 in 1952 (places less than 2,000 were 2.9% of the total urban population); and in 1960 it was 68 (places less than 2,000 were 1.6% of the total urban population).

Paraguay

URB. POP.: The 1950 urban population is estimated by assuming that the category, urban-minus-Asuncion, grew at a rate which was the average of Asuncion, 1950-62, and the total population 1950-62. The 1960 figure for urban was then interpolated from the 1950 estimate and the 1962 census figure.

Uruguay

URB. POP. '50: Montevideo's population was interpolated for 1950
from the 1941 census and the 1963 census. The category,
urban-minus-Montevideo, was assumed to have grown at a rate
halfway between that of Montevideo and that of the total
population, 1941-63, to find the 1950 urban-minus-Montevideo
estimate. The 1950 estimate for Montevideo was then added
to form the 1950 urban population.

URB. POP. '60: It was assumed that the 1963 urban-minus-Montevideo population grew at a rate that was the average of that
of the total population, 1941-63, and Montevideo (Santiago's
growth rate, 1960-63, was used to estimate the 1960 population
of Montevideo on the basis of the population of that city in
Uruguay's 1963 census). The 1960 estimate for Montevideo
was added to form the 1960 urban population estimate.

URB. DEF.: No definition available.

CITY POP. '60: See urban 1960 above.

EAST ASIA

China (Taiwan)

URB. POP.: Extrapolated to midyear for both dates from XII:1950
and XII:1955 estimates (UNDY:60).

CITY POP.: Estimates for both dates from Shao-hsing Chen, "Trend
of Urbanization and the Formation of a Metropolitan Area in
Taiwan During the Last Decade," J. of Sociology, No. 1 (Tapei:
National Taiwan University, 1963).

China (Mainland)

TOT. POP. '60: Growth of 2% per year applied to 1953 census (Nai-
Ruenn Chen, ed., Chinese Economic Statistics: A Handbook for
Mainland China; Chicago: Aldine, 1967; p. 124).

URB. POP.: Interpolated and extrapolated from 1949 and 1956
estimates (Ibid.).

URB. DEF.: Cities, suburbs and towns, including towns in the
suburbs of cities but excluding villages in such towns.

CITY POP.: For 1950 and 1960, individual cities were first estimated from 1949 estimates (UNDY:52), the 1953 census, and the
1957 estimates in N. Chen, op. cit. Later, when the 1970 projections were made, the results suggested the necessity of re-
vising the 1950 and 1960 figures. This revision was made with
the help of Morris B. Ullman, Cities of Mainland China: 1953
and 1958 (Washington: U. S. Bureau of the Census, 1961); U.S.
Department of the Army, Communist China: A Strategic Survey
(Washington: U. S. Army, 1966), Appendix H, Map 12; UNDY:67;
and a private communication in November 1968, from Professor
Sen-dou Chang, Department of Geography, University of Hawaii.
    The 1970 projections were made by assembling and chart-
ing as many figures for each individual city as were available. These included estimates for 1948 and earlier dates,
the returns from the 1953 census, and more recent estimates
from the sources mentioned above.
    Necessarily, the projections and the 1950 and 1960 esti-
mates are highly questionable. The best source is the census
of 1953, but even it is open to question. The further removed
in time one gets from the census, the more the figures are
sheer guesswork.
    Although the United Nations lists the Chinese cities as
CP's (UNDY:67), they seem more properly to be UA's. Ullman,
op. cit., p. 4, points out that they are in fact more akin to
metropolitan areas, hence at the opposite extreme from CP's,
because they include large territories and considerable rural
population. In recognition of this extended character of the
Chinese municipalities, the United States Army Map, op. cit.,
designates them as "Urban Areas." Ideally, one should remove
the rural population from the figures for the municipalities,
but this could not be done from our sources even for 1953.

Hong Kong

URB. DEF.: Hong Kong UA. Population 1,561,000 in 1950 and
3,075,000 in 1960.

Korea, North

URB. POP.: For North Korea we had very little information. However, we did have estimates for the three largest cities in
1960 (UNDY:65 and StY:63-64) and 1942 (UNDY:52). To estimate
the urban population in 1960, we assumed that the ratio of
the three largest cities to the urban population would be the

same in North Korea as in South Korea. We further assumed that the same ratio would hold for 1942. With the urban population thus estimated for 1942 and 1960, we obtained an estimate for 1950 by interpolation. Subsequently, in view of additional information, such as the addition of an extra city in 1960 (Kaesong, from Encyclopedia Britannica World Atlas, 1946), the 1960 urban estimate was judged to be too low and was raised by 22 per cent.

The projected urban population for 1970 gave too high an estimate, as judged by the city/urban ratio for that date. The projection was accordingly scaled down by half a million.

URB. DEF.: By implication, through analogy with South Korea, the urban category includes places of 5,000+; but no assumption should be made that the estimates come close to reality under any such definition.

CITY POP.: The 1950 and 1960 estimates were derived from the following data: A 1960 estimate for Pyong Yang (UNDY:65); 1963 estimates for Chungjin and Huengnam (StY:63-64); and 1942 estimates for Pyong Yang, Sinuiju, and Wonsan (UNDY:52). We adjusted the 1942 estimates for Sinuiju and Wonsan before calculating growth rates.

For 1970 the projections for Pyong Yang, Sinuiju, Wonsan, Chungjin, and Hamhung-Huengnam were calculated on the basis of the 1950-60 growth. Kaesong, Chinnampo, Haeju, and Kimchaek were given the same growth rate as these, to move them from 1960 to 1970.

Korea, South

URB. DEF.: Seoul city, and municipalities 5,000+.

Macau

URB. DEF.: Macau UA. Population 188,000 in 1950 and 169,000 in 1960.

Mongolia

URB. DEF.: Capitals and district centers.

Ryukyu Islands

URB. DEF.: Five largest "shi." Smallest was estimated in 16,800 in 1950 and 25,943 in 1960.

JAPAN

Japan

URB. DEF.:   Urban municipalities ("shi" and "ku" of Tokyo-to)
usually having 30,000+ and which may include rural as well
as urban clusters.

SOUTHEAST ASIA

Brunei

URB. POP. '50:   Given a 1960 census with an urban population, and
the growth rate of the four largest towns from 1947 and 1960
censuses, we applied the growth rate to the 1960 urban population to get an estimate for urban 1950.

URB. DEF.:   No definition available.

Burma

URB. POP. '60:   The ratio of cities to urban in 1950 was applied
to the city population of 1960 to estimate the 1960 urban.

CITY POP.:   Individual city populations estimated from 1953 and
1957 censuses, and 1958 estimates (UNDY:65).

Cambodia

URB. POP. '50:   An estimate from the Cambodian Ministry of Plan-
ning, Annuaire Statistique Retrospectif du Cambodge, 1937-57
(Phnom Penh, 1958) p. 11, with an estimate for Phnom Penh
(see city 1950) was accepted as urban population 1950.

URB. POP. '60:   Interpolation was made between our 1950 estimate
and 1962 census (UNDY:67). The figure 532,000 seemed too
low in view of other data and uncertain definition. It was
raised to 550,000.

CITY POP.:   A 1948 UA figure is calculated by applying the UA-CP
to CP ratio in 1959 (UNDY:62) to the 1948 CP estimate (UNDY:
52). The 1950 UA was then interpolated from the 1948 estimate and the 1962 census figure.

Indonesia

URB. POP. '50: The average of the growth rate of the total population, 1950-61, and the "selected towns," 1930-61 (Central Bureau of Statistics, Statistical Pocketbook of Indonesia, 1963; Djakarta, 1964; p. 12) was applied to the 1961 census figure for urban-minus-cities population to find the urban-minus-cities estimate for 1950. The 1950 estimate for cities was then added to find the total urban estimate.

URB. POP. 60: The growth rate of the total population, 1960-61, was applied to the 1961 census figure for urban-minus-cities to find the 1960 estimate for urban-minus-cities. The 1960 estimate for cities was then added to find the urban estimate.

CITY POP.: Interpolated and extrapolated from the 1955 estimates (UNDY:60) and the 1961 census data for individual cities.

URB. DEF.: Municipalities, regency capitals and other places with urban character.

Laos

URB. POP.: The capital city, Vientiane, was estimated for 1950 and 1960 as follows: We had a CP figure for 1958 (UNDY:52) and both a UA and CP figure for 1962 (UNDY:65). A UA was formed for 1948 by assuming that the CP/UA ratio was the same in 1958 as in 1962. The 1950 and 1960 estimates were then interpolated from the 1948 and 1962 UA figures.

    To find the urban population, the average ratio of the capital city to the total urban population in three similar countries (Malaya, Nepal, Cambodia) in 1950 and 1960 was applied to the estimates for Vientiane at those dates. Later the 1960 estimate was reduced by 22 per cent in order to give a more plausible city/urban ratio.

    The 1970 urban projection was also deemed to be too high in view of the city/urban ratio.

URB. DEF.: Towns.

CITY POP.: For 1950 and 1960, see urban above. For 1970 the curve-projection for the city population was low compared to the projection of Vientiane based on a 1962 estimate. A compromise figure was adopted.

Maldive Islands

URB. POP. '60: Interpolated from the 1946 census and the 1965 estimate (UNDY:65).

URB. DEF.: Mali, the capital city. Population 9,000 in 1950 and 10,400 in 1960.

Philippines

URB. POP. '50, '60: The 1948 census contained data on towns (poblaciones) of 2,500+. The population in all such places, together with the population of the Manila UA, was accepted by us as the urban population. However, for 1960 similar data could not be found. We therefore decided to use municipalities as a basis for estimating the population in places of 2,500+ at the time of the 1960 census. Since the municipalities in the Philippines often include extensive territory, we utilized a density criterion in estimating. We took the combined population of municipalities (municipios) having at least 20,000 inhabitants and a minimum density of 400 persons per square kilometer in 1948, and obtained the ratio of this population to the total in towns of 2,500+ at that date. The same ratio was assumed to hold in 1960, except that the density criterion for municipios was raised in proportion to the rise in the average density of the Philippines as a whole between 1948 and 1960. In 1960 a municipio had to have a density of 563 persons per square kilometer to be included in the calculation. With a census figure for the urban population in 1948 and an estimate for 1960, we obtained our 1950 estimate by interpolation.

URB. DEF.: Towns (poblaciones) of 2,500 or more inhabitants.

CITY POP. '70: With exception of Manila UA, the projections were made on the basis of 1960 census data and 1966 estimates (UNDY:67). The Manila UA projection was based on our 1950 and 1960 estimates for this unit.

Portuguese Timor

URB. DEF.: Capital city, Dili. Population 43,600 in 1950 and 52,200 in 1960.

Sarawak

URB. DEF.: Kuching municipality. Population 67,200 in 1950 and 112,000 in 1960.

Singapore

URB. DEF.: Singapore UA. Population 1,022,000 in 1950 and 1,634,000 in 1960.

Thailand

URB. POP. '50: The growth rate of Thonburi and Bangkok, 1947 and 1960 censuses, was applied to the 1960 census urban population to estimate the 1950 urban.

URB. DEF.: 54 cities and towns. Smallest was estimated at 1,500 in 1950 and 2,685 in 1960.

CITY POP. '50: The first UA figures we found were for 1955 (UNDY:55). In the census of 1947 there were only CP data (Ibid.); hence we had the problem of estimating the UA's for 1947. This was done by assuming that the growth rate of the CP's between 1947 and 1955 would also characterize the UA's. But we also had the question of allocating the UA population as between Bangkok and Thonburi in 1947, because the cities are side by side across the river. We assumed that the two had the same proportion of the total UA population in 1947 that they did in 1955 and 1963 on the average. With the 1947 UA's thus estimated, we interpolated between that date and 1955 to obtain the 1950 estimates.

Viet-Nam, North

TOT. POP. '50: Extrapolated from the 1955 estimate (UNDY:65) and the 1960 census.

URB. POP.: Lacking data on the urban population as such, we had to estimate it. Information for Viet-Nam and other Southeast Asian countries suggested a ratio of 2:1 for the urban population in relation to the city population. Consequently, for North Viet-Nam, this ratio was applied to the city population for 1960 (at which date we had census figures for the cities) to estimate the urban population then, and it was also applied to our 1950 estimated city population (see below).

CITY POP.: The 1950 populations of Hanoi and Haiphong were interpolated from the 1948 estimates (UNDY:52) and the 1960 census figures. For 1970, the population of Hanoi was projected on the basis of a 1948 estimate and the 1960 census figure, but the population of Haiphong could not be projected on that basis because the UA appeared to have a 1950-60 growth rate not likely to be repeated. An average was taken of the CP and UA growth rate of Haiphong between 1948 and 1960 as a basis of projection. Nam Dinh was arbitrarily given a growth rate of 4 per cent between 1960 and 1960. Thai Nguyen was given 110,000 on the basis of a footnote in Worldmark Encyclopedia of Nations, which said the town would reach 90,000 by 1964 due to the opening of new steel mills. Hon Gay was given 100,000 for 1970.

Viet-Nam, South

TOT. POP. '50: Extrapolated from 1955 and 1960 estimates (UNDY: 65).

URB. POP.: Due to the lack of other information, and because the available data suggested a city-to-urban ratio of 1:2, we estimated the percent urban at twice the city percent for both 1950 and 1960.

CITY POP.: For 1960, Saigon was interpolated from 1958 estimate (UNDY:60) and 1964 estimate (UNDY:65). For the two other cities, Hue and Da-nang, 1960 estimates (UNDY:62) were accepted. For 1950, Saigon, the only city, was estimated by taking the average of a 1958-64 extrapolation and a 1936-60 interpolation, the 1936 figure being from Annuaire Statistique de l'Indochine, p. 19.

West Irian

URB. POP. '50: Extrapolated from 1956 and 1960 (UNDY:62).

URB. POP. '60: Midyear estimate from UNDY:62.

URB. DEF.: Capital city, Kotabaru. Population 13,200 in 1950 and 14,100 in 1960.

SOUTHWEST ASIA

Bahrain

URB. POP.:   Interpolated and extrapolated from 1959 census and
1965 estimate (StY:66-67).

URB. DEF.:   Towns of Manama, Muharraq, Hidd, and Riga.   Smallest
was Hidd with 4,435 in 1959 and 5,230 in 1965.   Estimated
population of Hidd was 3,300 in 1950 and 4,600 in 1960.

Cyprus

URB. DEF.:   Six urban towns and Nicosia suburbs.   Smallest urban
town was 2,916 in 1950 and 3,498 in 1960.

Federation of South Arabia (Southern Yemen)

TOT. POP. '50, '60:   Estimates were made separately for Aden and
the Protectorate of South Arabia, which together once constituted the Federation.   For Aden, there was a 1955 census.
We assumed that the Aden population had grown at a rate of
1.2 per cent per year prior to this census.   For the Protectorate we assumed that no growth in population occurred
between 1950 and 1960, and that therefore we could use the
1960 estimated population for that date.   The 1960 estimated
population is from StY:66-67.

URB. POP. '50, '60:   The Aden UA was obtained by the usual procedures from the 1955 census and the 1964 estimate (UNDY:65).
The Lahej and Mukalla estimates for 1960 came from StY:60-61.
The 1950 estimates for these two towns were calculated by
using a growth rate one-half that of the Aden UA during 1950-
60 to project back from the 1960 estimates for the two towns.

URB. DEF.:   Aden UA plus the towns of Lahej and Mukalla.   The
smaller of the two towns had approximately 10,000 people in
1950 and about 15,000 in 1960.

CITY POP.:   The 1950 and 1960 estimates for Aden UA are based on
the MA figure for 1955 in The World's Metropolitan Areas and
the 1964 estimate of UNDY:64.   The 1970 projection was made
on the basis of the same growth rate, but was scaled down in
view of political unrest in the area in years prior to 1970.

Gaza Strip

TOT. POP. '50:   Extrapolated from 1955 and 1960 estimates (UNDY: 65).

Iran

URB. POP.:   The growth rate of the combined population of the eight largest cities in the 1956 census and the combined population of the nine largest in 1960 (estimates from (UNDY: 63) was applied to the 1956 census urban population, to estimate the 1950 and 1960 urban populations.

URB. DEF.:   Places 5,000+ and administrative centers of districts.

CITY POP. '50:   Extrapolated from 1956 census and 1960 estimates (UNDY:63).

CITY POP. '60:   Midyear estimates from UNDY:63.

CITY POP. '70:   The urban population of the district of Teheran was accepted as the Teheran UA, and the 1970 figure was obtained by extrapolating on the basis of its growth between the 1956 and 1966 censuses.

Iraq

URB. DEF.:   Cities and towns.

CITY POP.:   The Baghdad UA is composed of four Qadha centers (Karkh, Rasafah, Adhamiya, and Kadhemain) and three Nahiyas (Maamoon, Mansour, and Karradah-Sharqiya).   To estimate the 1950 and 1960 populations of this UA, we utilized data from the 1957 and 1965 censuses, by interpolation and extrapolation.   For the other cities in 1950 and 1960, we used the same sources and procedures, but in this case the Qadha centers were taken to be the city population.   The 1970 projections were made on the basis of the growth rates shown between 1957 and 1965.   With four new cities added between 1965 and 1970, the summary of the city projections came very close to the curve-projection for the city population as a whole.

Israel

URB. POP. '50: For 1950, there was no official estimate of the
total urban population, although a 1950 figure existed for
the Jews. There was a 1951 estimate (UNDY:60) for the total
urban and the Jewish urban; however, we assumed that the
Jewish urban proportion divided by the total urban proportion
was the same in 1950 as actually found in 1951 to estimate
the total urban for 1950.
   In 1950 the urban definition was different from that in
the 1961 census. The 1961 definition was first used in official Israeli estimates in 1957. We estimated by extrapolation
the 1956 percent urban, using the new definition. The ratio
of this estimate to the official percentage in 1956 was then
applied to correct the 1950 percentage as estimated above.

URB. POP. '60: Interpolated from the 1958 estimate (UNDY:60) and
1961 census.

URB. DEF.: All settlements of 2,000+ except those where at least
1/3 of the labor force is engaged in agriculture.

CITY POP.: The UA's for Tel Aviv, Haifa, and Jerusalem were defined by us in terms of subdistricts. The 1950 and 1960
estimates were derived from 1950 official estimates (UNDY:62)
and the 1961 census reports. Ramat Gan for 1960 was extrapolated from the 1961 census and the 1967 estimate (StY:68-
69). The 1970 projections were based on 1960 estimates
(Statistical Abstract of Israel, 1962) and 1967 official
estimates (UNDY:67).

Jordan

TOT. POP. '50: Extrapolated from 1951 and 1955 estimates (UNDY:
65).

URB. POP.: The 1950 and 1960 town figure was calculated from the
1952 census and 1961 census figures. The ratio of towns to
5,000+ in the 1961 census was then applied to the 1950 and
1960 estimate for towns to find the urban estimates for both
dates.

Kuwait

URB. POP. '50: The capital city was extrapolated from the 1957
and 1961 censuses. It was assumed that there was one other

place over 5,000 in 1950 and it was given 5,500 and added to the capital city population for urban 1950.

Lebanon

TOT. POP. '50: Extrapolated from 1955 and 1960 estimates (UNDY: 65).

URB. POP. '50: Estimate for six cities from <u>Columbia Lippincott Gazetteer of the World, 1952.</u>

URB. POP. '60: Estimate for eight cities for 1961 accepted as 1960 from <u>Encyclopedia Britannica World Atlas, 1964.</u>

URB. DEF.: Eight largest cities (1960). Smallest was 7,085. Six largest cities (1950). Smallest was approximately 10,700.

CITY POP. '50: See urban 1950 for source.

CITY POP. '60: For Beirut UA, a 1959 estimate from UN Technical Assistance Program, <u>Administrative Problems of Rapid Urban Growth in the Arab States</u> (New York: 1964), p. 111, was accepted for 1960. For Tripoli UA, a 1958 estimate was used for 1960.

Muscat and Oman

URB. POP. '50: Estimate from <u>Rand McNally World Guide, 1953.</u>

URB. POP. '60: Estimate from StY:66-67.

URB. DEF.: Two main towns, Muscat and Matrah. Smaller was 4,200 in 1950 and 6,208 in 1960.

Qatar

URB. POP. '50: Estimate from <u>Columbia Lippincott Gazetteer of the World, 1952.</u>

URB. POP. '60: Estimate from UNDY:62.

URB. DEF.: Main city, Doha. Population 13,000 in 1950 and 20,000 in 1960.

Saudi Arabia

TOT. POP.: Growth rate from 1958 to 1964 (UNDY:65, p. 114) was applied to the 1958 estimate (Ibid.).

URB. POP.: Using the Rand McNally World Guide, 1953, Merriam Webster Atlas, Worldmark Encyclopedia of the Nations, 1960, and the UNDY:65, we compiled data on all places 4,000+ for dates around 1950-52 and 1960. For those places for which we had populations at both dates, we obtained an average annual growth rate (for the combined population). Applying this average to the places for which we lacked data at one or the other date, we obtained populations for all places at both times. The totals gave us the estimated urban population for 1950 and 1960.

URB. DEF.: Places 4,000+.

Syria

TOT. POP. '50: 1950 figures (Syria Directorate of Statistics, Statistical Abstract, 1961; Damascus, 1962; p. 23), adjusted to midyear.

URB. POP. '50: A provisional 1950 urban figure was extrapolated from 1952 estimate (Statistical Abstract, 1956, p. 14) and the 1960 estimate (Statistical Abstract, 1961, p. 55). Since the Abstract and the census differed slightly for 1960, the same difference was assumed for 1950. The provisional 1950 figure was adjusted accordingly.

URB. DEF.: Cities or administrative centers of districts, Mohafaza centers and Mantika centers. Smallest in 1952 was 1,475 and in 1960, 2,185; estimated at 1,600 in 1950.

CITY POP. '50: Provisional figure extrapolated from 1952 and 1960 data (same sources as above). This figure was adjusted (as above) to make it comparable to the 1960 census.

Trucial Oman

URB. POP. '50: Extrapolated from 1956 and 1960 estimates for main city (UNDY:62).

URB. POP. '60: Estimate for main city from UNDY:62.

URB. DEF.:   Main city, Dubai.   Population 20,000 in 1950 and
40,000 in 1960.

Turkey

URB. DEF.:   Chief towns and cities; these are localities with a
municipal organization, i.e., administrative centers of provinces and districts regardless of size, and other agglomerations of 5,000+.

Yemen

TOT. POP. '50:   The 1960 estimate (see below) was used and a
growth rate of 1.4% per year assumed for prior decade.

TOT. POP. '60:   Interpolated from 1955 and 1964 estimates (UNDY:
65).

URB. POP. '50:   Estimate from Rand McNally World Guide, 1953 for
"main towns."

URB. POP. '60:   The average of the sums of the main towns from
two sources was used.   (International Yearbook and Statesman's Who's Who, 1966 and Worldmark Encyclopedia of the
Nations.)

URB. DEF.:   Six main towns.   Smallest was 5,000 in 1950 and
12,000 in 1960.

SOUTH CENTRAL ASIA

Afghanistan

URB. POP.:   To start with, we had for 1948, population estimates
for a list of towns, the smallest of which was over 20,000
(StY:63).   We also had 1966 estimates (StY:66-67) for the
same places.   For Kabul we had, in addition, a 1960 estimate
(StY:66-67).
     To get a 1960 estimate for the urban population, we took
the 1960 Kabul estimate, and added to it our estimate of the
1960 population of the other places of 20,000 or more which
was accomplished by assuming that these towns had reached
2/3 of their 1948 growth by 1960.

With the estimated population in places of 20,000, we then used a ratio drawn from other countries to give us an urban population. We took the average ratio of 20,000+/ 5,000+ in India 1951, Pakistan 1951, Burma 1931, Portugal 1950, Haiti 1950, and applied this average ratio to the 20,000+ estimate for Afghanistan in 1948 and 1960. With these two estimates, we could interpolate to get an urban population for 1950.

CITY POP. '50, '70: The Kabul CP for 1950 was interpolated between an estimate for 1948 (StY:63) and one for 1960 (StY: 66-67). The projection to 1970 could, fortunately, be made on a UA basis, because we had a 1965 estimate for the Kabul UA (UNDY:67). To find the UA for 1960, we assumed that the proportion of the UA lying outside the CP was only half of what it was later in 1965. The 1970 projection was made on the basis of our 1960 estimate and a 1967 official estimate (UNDY:67). The Kandahar CP, on the other hand, was projected on the basis of the 1966 and 1967 estimates.

CITY POP. '60: See urban for method and sources.

Bhutan

TOT. POP.: Interpolated from 1958 and 1964 estimates (UNDY:65).

Ceylon

URB. DEF.: Municipalities, urban council areas, local board areas. Smallest in 1946 was approximately 1,250; estimated as 1,400 in 1950 and at 1,800 in 1960.

India

CITY POP.: For sources from which to prepare our 1950 and 1960 estimates, we used the 1951 MA's as delineated in The World's Metropolitan Areas from India's 1951 census data and the UA's of the Indian report of the 1961 census (Census of India, 1961, Vol. 1, Part 2, "General Population Tables"). The latter publication defines UA's as "town groups" or large towns.
    The projections for 1970 were based on the same sources. However, since the curve-projection for the city population

as a whole gave a higher figure than the sum of our individual city projections, we pushed up the estimates, especially those of the larger UA's, in the process of rounding.

Nepal

URB. POP. '50, '60: The most appropriate lower limit of population for urban places in Nepal seemed to be 5,000. The
1953 census gave the data for towns of this size and larger,
but the 1961 census did not. The latter census did, however,
give the population in places of 10,000+. We therefore used
these data to estimate the places of 5,000+ in 1961; to do
so, we employed the ratio of population in places of 5,000 to
10,000 in relation to the population in places 10,000+ in
India in 1941. This ratio was applied to the 1961 figure
for places 10,000+ in Nepal to obtain the 5,000+ estimate for
that date. Our 1950 and 1960 estimates were then obtained by
interpolation.

CITY POP.: The Katmandu UA for 1950 (Katmandu and Patan) was
extrapolated from the 1952-54 census and the 1964 estimate
(StY:66-67). In 1960, the Katmandu UA (Katmandu, Patan, and
Bhatgaon) was interpolated from the 1952-54 census and the
1961 census data, and for 1960 it was extrapolated from the
1961 data and the 1966 estimate (StY:68-69).

Pakistan

URB. DEF.: Places of 5,000+ and places of less than that if they
have urban characteristics.

CITY POP.: The 1950 and 1960 estimates were obtained by the usual
procedures from the MA's derived from the census of 1951 (The
World's Metropolitan Areas) and the census figures of 1961
for apparently the same units (UNDY:65). The only exception
was Dacca, whose 1960 population was estimated on the basis
of the 1961 census and the 1967 estimate. The 1970 projections were made with the 1961 census and 1967 estimates
(UNDY:67).

Sikkim

URB. POP. '60: Interpolated from 1954 estimate (UNDY:63) and
1961 census figure.

URB. DEF.: Capital city, Gangtok. Population 2,700 in 1950 and 6,800 in 1960.

NORTHERN EUROPE

Channel Islands

URB. DEF.: St. Peter Port and St. Helier. Smaller was 16,741 in 1950 and 15,906 in 1960.

Faroe Islands

URB. DEF.: Capital city, Torshavn. Population 5,600 in 1950 and 7,400 in 1960.

Finland

URB. DEF.: Non-administrative agglomerations, i.e., almost all groups of buildings occupied by at least 200 people and with usually not more than 200 metres between houses.

Iceland

URB. DEF.: Kaupstadir--all towns: Reykjavik and "other towns." Smallest was approximately 760 in 1950 and 750 in 1960.

Ireland

URB. DEF.: Cities and towns, including suburbs, of 1,500+.

Isle of Man

URB. DEF.: Castletown, Douglas, Peel, and Ramsey. Smallest was Castletown with 1,749 in 1951 and 1,549 in 1961. It was approximately 1,788 in 1950 and 1,600 in 1960.

Norway

URB. POP. '50: The ratio of "towns and rural localities 2,000+" (Central Bureau of Statistics, Population Census, 1960,

Vol. I; Oslo, 1963; p. 10-26) to the total urban population
in the 1960 census was applied to the 1950 census figure of
"towns and rural localities 2,000+" (Norway Central Bureau of
Statistics, <u>Population Census, 1950</u>, Vol. III; Oslo, 1956;
pp. 20-34) to find the 1950 urban estimate.

URB. DEF.: Localities or population clusters of 2,000+ irrespec-
tive of administrative divisions, with usually not more than
50 metres between houses but including smaller groups of
houses naturally belonging together even if they are more
than 50 metres apart.

Sweden

URB. POP. '50: The ratio of towns 2,000+ to the total urban in
the 1960 census was applied to the 1950 census urban population to find the 1950 estimate for towns 2,000+.

United Kingdom

URB. DEF.: Areas classified as urban for local government purposes, i.e., county boroughs, municipal boroughs, and urban
districts. Smallest was estimated at 630 for 1950 and 590
for 1960.

CITY POP.: The UA's in this country refer to metropolitan areas.
These areas were delimited twice at IPUR, once for 1951 as
published in <u>The World's Metropolitan Areas</u> and again for
1951 and 1961, by Valerie Herr while she was on IPUR's staff.
The estimates given here for 1950 and 1960 are based on Mrs.
Herr's delineations, as are the projections to 1970. There
was no search made for new MA's between 1960 and 1970, because it appeared that the old MA's covered so much of the
country that there was little chance for new ones to arise
having as many as 100,000 people.

WESTERN EUROPE

Austria

CITY POP.: The UA's are tantamount to MA's. The 1950 and 1960
estimates were derived from the MA's delimited in <u>The World's</u>

309

Metropolitan Areas with data from the 1951 census and from comparable data in the 1961 census. The 1970 projections were based on the growth rates between 1951 and 1961.

Belgium

CITY POP.: Cities, except Charleroi, interpolated from 1947 census and 1961 census data. Charleroi had given only a 1961 population, so it was estimated for 1960 by taking the ratio of its 1961 population to the population of the four other cities and applying that ratio to the estimated population of the four cities in 1960. The same ratio was applied to find its population in 1950.

France

CITY POP. '50: First, Paris was extrapolated from the 1954 census figure for "le grande Paris" and the 1962 census figure for "l'agglomeration etendue." Then for six cities--Toulouse, Nice, Toulon, Rennes, Limoges, and Marseilles--the CP's were extrapolated from the 1954 and 1962 census data. The UA's of these cities were estimated for 1950 by applying the UA/CP ratio of 1962 to the 1950 CP estimates. The rest of the UA's were calculated for 1950 by first extrapolating the CP's from the 1954-62 data and then extrapolating the UA/CP ratio from the same years. These extrapolation ratios were then applied to the estimated CP's to find the 1950 UA populations.

CITY POP. '60: Paris was interpolated from the 1954 census figure for "Greater Paris" and the average of the 1962 census figures for "le agglomeration etendue" and the "complexe residentiel de l'agglomeration de Paris." The other UA's were interpolated using the 1954-62 data. Where there was only CP data in 1954, the average UA growth rate was used with the 1962 UA figure to estimate the 1960 UA's. One CP was interpolated from the 1954-62 populations.

Germany, Federal Republic of

URB. DEF.: Cities 2,000+ and West Berlin.

CITY POP.: The UA's for West Germany are delimited on a metropolitan basis. For 1950, we utilized the MA's derived from the 1950 census and published in The World's Metropolitan

Areas, and for 1960 we made use of similar data from the 1961 census. We treat West Berlin and East Berlin as separate cities although, in a purely geographic sense, they are one urban complex.

Liechtenstein

URB. DEF.: Capital city, Vaduz. Population 2,700 in 1950 and 3,500 in 1960.

Luxembourg

URB. DEF.: Communes having 2,000+ in the administrative centers.

Netherlands

URB. DEF.: Municipalities with a cluster of 5,000+, and municipalities with no more than 20 per cent of the economically active males engaged in agriculture.

CITY POP. '50, '60: The 1950 census figures were used for that date except when no UA population was given for cities for which UA data did exist in 1960. In such cases, the ratio of the UA/CP in 1960 was applied to the 1950 CP figure to estimate the UA for that date. In the case of the Enschede-Hengelo UA, however, the 1950 and 1960 populations were interpolated from the 1947 census and the 1967 estimate (StY:68-69).

Switzerland

CITY POP. '50: The UA/CP ratio in 1960 was applied to the 1950 census CP populations to estimate the UA's for 1950.

EASTERN EUROPE

Bulgaria

URB. DEF.: Towns, i.e., localities legally established as urban.

Czechoslovakia

URB. POP.: The ratio of communes 2,000+ to the total urban population in 1961 was applied to the 1948 census figure for communes 2,000+ to find the urban estimate for 1948. The 1950 and 1960 urban populations were then interpolated from the 1948 and 1960 figures.

URB. DEF.: Towns that are seats of a regional or district national committee and communes of 2,000+ (approximately) which either a) are part of an urban agglomeration or b) in general, have specified urban characteristics (relating to density, availability of certain facilities and percent of population in agriculture) and perform specified urban functions for surrounding rural areas.

Germany, East

URB. POP. '60: Extrapolated from the 1950 census and 1959 estimate (UNDY:63) with a 1960 estimate for East Berlin (UNDY:62) added.

URB. DEF.: Communes of 2,000+ and East Berlin.

CITY POP. '60: Interpolated from 1960 estimates (UNDY:62) and 1962 estimates (UNDY:63).

Hungary

URB. DEF.: Budapest and all other legally designated towns. Smallest, estimated at 3,800 in 1950, had 9,818 in 1960.

Poland

URB. DEF. '50: Towns with urban administrative organizations with president or mayor. Smallest was estimated at 2,700 in 1950 and 2,975 in 1960.

URB. DEF. '60: Towns of urban type; e.g., workers settlements, fishing settlements, health resorts.

CITY POP.: The UA's for Poland are delimited on a metropolitan basis. The 1950 data were taken from The World's Metropolitan

312

Areas, where MA's were delimited on the basis of 1950 census data. For 1960, comparable data were derived from Rocnik Statystyczny, 1966.

Romania

URB. DEF.: Cities and towns and 183 other localities (comprising 13% of the urban population) having urban socio-economic characteristics. Smallest was estimated at 1,200 in 1950 and 1,700 in 1960.

CITY POP. '50: Interpolated from 1948 and 1956 census data. For those with UA data only in 1960, we estimated the 1950 UA's by applying the UA/CP ratio of 1960 to the 1950 estimates for CP's.

SOUTHERN EUROPE

Albania

URB. POP. '70: The projected urban population was scaled down from 902,000 to 750,000 because it yielded an unlikely city/urban ratio.

URB. DEF.: Towns and industrial centers with more than 400 inhabitants.

Andorra

TOT. POP. '50: Since the UNDY:65 midyear estimates show little growth from 1946-57, the 1954 census figure was rounded down, and accepted as the 1950 estimate.

Greece

URB. POP.: Percent urban figures are given in the report of a field survey by V.G. Valaoras, A. Polychronopoulou, D. Trechopoulos, "Control of Family Size in Greece," Population Studies, Vol. 18, March 1965, p. 268.

URB. DEF.: Communes 2,000+ and 12 multi-communal agglomerations.

Italy

URB. POP.: The 1951 urban population was estimated by using the growth rate of the size-class 10,000+ during 1951-61 and applying it to the urban population in the 1961 census. The 1950 and 1960 urban estimates were then derived, by interpolation and extrapolation, from the urban population in the 1961 census and our 1951 estimate.

URB. DEF.: Communes with less than 50% of the economically active population engaged in agriculture. Smallest was estimated at 24,100 in 1950 and 27,800 in 1960.

Malta and Gozo Islands

URB. DEF.: Built-up areas where streets are continuously fronted by buildings. Smallest was estimated as 2,100 in 1950 and 2,000 in 1960.

San Marino

URB. POP.: The population of the capital town (UA) declined slightly according to estimates (UNDY:63 and UNDY:65). Accordingly, we gave it no growth between 1950 and 1960. Since the UA appears large in relation to the CP (for this kind of place), we rounded the town's population down to 3,800.

URB. DEF.: Capital town, San Marino (UA). Population estimated at 3,800.

Spain

URB. DEF.: "Urban"--included in an urban nucleus of 10,000+ and without regard to municipio boundaries. "Semi-urban"--nucleus of 2,000-10,000.

Yugoslavia

URB. DEF.: All localities with 15,000 or more inhabitants; localities of 5,000 to 14,999 if 30 per cent or more of the population are non-agricultural; localities of 3,000 to 4,999 if 70 per cent are non-agricultural; and localities of 2,000 to 2,999 if 80 per cent are non-agricultural.

NOTES: OCEANIA (continued)

CITY POP.: The 1961 census gave data for cities and their suburbs (StY:68-69), but our information from the 1953 census
included only CP data. To obtain an estimate for the suburbs
in 1953, we assumed that the growth rate of the suburbs between 1953 and 1961 was 1.5 times that of the central cities.
The estimated population of the suburbs in 1953, added to
that of the central city, gave us the estimated population
of UA's at that date. The 1950 and 1960 UA's were then obtained from the 1953 estimates and the 1961 data by the usual
procedures. The 1970 projections were based on the 1950 and
1960 UA estimates.

AUSTRALIA AND NEW ZEALAND

Australia

URB. DEF.: Cities and towns of 1,000+ and contiguous urban de-
velopments.

New Zealand

URB. DEF.: Cities, boroughs, and town districts. Smallest was
estimated as 200 in 1950 and 150 in 1960.

CITY POP. '50: The average of interpolation from 1945-51 census
data and extrapolation of 1951-61 census data.

CITY POP. '60: Interpolated from 1956 census and 1963 estimate
(UNDY:63).

OCEANIA

American Samoa

URB. DEF.: Capital city, Pago-Pago. Population 1,600 in 1950
and 1,300 in 1960.

Fiji

URB. POP.: First, Suva was interpolated for 1950 from 1946-56
census data and for 1960 from the 1956 census and 1963

estimate (UNDY:64). Then it was assumed that the Suva-to-total-urban ratio in 1956 was the same in 1950 and 1960, using the Suva estimates.

URB. DEF.: Suva city, towns, and townships. Smallest was estimated at 480 in 1950 and 690 in 1960.

French Polynesia

URB. DEF.: Capital city, Papeete. Population 14,100 in 1950 and 19,000 in 1960.

Gilbert and Ellice Islands

URB. POP. '60: Extrapolated from the 1963 census and the 1965 estimate (UNDY:65).

URB. DEF.: Capital city, Tarawa. Population 7,200 in 1960.

Papua

URB. POP.: A 1956 estimate of 14,250 for Port Moresby (UNDY:65) was rounded to 14,300 for the 1960 estimate of the urban population. The 1950 figure was estimated by assuming the same proportion urban in 1950 as in 1956.

URB. DEF.: Capital city, Port Moresby. Population estimated (see above) as 11,800 in 1950 and 14,300 in 1960.

Solomon Islands (U.K.)

URB. POP. '50: The percent urban in 1956 was applied to the 1950 total population to find the urban estimate.

URB. POP. '60: Extrapolated from the 1956 estimate (UNDY:60) and the 1959 estimate (UNDY:64).

URB. DEF.: Capital city, Honiara. Population 2,200 in 1950 and 3,800 in 1960.

Tonga

URB. POP.: The average of three methods was used. 1) Applying the ratio of the capital city to the total population in 1956 to the 1950 and 1960 total populations. 2) Applying the growth rate of the French Polynesian capital, 1950-60, to the 1956 estimate of Tonga's capital city. 3) Applying the growth rate of Gilbert and Ellice Islands' capital city, 1950-60, to the 1956 estimate of Tonga's capital city.

URB. DEF.: Main city, Naku' Alofa. Population 7,700 in 1950 and 10,200 in 1960.

Western Samoa

URB. DEF.: Apia urban area. Population 11,800 in 1950 and 20,900 in 1960.

U.S.S.R.

U.S.S.R.

URB. POP. '50: Two interpolations could be made for 1950 on the basis of the 1939 and 1959 censuses. One was an interpolation of the _percentage_ urban, which was then applied to the estimated population of the Soviet Union in 1950. The other was an interpolation of the absolute urban population. These gave different results, presumably because of the difficulties of estimating populations. For our estimate, we averaged the two interpolated values.

URB. POP. '60, '70: The 1960 urban estimate was on an extrapolation from the 1956 estimate (UNDY:60) and the 1959 census (UNDY:64). The 1970 urban population projection was scaled down by slightly less than 1 per cent in view of the city/urban ratio.

URB. DEF.: Cities and localities of an urban type officially designated by each of the republics, usually according to criteria of the number of inhabitants and the numerical dominance of agricultural over non-agricultural workers.

CITY POP. '60, '70: Our estimates were derived from the 1959 census figures (UNDY:63) and the 1967 estimates compiled

by Chauncy D. Harris, University of Chicago, from the U.S.S.R.
Prezidium Verkhovnogo Soveta, <u>SSSR, Administrativno-Terri-</u>
<u>torial'noe Delenie Soiuznykh Respublik na 1 iiulia 1967 goda</u>
(Moskva, 1967, "Parechen' gorodov s ukazaniem chislennosti
naseleniia," pp. 592-604. Professor Harris kindly furnished
the data by personal communication.